RONAN O'GARA

UNGUARDED

www.transworldireland.ie

www.**transworldbooks**.co.uk

UNGUARDED

My Life in Rugby

Ronan O'Gara
with Gerry Thornley

TRANSWORLD IRELAND

TRANSWORLD PUBLISHERS
61–63 Uxbridge Road, London W5 5SA
A Random House Group Company
www.transworldbooks.co.uk

First published in Great Britain
in 2013 by Transworld Ireland
an imprint of Transworld Publishers

A CIP catalogue record for this book
is available from the British Library.

ISBN 9781848271784

Addresses for Random House Group Ltd companies outside the UK
can be found at: www.randomhouse.co.uk
The Random House Group Ltd Reg. No. 954009

The Random House Group Limited supports the Forest Stewardship Council®
(FSC®), the leading international forest-certification organisation. Our books carrying
the FSC label are printed on FSC®-certified paper. FSC is the only forest-certification
scheme supported by the leading environmental organisations, including Greenpeace.
Our paper procurement policy can be found at www.randomhouse.co.uk/environment

Typeset in 11.25/16pt Berling by
Falcon Oast Graphic Art Ltd.
Printed and bound in Great Britain by
Clays Ltd, Bungay, Suffolk

2 4 6 8 10 9 7 5 3 1

MIX
Paper from
responsible sources
FSC® C016897

'Adversity causes some men to break; others to break records.'

– William Arthur Ward, American writer,
often quoted for his maxim

Contents

PROLOGUE

I remember the day vividly. It was lunchtime on Sunday, 3 March 2013. Myself, Jessica and the four kids went to Luigi Malone's for pizza and ice cream. We had tickets booked for *The Gruffalo's Child* in the Cork Opera House at three that afternoon so we headed over there. *The Gruffalo's Child* will never be the same again.

I was relaxed in my own head. I wasn't expecting a call because the Munster game against the Ospreys the night before had gone quite well from a personal point of view, and I'd just needed to show that. My gear was still in Carton House outside of Dublin where the Irish squad had been based for the Six Nations. In fact, as I write these words, over seven weeks later, it's still there.

I was due in Carton House that night so my day was revolving around that. I was going to travel with Donncha O'Callaghan, as always. I don't remember whose turn it was to drive but we collect each other around six o'clock to be up there for around 9.30, so I had plenty of time.

Because of where we were, I had the phone on vibrate in my pocket. When it rang I had a look at the name. Declan Kidney. Fuckit. Ignored it. Deccie obviously wasn't ringing me to tell me I was captain against France the following Saturday at the Aviva.

About halfway through *The Gruffalo's Child* I took JJ to the toilet and the phone went again. I was going to answer it but that wasn't the time or place so I just let it ring.

After we walked out to the car, which was parked about two hundred metres from the Opera House, I rang him back.

I said, 'Howya.'

He said, 'I need to meet up with you. I need to speak with you.'

'OK, yeah, grand, no hassle. I'm not around though, Dec. I've just left the Opera House with the family.'

'When will you be finished there and I'll meet you?'

Sometimes the management stay in Carton House because they're so busy, but Deccie was in Cork. He bent over backwards to try and meet me but I just said, 'Deccie, it doesn't make any difference to me what you say to me, whether it's over the phone or to my face, I'm not going to look upon you any less as a man. It's obvious you've something to say.'

I've learned over the years that the key with Deccie is not to speak too much because that's what he loves. He's happy to leave forty-second silences on the phone if you let him.

He said, 'No, I can't do this over the phone.'

'Well sure it's not good news so, Deccie. I'm not fucking stupid. I realize what's going on.'

He was humming and hawing, and kept trying to arrange a meeting; it felt like he was having difficulty holding back his emotions. I was obviously feeling hugely disappointed because I thought I'd weathered the storm with the game against the Ospreys, but he just said to me, 'I don't have a place for you this weekend.'

'OK,' I said. 'That's all right.'

'Do you want to ask me anything about it?'

I said, 'Can I ask you, for my own head, why?'

'I don't think your form at the minute is good enough,' he replied.

I snapped. 'Did you see the game last night?'

'Yeah, I was at the game.'

'How did you think I went?'

'You went very well.'

'Is that not the latest form?'

'It is, it is, but I thought Paddy went really well against Scotland,' he said.

'You thought he went really well against Scotland? Well, if that's how you think that's fair enough, you know. That's your opinion, but I wouldn't necessarily agree with going really well at Test level.'

And he said, 'Well, that's where we are.'

'Grand,' I said, 'that's fine, I've nothing else to ask you.'

'I wanted to say it to you before you got in the car and you came up to training and I spoke to you in Dublin,' he added.

'Yeah, I appreciate that. That's very important to both of us, how it's handled.'

We hung up. It had been as amicable as it could be. Deccie had been my coach on and off – mostly on – since making me captain of the Under-14s in Presentation Brothers College. Now I was being dropped from a match-day squad for the first time in fourteen years playing for Ireland. We'd had our conversation on speaker, with Jessie and the kids in the car. I talked with Jess for a little while and a swirl of thoughts went round in my head.

I was very conscious of the bigger picture at this stage. I was looking at coaching and issues like that because I was top dog for ten years, then I was sub, and I was always trying to gain experience, or learn about how important the squad is, and how you treat people. I wanted to make sure that I wasn't named in the squad and then have people perceive me as 'the difficult Corkman' – he got named in the squad and then he didn't show up. As disappointments go, this was huge, but I think the more mature and experienced you are, the better you can handle these things.

So I rang him back – just to clarify, as I said, that he had dropped me altogether, that when the squad was announced at tea-time or in the evening, my name would not be there. I told him that if it was a case of me being named in a squad and then omitted on Tuesday when the team and replacements were announced, I'd make my way to Carton House. I just didn't want my team-mates thinking 'this fella is sour now that he's not named in the thing'. I told Deccie, 'If I'm in the thirty-man squad I'll be there, nothing surer.'

He clarified that he was not naming me. That was it. It was courteous enough. He'd made his decision.

I was driving us to my parents' house and was glad to be with my wife and kids and family. I called one or two people whose judgement I trust, but they got it wrong. They advised me to issue a statement that night officially retiring from international rugby. But something inside me said 'don't do that'. It would have seemed petulant. It would have been a horrible way for it to end.

CHAPTER 1

The Final Road

Wednesday, 24 April 2013

It's fascinating really because part of me believed I could easily get back on the Ireland bench if I absolutely wanted to. I fully believed that – not that I needed to prove anything to anyone. Not me. Not after all these years. I think Munster's Heineken Cup quarter-final win against Harlequins five weeks after that conversation with Deccie showed what I could do. My cup rugby performances had demonstrated that all season, so the way it ended was, I suppose, the one time I'd never been backed in my career. Every coach had backed me. Deccie was under intense pressure for his own job but he didn't back me. And I hadn't played well in the Scotland game.

My first touch in Murrayfield was the restart after Greig Laidlaw's penalty had put them 9–8 ahead. We nearly scored off my next touch, which was a good cross-kick, but then my other big contribution was a horrific cross-kick – a mishit off my shin. It just summed up the day: when it fucking rains it pours.

I watched the video and two or three fellas could have cleaned it up, and even then I could have found touch.

With the last play of the game I threw a pass to Luke Marshall and he dropped it. I always throw the ball out in front of people but maybe it was just a little bit too far, and then came the final whistle. Game gone.

I came into the dressing-room and I put my hand up and said, 'I take responsibility for a stupid cross-kick out there, lads.'

A few of them said to me, 'Don't you put your fucking hand up and take responsibility for that. They'll use that stick to beat you.'

I couldn't believe it. That summed up where the team was, because in honest dressing-rooms that wouldn't happen. My gut instinct always tells me when you're wrong, put your hand up and you'll get respect for that. I think at that stage it was a survival changing-room with a lot of pressure on coaches and players, which is a bad place to be for Irish rugby. That shouldn't be the way.

Perhaps because of the public backlash, two days later the Irish team manager Mick Kearney said that this didn't spell the end of the road for Ronan O'Gara in Test rugby for Ireland. But deep down I knew it was the end of the road.

There's no doubt these boys have big futures, but I questioned Paddy Jackson being ready for international rugby at that stage. If I'd started against Scotland we would have been out of sight before they came into the game. Goal-kicking is crucial. For a head coach to say goal-kicking is a secondary role for an out-half is not an accurate comment.

It wasn't Paddy's fault he was selected. He along with Eoin O'Malley have been the two who have stood out at Irish train-ing when new players have been brought into the squad.

I watched the game against France at home on my own. The

kids were floating around but I was glued to it, and I didn't feel too bad. But then a week later I watched the Italy match at home in the same spot – I have my nice little chair – and I was angry. I was angry, yeah. I was freaking. I was thinking 'this is bullshit'. Against Scotland, Paddy's general game had been good and he had been playing nice and flat. But by the Italy game he was playing deeper and deeper. I was watching a different game. I didn't really understand what the thinking was.

You have to be careful how you blood young players. There are a lot of risks. There's a big difference between Magners/Rabo League, Heineken Cup and Test rugby in terms of comfort zones and how you get the best out of our players in the international jersey. It's a fascinating topic in its own right. At this time in Irish rugby the club, or province, definitely ruled over the national side – since, I would say, the Grand Slam in 2009. Up to then there wasn't that much change.

I think Conor Murray will be a very good player for Ireland, all the more so as he is starting to believe in himself. But not only was Eoin Reddan the established scrum-half in the Irish squad, he is also a very good talker. And when Conor heard Eoin contribute in meetings, it probably intimidated him. This is all part of the games within games in Irish camps. You're taken out of a comfort zone.

Even before that phone call from Deccie, I'd made up my mind. Jess is the one person who knows this Saturday – the Heineken Cup semi-final against Clermont – could be my last game. Mates want me to play on, and I suppose one reason to play on is for my boys. They are now at an age when they are starting to get it. In fact, Rua gets it now. But that can't be the deciding factor.

I haven't told our coach Rob Penney. I haven't told our CEO Garrett Fitzgerald. I haven't told anyone yet really. I'd say they're fully convinced I'm playing on for Munster. They're going to get a shock because I've been keeping my options open. There's no point in rejecting a contract if I've nothing else nailed down, and it wouldn't necessarily bother me if something else came up outside rugby.

Informing everyone after winning the Heineken Cup final would be the dream scenario, but it could all end this Saturday if we lose in Montpellier. Marcus Horan stood in front of the entire squad a few weeks ago and told us he was retiring. Most players do it that way. I won't do that. I'd need to ring twenty people because I'd care as much if not more about twenty fellas not in the room as the thirty fellas who were in the room. Former team-mates, loads of them, like Killian Keane, Dominic Crotty, John Kelly, Anthony Horgan, John O'Neill; fellas like Ian Murray, Peter Clohessy, Des Clohessy, Mick Galwey (Gaillimh), David Wallace, Frankie Sheahan, Mick O'Driscoll, Eddie Halvey, Alan Quinlan . . . Jim Williams, John Langford, Jerry Flannery, Denis Leamy, Peter Stringer, people like that. I have a nice bond with this current group but I have a deep bond with their predecessors.

Looking around the Munster dressing-room now my closest mates would be Paulie and Donncha, and Donnacha Ryan is a good fella. I'd be very close with Keith Earls. Simon Zebo is a good buddy, but I'm not their era. I've had the chats with Zeebs to get his act in gear, and I gave it to him eighteen months ago. It's unbelievable how quickly he's turned it around. I said to him – and this was when he was out of shape – 'You have it but you're not pushing yourself.' I said, 'I want you on the team, on the team I play with.' Munster is about hard work, with high standards; it's even a little regimented. That's our perception of it, but he has a completely different approach to life, and we didn't respect that. Now I know what makes him operate to the best of his ability, and that's to dance and listen to music and wear his cap backwards in the gym. And he's been our best player this season.

Who's to say that we're right? I wasn't right about him. That's man management, understanding how to get the best out of a player like Simon Zebo. For the first six months I hated him in the gym. But he actually gets his work done in a different way so you respect that – but only when you're wise enough to see it.

Today was our latest start of the season, eleven a.m. training in the Cork Institute of Technology, so we were all in at 10.15. We've a good breakfast crew and we met in a café: myself, Paul O'Connell, Damien Varley, Peter O'Mahony and James Downey. The boys sent out a text on the way down so we all just met there at about 9.20.

It's amazing how much the game has changed. You're gone first thing in the morning, and you don't come back till five o'clock. It's crazy. Meetings about meetings, and I don't know why we have some of them. It's something that has to be looked at. There are just not enough hours in the day. It's hugely time-consuming, and you wonder about the productivity. There's only so much you can take in.

Breakfast is always good when Paulie is there. I wasn't expecting him to be there. Paulie travels the furthest. Everyone thinks he's serious, cracking the whip all the time, but he has a good sense of humour. I have a role, an important one, but the thing would fucking collapse if he wasn't there. Aside from his presence it's his knowledge and his standards and his execution. No one else has all that.

Paulie pulled up in training yesterday in the University of Limerick, and although a scan has shown only a minor groin strain, he's still a serious doubt for the Clermont game. He didn't train today and it was shite. We literally got four plays in a row wrong on the eve of a Heineken Cup semi-final! It would have been very interesting if yer man had been on the pitch. It's just the look he would have given fellas. But subconsciously they knew he wasn't there.

Myself and Paulie have been around longer than any of them so we have a fair idea of the Munster style. I suppose our biggest asset down here is crazy intensity, and a bloody good mixture of a kicking game, a running game and an offloading game when we play. The perception of Munster sometimes annoys me it's so inaccurate. We were scoring tries, good tries, against Toulouse in the semi-final in Bordeaux in 2000. That's fourteen seasons ago!

I'd just turned twenty-three then. Coming into the 2012/13 season I was thirty-five; I turned thirty-six two days before the Ireland–France game. People were questioning my form going into Munster's first Heineken Cup pool match with Racing Metro in October on the basis of a few Rabo games. They are warm-up games in my mind. For other fellas they are important games because they're not proven players. I was seven years on that road before getting established.

Then I did my hammer against Racing and missed the Edinburgh game at home. Saracens home and away in December were good. I was on top of my game, and Edinburgh away in January was another good game, but Rob Penney took off 8, 9 and 10 – James Coughlan, Conor and myself – with sixteen minutes to go and we conceded fourteen points. That's when I had an outburst in the changing-room with Simon Mannix, our backs coach. 'Why would you make these changes?' I asked. 'Changing three decision makers! You and the coach are on about us trusting this new game plan, but you've got to trust your players a little more.' We had sixteen minutes to get two more tries for a bonus point but we ended up conceding two tries and soaking up pressure for the rest of the game. To make it worse, I was suspended for the final pool game at home to Racing a week later for stupidly kicking out at Sean Cox. So I missed the two easiest games, at Thomond Park against Edinburgh and Racing!

Even though I was approaching thirty-six I felt good mentally and physically. I was very happy as a rugby player, but I have seen standards slip in Munster and it wrecks my head. It isn't public, or even 100 per cent decided in my head, but myself and Dougie Howlett are retiring this year and Munster should have been doing everything in their power, from their point of view, to keep us on the pitch. I don't want to go back on the pitch, and I know there has to be a succession, but they are in for a rude awakening losing Dougie and all his experience.

For fourteen years there has always been plenty of Test rugby but this season there has been sod all for me. In the back of my head I've been thinking this might be my last season. But I also thought I had an outside chance of making the Lions, given my experience. So I said that could be a realistic goal. 'If you want somebody to kick a penalty with ten minutes to go, it's going to be me or Jonny Wilkinson.'

I could still carry on, but I just don't see the point. The coaching thing is ticking away inside me. I miss so many of the boys that played and I feel now is the time for the younger fellas to have a go. I could easily hang in there but I don't see what the point of that is. I want to get out at the top. You could be stubborn and try and prove a point and get one more Irish cap. But I don't really see what difference that's going to make.

There's been no one moment. It hits you over a period of time. I've been thinking about it since virtually the start of the season. I feel like I've given everything now so I want to go. I don't feel it's a tough decision. I've probably reached the stage where it's been so good that I want the memories to be as they are in my head today. It feels right to go. It feels very easy for me to go now, which is strange.

Thursday, 25 April

Three of the kids are in pre-school – Rua, JJ and Molly. Zac is not yet one. They're meant to be in by nine but it's usually 9.30 when I drop them off en route to training. Jess also does the run. They're there until 12.30, so they were home before I left.

We've an au pair in the house, so I'm firmly in third place. They were having lunch and were busy as usual. They have their wraps with ham, cheese and everything else in them. It's a joke – creatures of habit already. I'd been for a late breakfast on my own, chilled out, made sure I had my game plan in the head, checked the notes and packed the bag.

Jess and Rua were coming to Montpellier so there was big excitement. Every day that week Rua was going, 'Da, am I going in the airplane today?' And I'd say, 'No, no, I'll be going to

Limerick first and I have to sleep over in Limerick and then after that you go.'

He was on the Saturday day trip, out of Cork, with my mum and dad and Jess. Molly, the other twin, doesn't have any interest, and JJ doesn't yet get it. Rua gets the score and he knows the players. He loves Earlsy and Conor. A few months ago I contacted Paul Maloney in adidas and had a couple of kid-sized Munster jerseys sent down. When they arrived I went into the Munster Rugby Store in town and had the number 10 printed on both jerseys because Rua is always asking for one. I came home and gave him his jersey and he looked at it in awe for ages. He was delighted, and he put it on.

I gave JJ his package, and after he opened it, he looked at it and went, 'That not my number!'

And I said, 'What? There's your number 10.'

He got the jersey, threw it on the ground and said, 'That not Simon's number!'

The little . . . I couldn't believe it. Myself and Jess were in stitches.

'You should tweet that,' she said.

Unbelievable. It couldn't happen. My son got the Munster jersey, rolled it up in a ball, and chucked it on the ground, shouting, 'That not Simon's number!' He's fascinated with Zebo. To this day I don't think he's worn it. Stubborn, like his oul fella!

Rua was absolutely thrilled with his. He has the full kit – socks, shorts and jersey – and this semi with Clermont is his first Munster away match. He knows he's coming on the plane and he can hardly contain himself. As a father it's lovely. So saying goodbye to him and Jess was slightly different from a normal Thursday pre-match farewell. Sure it could be my last match, but sport has taught me that anything can happen, and in my head I'm going 'I'm winning this'.

There was some chat between management and players about when we should go. I would have preferred to go that Thursday, have the night in bed in France and then focus on a good kicking session on the Friday at the ground. Instead, we travelled to Limerick on the Thursday to train in Thomond Park, did some kicking there in the evening and stayed in the Clarion before an early Friday morning flight from Shannon.

That Thursday was different because Donncha O'Callaghan and myself have been Cork–Limerick buddies for all our careers but he'd been ruled out of the game with a knee injury. I'm only two years older than him and we've always been there for each other. We'd lost the third member of our Cork–Limerick drive, Denis Fogarty, to Aurillac a year before and Fogs was a big loss. Denis was never a regular on the first team but he was a great, great squad man. He trained hard and he is a good person. He has a great attitude about life, he has good values and he's good company, bar in the morning, when he can be a bit grumpy. There's no problem between me and Donncha when there's silence, but for the first hour Fogs wouldn't say anything anyway and we'd be shouting to get him going. Plus, he hadn't driven to Limerick for two years so he won't be getting any wedding presents.

Not only had Donncha been sidelined, he wasn't even invited along. I know it was a semi-final and there could yet be a final, but I always feel when you've got a tight team and a tight squad you bring someone like him, with his experience, to have him around. I suppose there's always two sides to every story, and does someone like Donnacha Ryan want him around when he's injured? But I still think it would have been nice if Donncha had been asked to come.

Dougie Howlett, as the captain, was there. Peter O'Mahony sent me a text that morning offering me a lift because myself and Donncha had once brought him, but then 'the bros', Casey Laulala and Dougie, intercepted him and took the freebie lift from Peter. So the three of them picked me up.

We were meant to be in Limerick for 4.15 but the lads were way late. Dougie had forgotten his passport. We had to ring his wife Monique and get her to meet us on the road. As we waited for Monique, Dougie was freaking with her.

'Hey Dougie, you're after forgetting your passport!'

But sure it's always the wife's fault. 'Will she ever just get here?' he kept saying.

The traffic was bad so Peter floored it all the way to Limerick. Ridiculous driving. But we were still late. All thanks to the non-playing captain. We had also been late for the Harlequins game when Donncha was driving me and he was late. I hate being late. The moral of the story is don't hand over control to someone else; but you can't be a loner either. I was relaxed about this one really. We were having great craic with Dougie, because it's a €50 fine for being late.

'Dougie boy, get out the two hundred quid!'

Me and Casey dragged in Peter to pay up some of the fine too.

'I'm the driver,' he complained.

'Yeah, but you were late for me,' I said, 'and if I'd been late for you I'd pay up.'

Casey's a really good fella, a very likeable lad. I think he's a big-game player who's just begun to show what the real Casey is all about in the knockout games. As I've gone through my career I've realized how confidence affects even proven professionals who come into a new set-up. If things don't go well immediately they question themselves. Look at some of those Clermont backs we would be facing in two days' time, like Sivetini Sivivatu, Regan King and Napolioni Nalaga. Unbelievable athletes, but perhaps their one Achilles heel – and I saw it when we played the All Blacks once or twice – was that they could become a little stressed if things went against them. Maybe I was just trying to give myself confidence that they might crack before me if we could get them into a dogfight, because if you give Sivivatu, King or Nalaga the ball they're brilliant with it, whereas I can't do a goose-step and skin a fella for thirty yards or do reverse, out-the-back offloads. Certainly with their captain, Aurélien Rougerie, ruled out of this game I was saying 'these boys are beatable'.

Dougie is special. After Brian O'Driscoll, I would place Dougie as probably the best back I've played with – it's just his vision and ability to read a game, and to call the correct shots. He's the model professional too. The two best communicators I've played with are Dougie and Rua Tipoki. Rua just made the game unbelievably simple. All he ever talked about was plus and minus. A plus would be to push him on an outside pass and a minus would be he wanted more of 'an unders' – a pass inside. He could talk on the run. 'ROG, you get to him,' and then it would be 'plus' or 'minus'. It was just so easy for the season he was with us. Similarly, if we had a scrum on the right-hand side of the pitch, Dougie's ability to call on the run was brilliant. Sometimes he'd be ten yards deeper than me so he had the ability to confirm or overrule what I was seeing. Dougie just has a huge understanding of the game.

Dougie has seen other cultures, teams and experiences in the southern hemisphere with the Auckland Blues and the All Blacks, and now for six seasons in Europe with us. I think he's an ideal fella to get the best out of the young players in Munster. Maybe his communication skills wouldn't be as good as someone like Paulie or myself in terms of having the local knowledge or insight, but if Munster had any foresight they'd get him working straight away. Some people say you shouldn't coach your peers, but everybody respects Dougie hugely. In Toulouse, Guy Noves brought in Yannick Bru, William Servat and Jean-Baptiste Elissalde straight from retirement on to the first-team coaching staff. People don't understand, but Dougie is a once-in-a-generation type, and these fellas are very hard to find.

I think Dougie is very happy to retire, even though it's horrible that injury forced it on him. He damaged his shoulder scoring a late try when we were hammered in Glasgow in March, hasn't played since, and won't play again. He is going to stay around a while in Cork, and he bought into the whole Munster thing as soon as he came. He's been a model pro for six seasons, and this season he was a good choice as captain, although when Paulie is in Munster, Paulie is the captain. I'd be biased, but it's the same in the international arena: when Brian is with Ireland, Brian is the captain. Presence in sport is huge, and you either have it or you don't. Don't get me wrong, Jamie Heaslip and Dougie have presence, just not like Brian or Paulie. No one in Irish rugby has presence like theirs.

Dougie would agree, and I remember him saying that Paulie was going to be out for a while and Paulie wanted to concentrate on getting himself right before Dougie handed back the responsibility. It was brilliant in that regard because Dougie is hugely capable. But the way it worked out in the quarters against Harlequins, with Dougie injured and Paulie captain, was a pity. Dougie deserved to have the honour of captaining us that day. We probably would have got the same result anyway.

The night before that game, Dougie sent us all an email along the lines of a soldier's poem. I was lying in bed at around 11.30 when the email came through. After reading it, I was ready to play that night! I couldn't get to sleep for an hour. It was in relation to Anzac day, and being brothers and all that.

Dougie spoke very well in the hotel, too, when we assembled about an hour and a half before the game.

But back on that car journey to Limerick, I was thinking about Donncha, not Dougie. I've great time for Donncha. He's hard-working, loyal, so professional, and just loves Munster. The young fellas need to see what it means, and they need only observe him. He's an absolutely perfect role model in terms of how to live your life and be respectful. He works his arse off. He has had plenty of disappointments but just takes them, puts his head down and works on.

It's strange how the two of us get on so well. He has a great sense of humour but I suppose what I like about him is that he takes the game as seriously as I do. Sometimes I'd be thinking 'Am I not seeing this right?' but then I'd bounce things off him and he'd confirm it. He's a diehard. Sometimes the lads slag us for being comfortable together in silence. 'I'd say there was great chat in that car this morning, lads, was there?' But that's better than fellas talking bullshit for an hour. With me and Donners, there's no need to do that. We've been through our whole careers together, all the World Cups together, and there were some lonely days during them and there were some great days together too. I always roomed with Donners when we were with Ireland, whereas with Munster it was usually Quinny – Alan Quinlan.

I put value on the person as opposed to the player. I think when you have a happy person you'll have a happy player, and on that journey to Limerick I was wondering in my coaching head – which I've been moving into more frequently of late – 'Have Munster even approached Donners by now regarding next season?'

I texted him: 'No invite?' He came back with 'Spot on', which I'd like to say surprised me, but it didn't.

So we arrived in Thomond Park late, the last four to arrive, and were clapped in by the boys. Usually you'd be there half an hour before the 4.15 start, to do your 'markers': your hamstring flexibility, ankle stiffness, sit and reach, weight, how you slept, what's your mood like, any other unusual stiffness.

We've all been independently analysed throughout our careers, which has definitely been crucial to my longevity. The strength and conditioning staff have a huge role. Your team will function and thrive if you've a good head coach, a strong manager and a good 'S and C'. They're the pillars of the whole organization, and in Munster we've always had really good S and Cs. The current ones are Bryce Cavanagh and Aidan O'Connell in Cork, then Aled Walters, a Welsh fella whipped out of the southern hemisphere, and Will Cuddihy in Limerick. I would always do Cork, so Aidan O'Connell has been there for an awful long part of my career and he understands me. He gets me. He's great for me. He does the science behind it, the theoretical and practical side of it, and Bryce is the Aussie master planner. These are the boys who came up with Project Maldini. Due to the age profile in Munster, they went to Italy to research the AC Milan team, the club Paolo Maldini famously played for until he was forty-one, after which we were all given folders and handouts – essentially a bible on how to prolong your career and how to excel.

But this day, by the time we arrived the forwards had gone into another room and the backs were in the changing-room waiting to go through their analysis meeting. 'Sorry boys,' I said, but it was fine: it was on the button of 4.15 and they hadn't started. We went through the five key areas we felt were important going into the game.

I'd spotted Fla – Jerry Flannery – lingering in Thomond Park when I came in and I knew he wasn't there to watch training. There was a break with tradition in that he presented the jerseys to us, in the media room, and it was powerful, as he is, because Jerry is a special person. He's crazy, but his key attribute is that he got huge reward out of Munster. He loves Munster. He was good to listen to, particularly for the younger fellas. He gave Tommy O'Donnell a good plug. Having seen the shit the younger players had had to put up with all year, they showed him what they could do against Harlequins, and now that they had the momentum they had to keep it going. He could see fellas like Killer (David Kilcoyne), Mike Sherry, Varley and O'Donnell growing in the jersey. He spoke for five or six minutes, and he'd obviously done a fair bit of research.

Jerry is convincing. He leaves you in no doubt. He's not saying it for the sake of it. He genuinely believes in what he's saying, which is very important. I think when you see that you appreciate it. He would have had at least a couple more big years in him with Munster, had the calf injuries not ended his career. When he was injured before the Lions tour in '09 he was the best hooker in Europe, and so much of it was down to hard work. I can remember years and years ago when I used to go to Con to practise my kicking. The weather might have been horrible but he was throwing balls up against the post, and this was before he was even playing for UCC. It smacked of a Junior 2 player. A brutal day, but serious determination.

I think he is all right though because he's thriving in retirement with Barry Murphy and Ian Dowling. They were the three boys that drove standards in Limerick, along with John Hayes, Axel, Quinny and David Wallace. It was so competitive and they were the three new guys – Mossie Lawlor was in the mix as well – that challenged the older fellas. They were so passionate about it, and they still train together nearly every day. Jerry loves himself so Jerry's doing it to look good! But it's like an old club, and it's nice to see.

Now that I'm retired from playing, I'd say I'll miss being fit as much as anything. I get itchy. I just have to go training. That's something you have to keep because you'd be surprised how quickly you waste away. I'd be keen enough to train anyway but you've got to find something as an outlet or a reason – perhaps an old club like that.

I love training, but in the gym I'm not the most explosive or the strongest or the fastest, so I always have to be nearly at my competitive best to find a way to cheat or train, to try and keep up with the rest of them. When a ball came into it, that's when I came into my own. Still, I loved the raw training. The boys would kill me in a one-off endurance run, but by reps four or five I'd have them rowed in.

After Jerry's presentation, training was very frustrating because we had a few changes in the squad from the Harlequins game. Training in Cork on Wednesday had been a very average session. Some players didn't know the calls, didn't know their roles, and I was finding that very hard to accept, but I could see why they didn't because they hadn't been in the team for a while. One of the good things our coach Rob Penney does is ensure that the twenty-three-man squad virtually get equal reps. It wrecks my head because I want the first fifteen to get it right first, but I can see exactly what needs to be done to run a team. The 'run-ons', as he calls the replacements, will have their chance, but it was sloppy.

Ironically, against Harlequins, apart from Donncha O'Callaghan replacing Donnacha Ryan, we didn't use our bench until the 76th minute, and I agreed with the use of the bench in that game – I thought it was perfect. I might have questioned why Munster had signed up BJ Botha for two years but I was reminded in that match that he's a big-game player. I love that in BJ. I was proud of him. I've huge respect for him as a result of that because, like everything else, your memory some-times needs to be jolted, and the proof is doing it in the big games.

Training that Thursday was shit, and then when I kicked there was a tricky bloody wind and that was wrecking my head a bit. Knowing it was my last kicking session before the game I stayed out there longer than I needed to.

Tony McGahan was big on the content of the week and how you train and how that leads to a good performance, but I don't really see that in Irish people. I don't think it really applies because the great thing about the Heineken Cup is that an animal comes out on match day and you need to keep that coiled a little. In saying that, though, I think you need to be hitting 80 per cent every time. You never hit 100 per cent, but if you can have your general standards above, say, 70 per cent you're in the right zone. We weren't anywhere near even 70 per cent that week.

We trained until about seven p.m. and that night we went to the Cornstore in Limerick for a meal. I didn't pick any social clothes so they were all laughing at me. I was in a black track-suit and a black hoodie and black runners. They were very comfortable but they looked like they came off the side of the street. But I'd no problem with that. 'Jesus, I never knew the Heineken Cup semi-final was an all-social event, lads!' I was slagging the younger fellas. They were all done up – skinny T-shirts, jeans, all the gel in and everything. A gas crew. They began to call me Monty, from *The Simpsons*. Monty Burns, the oul frail fella. They were getting a great kick out of it, Conor Murray, Killer, Sherry, all those fuckers, calling me Monty. They came up with it in Irish camp when they called Paddy Jackson Smithers, Monty's personal assistant. It's good humour. I don't watch *The Simpsons* so I didn't have a clue. I Googled it and said, 'Ah for fuck's sake, lads!' So they think I'm old and frail. They probably have a point.

It was random tables, and I had Simon Mannix, Dougie and Paulie nearest at our table of ten. I had prawns in piri piri sauce, recommended by Mr O'Connell, and then the fillet steak. Prawns followed by steak – you can't go wrong, although the night before a game I wouldn't have a steak, I'd have the fish or chicken, and always chicken on match day. I won't miss chicken on match days. Paulie opened the batting with, 'Well Dougie, what's he up to?' Meaning me. 'What's he going to do about next year?' and stuff. So there was a bit of slagging, but we talked mainly about Paulie's wedding.

I roomed with Dougie. Early to bed, by 10.30, and got a good sleep.

Friday, 26 April

Up early enough, a good breakfast, and out to Shannon. There was a big crowd at the airport heading to the game. Garrett Fitzgerald, the chief executive, texted me before the flight – 'Call in to me Monday, we must talk', or something. On the flight over I sat beside Keith Earls and Ian Keatley and I had a great chat with Earls. I've a big soft spot for him. He's still young, honest and humble, and still a little insecure. Criticisms had got to him. I'd love to work on Earlsy over the summer, and if I wasn't going into coaching I'd manage all these players.

I had a heart-to-heart with him. The talk then was of Zebo, Murray and Peter O'Mahony for the Lions. Earlsy was not even being mentioned. He was a Lion four years ago and he's at a better age now. Is he a better player than Zebo at the minute? No, he's not, but does he have the capability? Without a doubt. I think he's so good that he'll be played anywhere, and that's no good to him. He's literally international class in five positions: inside and outside centre, both wings and 15. That's the reality of it. He's the one fella that troubles Brian every time in training when he plays there and I haven't seen anyone else do that. He just has that searing acceleration that no other player has. You can play with plenty of width in your game with him as a 13 because you can throw him a missed pass and he can whip it again.

What frustrates me is that Earlsy doesn't always translate his training form to matches, whereas someone like Danny Barnes is a way better player than trainer. People talk about Earlsy's passing at 13 but Earlsy has lovely width on his pass. Earlsy's passing would be as good as Drico's. We haven't seen it enough in matches but I think he's on the road back. Watch Earlsy under Joe Schmidt and we will see what I saw every day in training. This guy will be a superstar.

That's what I find anyway with people when they address an issue; you can find a solution but not if you brush it under the carpet. Earlsy opened up, because he is always honest, and I was telling him that I wouldn't be playing on.

'Oh Jeezus, Rog, no, no.'

I said, 'No, Earlsy, I think I'm done.'

'It'll be very odd without you here.'

I said, 'Yeah, well, I know, but hopefully now we'll have a fine week.'

'Yeah, come on,' he said, 'we'll get our shit together.'

We arrived in Montpellier around noon. Our hotel was grand. They don't mean anything to me any more. Had lunch, and then it was a bit of a journey to the ground. It was wet, and I was thinking, 'Jesus, I've two pairs of boots but I didn't bring my bloody studs.' I hadn't brought the steel-capped blades and it was worrying me: the pitch was lovely but there had been a lot of rain on it the day before and there was more forecast for the morning of the match. I was like, 'Oh fuck, what am I after doing here?'

As I got older I tended not to practise kicking on travel days because I felt it took too much out of me. When I kick, I like to kick at match intensity, which means it takes me a bit longer to warm up. Also, I've had a chronic nerve issue in my right glute for about six months. I can't shake it. It's perfect on game days because of the adrenalin, but I didn't kick the day before Harlequins and I didn't in Montpellier. I went there and did my mental imagery and my visualization. You can genuinely pick out targets. The posts are big targets themselves, but I like to pick my own. In Montpellier they had tiles behind the goal way up, and the higher the target the easier it actually is. 'Beautiful, I have them now for tomorrow, boxed off.'

For the line kicking, the stand was quite far back. It's easier when the stands are closer to the sidelines. You always have to aim much higher than you think. If I was looking to kick a drill spiral (I suppose the ones I'm good at) at, say, the height of a door, my eyeline would probably be nearly twice the height to get that carry. So if you had a kick on the ten-yard line or halfway line you'd nearly be looking at the crown of the stadium to get more travel. It's something I've learnt as I've gone along.

We'd been getting huge return out of restarts all season, with the focus on trying to win the ball back. It's great having players like Felix Jones, Tommy O'Donnell and Paulie O'Connell and we have five different zones across the pitch for a twelve-yard kick so I just say to them, 'Who's going after this one?' and then it's instinct on the day. So that was the kicking done.

Paulie called us in and we went down the pitch and went through strategies and all our mental 'prep' in terms of plays here, plays there, and that was smooth. Then it was back on the bus into Montpellier. Some of us went for a stroll but there were fans everywhere so we just had a coffee and returned to the hotel.

Considering we arrived there only that day, it was a bloody long build-up to the game. We were nervous. I was nervous. A lot of players were nervous. Damien Varley and myself were chatting. The game itself wasn't until six p.m. local time the next day so there was plenty of time, and it was also dragging because we knew we could get thrashed. That's what Clermont can do to you. But when Munster have that fear factor we always play our best. It was just a case of trying to kill time.

Paulie spoke that night at the team meeting and dropped the bombshell that he still only had a slight chance of playing. I knew because he had told me, and when we returned to the hotel after coffee Rob Penney had called me aside.

'Paulie could be doubtful so in relation to the captaincy I've two options, you and Peter O'Mahony, and I'm thinking you've so much on your plate that Peter would be a good choice.'

I said, 'I haven't even thought about it, Rob. I'm happy with that.'

And he went, 'All right, cool. Thanks.'

Rob then grabbed myself, Paulie, Peter, Murray and Donnacha Ryan and said, 'You are the drivers of the team. If Paulie is out, Donnacha, you will be calling the line-outs. Peter will be captain. Rog, you'll be running the show, so, Conor, you need to take responsibility.'

It was good, and then just at the end Paulie said, 'To be honest, I'm fifty-fifty, lads. I don't know.' That would be a killer blow for us, a psychological boost for Clermont. It was too much, especially with Donncha out.

I watched Stade Français away to Perpignan in the Amlin Challenge Cup semi-final that night. Our former team-mate Mafs – Lifeimi Mafi – was carving it up, and the camera zoomed in on the president of Stade Français, Thomas Savare, who was in the crowd. Through Diego Dominguez there had been discussions with Stade about me joining their coaching staff. I thought to myself, 'Jesus, I must make contact with him.'

I guess that was the beginning of the end.

CHAPTER 2

The Magnificent Obsession

Wednesday, 15 May

All the Munster lads know by now, but I need to finalize my plans for the 2013/14 season before I announce my retirement. I'm trying to rule things in and out. I've left it late but I'm not too worried. Something will turn up, but I definitely won't be playing again. No second thoughts. I'm very happy in my decision. Garrett Fitzgerald is hunting me down but I told him that even if he offered me half a million only then maybe I'd have a decision to make. But it genuinely isn't a financial issue. The exit is nearly as important as the previous sixteen years, and I believe now is a perfect time to go.

I won't be having a formal retirement party. There have been enough end-of-season events anyway. Last Friday we had the Munster annual awards lunch in the Maryborough House Hotel. Great venue, great staff, and emails had been circulating in advance. This was going to be a big one. There were two players per table and myself and Scott Deasy were paired with the Hall of Fame table. Liam Coughlan of Cork Con won that and he had all his buddies with him. We were slagging and messing, although as Liam's wife was there the stories had to be tamed.

Simon Zebo won Young Player of the Year and Tommy O'Donnell won Player of the Year. In his acceptance speech Tommy admitted that if somebody had told him the previous October he'd be standing there receiving that award he wouldn't have believed them. He had to bide his time behind other back-row forwards like Dave Wallace, and Dave Wallace is an unbelievable player. We'll rarely see his like again.

He was a freak, but David trained his arse off too. People don't see that. They think of him as a nice guy, which he is, but he's as focused as any player I've ever known. In pre-season training no one paid more attention to detail. His fitness tests were more extensive than for any Test match because I think he needed to prove to himself that he was very quick, very powerful and very strong, and then the rugby side of his game followed from that. I'd focus more on the ball and skill and vision, but that's what makes rugby so great. You've all shapes, sizes and mentalities.

This was the first end-of-season awards without David. All the current squad were in attendance – in Munster suits – and we agreed that we'd keep the formal wear for the races afterwards. Paulie and a few others were moving on to Mike Prendergast's going-away party – he's coach in Grenoble now – but twenty-five of us took a bus from the Maryborough to Mallow racecourse, all the young fellas with their shades on of course. The place was dead. Empty. No one around. I organized the top level for some finger food and a few pints. Flat racing isn't the most interesting. The jumps are more exciting, and last longer too.

We met Dermot Weld, Tommy Stack, Tom Hogan, Joe Murphy and all the trainers, as well as Eimear Mulhearn, Charlie Haughey's daughter, who has a stud farm up the country. I know the head lad there, Buzzer (that's what he's in the phone as), who was involved in Kevin Prendergast's yard and now works for her.

Kanturk had won the Munster Junior Club of the Year and Pat Geraghty, who was running the show, thought going there would be a good idea. He's a beauty, and great fun with a few glasses of wine. 'C'mon, lads, we have to do this. We have to do this.' We were well up for it. We had a sing-song on the way from Mallow (it's about twenty minutes to Kanturk). Mike Sherry's song was so bad he was thrown off the bus. He took Billy Holland with him, and the two boys were left at the side of the road. We thought it was hilarious, but the two of them were sipping pints in the Alley Bar when we arrived. They'd hitched a lift in the back of a lorry box from the horse trainer Eugene O'Sullivan. We were treated like kings. Pints, pizzas, kebabs, burgers – an unbelievable feast.

On to the bus and back into town to the Castle Bar, a traditional pub with a snug. A few of the boys went to my pub, Bob Fox's off Washington Street. I own a third of it with two buddies, John O'Driscoll and Michael O'Flynn. We went on to Riordans, a night club, for lashings of pints, where I had the bright idea we'd all go back to my place. The boys went through the twenty-four-hour McDonald's en route and brought back a good feed to the house, and we opened a few bottles of whiskey and vodka. There was a mixed bag: Donnacha Ryan,

Casey Laulala, Zeebs, myself, Felix Jones, Wian du Preez, CJ Stander, Dave Kilcoyne and Sean Scanlon. Casey, a great man for the beats and for a party, was on the iPod. I bailed out at about seven a.m. I think Donnacha and Casey were the last two standing.

Jess came down with Molly at around five in the morning. Jess is cool about stuff like that, but Molly was shocked that people were in her house with their feet on the counter. But I knew it was my last big shindig with them.

Looking back, Munster is unrecognizable from when I started. The improvements have been slow and gradual. I first sat on the bench for Munster in 1997 against Connacht in Temple Hill, and with each and every passing year it has become bigger. The interest in rugby in Ireland now is incredible. That wasn't the case back then. I'd say they'd have been lucky if a thousand were at that Connacht game.

Ireland were always well supported, but the provincial game has become so competitive that there has just been a huge buy into it. As with Ireland, there's probably a warped sense of reality about Munster too, but the most pleasing achievement for me is ten semi-finals. That takes serious consistency of performance. I remember chatting with Brian O'Driscoll about this. What's most important for me is that we were part of the first group to do something. We were part of the first Munster team to win the European Cup. It showed the other provinces what was possible; it's the same winning Triple Crowns and a Grand Slam. Maybe it sounds a bit cocky, but from a purely selfish point of view, to be part of those breakthroughs, to be one of the trailblazers – it was the best of times.

We took it very seriously and accepted massive responsibility for our performances but it wasn't easy. I would have taken it all very personally. There would have been times when I hated myself, or hated a TV pundit if there was personal criticism of me. That's the depth of feeling I had for the game. The perspective from outside is very different. People from outside aren't aware of the team's tactics, or the approach they want to take to a game. There's also a human side to it. Some days you feel great and others you don't feel so great, yet commentators make no allowance for that. There were times when I was very close to saying, 'I'm done with this. I don't fucking need this hassle. This is killing me.'

I suppose the big thing for me over my career is that every time I played I felt I had a direct influence. I could chat to Brian about this as well. In some games, by the nature of his position as a 13 even Brian mightn't have that much influence. But every single time an out-half has to analyse his game, and especially his kicking. And I had bad games. I know it too well. By God, I had them, but I think I could always come back from a bad game, or bad moments in a game, and produce a positive out-come in the next play or the next match. That's what fuelled my love for the game.

In 2000, moments after losing the Heineken Cup final in Twickenham, the entire squad gathered in a circle on the pitch. I can picture being in that circle perfectly to this day, and my memory is poor enough. But that was incredible sport, and that was the start of it. I remember it so well primarily because we were beaten and I had essentially cost us the game. That's the reality for a kicker. I'd missed four kicks at goal, including a tricky one late on to win it, and I didn't have anything like the leg strength I'd have now. I was a talented kicker but I hadn't yet established a bulletproof technique. Whatever Deccie or Gaillimh or anyone else said in that huddle I'll never know, because I was in a world of my own. I was devastated.

Even though Northampton had won, the ground broke into 'The Fields of Athenry'. It takes a special mindset to do that. It wouldn't be done now because our standards are way higher, but at that time it was a hugely significant and inspiring moment for the road ahead. If the crowd had gone sour that day, that could have been the end of the Munster story. Instead, that was the moment when the magnificent obsession started. From that day on we had to win a Heineken Cup.

Other people may not like this, but Munster have made the Heineken Cup, because they gave it such impetus. We've targeted it every year, and while ultimately we've had our success and our rewards, what's been hugely satisfying from my point of view is that we've constantly been there or thereabouts. You can live with yourself as a professional if you have been contenders every year. Ten semi-finals, in such a prestigious competition!

We've been unlucky too when you consider we've been drawn away in seven of those semi-finals, and that six of them have been in France – Toulouse (2000), Stade Français (2001), Castres (2002), Toulouse again (2003), Biarritz (2010) and Clermont (2013). You can be sure that if we played Clermont not even in the Aviva but in a truly neutral venue such as Geneva, where we played Bourgoin one year, we might have had five thousand more fans present, and Clermont might have had five thousand fewer. In that scenario there'd be a better chance of that attack near the Clermont line at half-time leading to a penalty, and with those three points we could have kicked the penalty with four minutes remaining to force extra time. These are the little things that matter. I know one incident in a game doesn't define the scoreline, but at home you do get the rub of the green. That's the reality. Referees are human beings. As much as we like to think that they're not, they are influenced by crowds. It's happened to our benefit in Thomond Park before.

The primary reason for our success has been the quality of player, allied to a huge desire to do well for your home province. Over a sustained period of time Munster has without doubt been the best-supported rugby club in the world. The passion of the fans, the Limerick people especially, can come only from a real love of rugby. The biggest compliment I can give them is that they accepted me as one of their own. They don't necessarily do that for Cork people!

The new Thomond is a legacy for all those who played a part during those years, but the old Thomond was a fortress. It suited Munster. It was grey. Teams didn't like coming there. The terracing around three sides of the ground, and even in front of the stand, intensified the team's support. Health and safety and fire regulations weren't such a consideration in those days. The new stand is completely different. The playing surface is better though. I had issues with the old pitch, and due to the Heineken Cup's growth we've played on some very good soccer surfaces. The game is so different on a soccer pitch. Generally the grass is shorter and, as any kicker will tell you, that makes kicking so much easier.

When I made my Heineken Cup debut away to Harlequins we were playing against superstars, Keith Wood among them. We wore O'Neills tracksuits back then. That was a young Munster team formed from the best All-Ireland League club players. The Munster model, as it would become, had not yet been established. There had been serious history in the province with one-off wins against touring teams but this was different and people were unsure how it would work out – a full-time professional set-up with players sacrificing jobs in banks and so forth for relatively modest rewards. My first contract in 1997/98 was 7,500 a year. From there it rose to 18K, and then to 27,500.

For all the quality players we had, success wouldn't have been possible without a good coaching set-up. Deccie was the head coach, Niall O'Donovan did the forwards and 'Holl' – Jerry Holland – was the manager. A slimline staff by today's standards, but that was the norm then, and they were three shrewd rugby brains and three passionate Munstermen. They made us feel good about what we were doing. They were a local and highly ambitious young management team. Deccie's preparation would be meticulous. Niall had all the skills and winning mentality of playing and coaching with Shannon. The AIL was a serious league and he had the Munster pack humming in those years. Holl had presence as a manager. We were afraid of him and I think that's always the best way. He was a gentleman, but what Holl said stood and you didn't question him. If he said it, you did it. End of.

I was a young fella and, I would like to think, respectful. I mostly kept my mouth shut, and rightly so, because I was still very much a junior player in the pecking order. I wouldn't question authority. You watched the senior players and how they operated, and everything seemed to be running smoothly, so you made sure that you weren't late and you had high standards.

There was terrific talent, in the pack especially: Axel, Wally, Quinny, Halvey, Gaillimh and Claw – prop Peter Clohessy – with Paulie and Donncha to come through. Fester – Keith Wood – was a big factor that year in bringing more professionalism to the organization. But Woody, to be fair, knows that he's done only one year in Munster. He knows relatively little about Munster. You have to be within the four walls more than a year to know exactly how a place operates.

Woody definitely helped raise standards. His attitude to training was impressive. He came from a much more professional and confident set-up in Harlequins and that gave our players more belief to kick on in the year he was there because he was, in truth, the figurehead. He was a very important player in our game. Every team needs one, probably two, and preferably three or more big carriers. That season, Woody, Wally and Mikey Mullins were the three players who regularly gave us go-forward ball. But still I think it's an accurate assessment to say that Woody knows very little about Munster.

I was fortunate too in that my early career coincided with the most professional player of that era – Dominic Crotty. He was the first player to be offered a national contract and he took me under his wing. I had a bicycle and he had a moped, and on week nights we met up in the Mardyke for him to practise his catching from my kicking. What we're doing nowadays, Dominic was doing fifteen years ago. The only flipside of his search for perfection was an element of paralysis by analysis, but what an attitude. No one had a bigger influence on me in those early years until I went on the Lions tour in 2001 and witnessed Jonny Wilkinson's work ethic.

They weren't just good players in Munster, they were good characters too. I don't think a young player could have experienced a more honest or welcoming dressing-room. At that stage we were having pints after games and some fellas wanted to continue on Sundays, but some of us younger players realized that if you wanted to make the cut, you had to cut that out.

The slagging was merciless and the craic constant. You never got above your station, and the older guys were ruthless in that sense, but it wasn't excessive. Fisticuffs were rare because although the line of respect was pushed on many occasions, it was never overstepped. That's a subtle difference. It was taken to the max plenty of times but that line of respect among players was always maintained.

As well as being a turning point, the 2000 final was also a reference point. What we all learned most from Twickenham in 2000 was that by the time we got to the final we were emotionally drained; we had overestimated the size of the task as opposed to continuing what we had been doing. But none of us had had any experience of that before. You live and learn.

The lessons for me would take longer to sink in, but were hammered home two years later in New Zealand, when Ireland played two Tests with the so-called 'pig' – a yellow adidas ball. Andrew Mehrtens and myself actually talked about that 'pig' after the Clermont game. I kicked poorly on that NZ tour. It was very cold and wet, and the ball wasn't good, but we could have beaten them. I went on holiday with Jess after, but about four days in I nearly had a breakdown because I couldn't think of anything bar rugby and I was just waiting for the first game of the 2002/03 season. I wanted to kick to get those performances out of my head. I had to ring Keith Wood from the lounger in Crete.

I remember his exact words. 'Rog, you've got to address this. You've got to establish a technique that you know will work. If you brush this under the carpet it will come back to haunt you in a semi-final or final again.' Woody was the Irish captain and I was probably reaching out for some comforting words of security and assurance, but he gave it to me straight between the eyes: 'You've just got to address this. You've got to work on it.' They were wise words. He was coming from the perspective of having mastered a specialist skill, and he would have had issues with his line-out throwing too, so I could relate to him as well.

By then Munster had lost a second Heineken Cup final, but in some ways the 2002 defeat to Leicester in Cardiff was far easier to accept because it felt like we played in that final, whereas the Northampton game was there for the taking and should have been won. We came up against a good Leicester team that day. We had chances but Leicester were a better team than Northampton and it was a far better game, a far higher standard. As difficult as defeat was, it didn't feel like you'd left it behind you, and as a sportsman that is easier to accept.

Besides, who knows, had Munster won the Heineken Cup in 2000 it's conceivable that the players and fans would have been not only sated but bloated. The pain of that defeat spurred us on for years afterwards. I also think Munster were different from every other team back then in that we were playing with friends. We genuinely cared about each other.

Admittedly it's a difficult subject for me to comment on because I'm a one-club man, but there have definitely been times, in latter years, when I've felt that the whole thing has become diluted. It's become dominated by people who aren't from the province, and I think that needs to be addressed. There are some great rugby brains in Munster yet at times we're happy to pass the coaching responsibility to outside coaches. Maybe they are the best, but there should always be a strong local manager and at least 50 per cent of the coaches should be if not local then Irish, men who are in touch with the history and understand the ethos.

As significant as any coach in our finally winning two Heineken Cups in '06 and '08 was the emergence of new young players. Jerry Flannery, Ian Dowling and Barry Murphy added an impetus, raising standards in training and everything else off the pitch. Foley, Wally, Quinny, John Hayes and Marcus Horan were established, but the younger brigade drove it on. They probably antagonized the older people but that got the best out of them. Jerry is full of self-belief, and that rubbed off on people around him.

I can remember walking out on the pitch in the Millennium Stadium for the '06 final and players were calm. Paulie said, 'Lads, we can't just go and play. We've got to go and win this.' Simple, calm words, but there's a difference between going out to play and going out to win, and that was evident in the Harlequins and Clermont games in 2012/13. We attacked Harlequins, whereas we waited to see what Clermont had.

Strange as it may sound, we attacked Biarritz in the '06 final in the Millennium Stadium yet within two minutes Sireli Bobo scored in the corner and Dimitri Yachvili converted from the touchline. Seven points – that's a big start to give a team, especially after losing two finals. Yet there comes a stage in your career when you believe, 'I have more to give than the opposition on this day'.

Sometimes too you reach a crossroads. 'Are you pretenders or are you going to be taken seriously?' Most of us had been going well for both Munster and Ireland, and been on Lions tours, but you've got to win something if you want to be considered a winner, and we hadn't. In '06 it was a case of 'this year or get off the stage because you're a fraud'. That was exactly our thinking. There is no point in being a journeyman, or a collection of nearlymen, all your career. That's what we were in danger of becoming. It's all about winners' medals.

Maybe after winning it in 2006 we fell in love with ourselves. We had a shocking season in 2007, although at least we had the capability to turn it around again, because to have won it only once would have been an underachievement.

Beating Toulouse in the '08 final was the best day of my career in a Munster jersey. When you beat a team like Toulouse, or any of the other giants of the competition, you know you've tested yourselves against the very best. We had won a group containing Wasps (then the European champions) and Clermont before beating Gloucester and Saracens away in the quarters and semis. We were proper European champions that year.

There's competition to get on the team within Munster, so to have been the Munster number 10 for such a long period is enormously satisfying. That entails a huge amount of preparation, and I do prepare well. I make no secret of that. You set goals for yourself. You set training sessions for yourself. You watch training. You watch where you can find weaknesses in the opposition and you take satisfaction from that because these things don't happen by accident. I always remember my mum telling me that 'you get out of it what you put into it', and I've invested a lot into my career and got a massive return. And that's probably why it's so easy to walk away.

I have played 110 Heineken Cup games, but that's a reflection on Munster; I'm just a small part of the story. I've played more games for Munster in the Heineken Cup than any other player and scored more points than any other player in the competition's history. I was fortunate to play for sixteen years, and it wasn't as if I was given a hard time. I received plenty of compliments and was honoured as the best player in the first fifteen years of the competition. I'm not going to lie: that really does give me massive satisfaction. But it's a team game, and that's what I enjoy the most. In Munster you have so much craic, enjoyment and satisfaction because of who you're playing with, as opposed to, say, playing with a rich French team. Though I should be careful what I say here!

I thought about leaving Munster, but I never had to think too long about it. I'm absolutely delighted that I played my whole career there because I think loyalty is an important trait. I was one of the senior players, and I suppose a strong personality too, along with other people as motivated as me, so if I had walked away, what kind of an example would I have set?

Munster challenged me in every way but I always felt it was going in the right direction because of the players, coaches and management we had, as well as the set-up and our supporters. To go anywhere else would have been a backward step for me, and certainly would not have been as rewarding.

Even though it rankles, I suppose I shouldn't be too hard on myself or my team-mates or my coaches for having won only two Heineken Cups. We came from so little, from humble origins, and we were part of the original journey, from 1997 to 2006. That first cup was a decade in the making. Everybody who contributed was part of that journey, not just the twenty-three in the '06 match-day squad. It's like the first landing on the moon. Everyone knows the first man to do so was Neil Armstrong; but who knows the names of those who paved the way, and how many can recall the names of all those who sub-sequently walked on the moon? Nowadays, for the Rob Kearneys, the Sean O'Briens, the Johnny Sextons and Keith Earlses, it's expected of them. For those players and the supporters, to have and to maintain such high expectations requires an awful lot of groundwork, preparatory graft to bloody convince yourself that you're going to be good enough to take on the best of the English and the French. But to boldly go where no other team has gone before in the history of the competition is why it's so special.

Moving into the 2008/09 season, Dumper – Tony McGahan – moved up from defensive coach to take over from Declan Kidney. We were the kings of Europe. We breezed through the pool stages. We absolutely filleted a good Ospreys team 43–9 in the quarter-final in Thomond Park. That week eight Munster players were selected in the Lions squad. But then we ran into Leinster in the semi-finals in Croke Park – a day which marked a shift in the balance of power.

Munster were never quite the same again, until this year. After a decade of almost continuous progress it was a tough period to go through, especially losing in Toulon in 2011 and not qualifying for the knockout stages for the first time in thirteen years. That was low, very low. We were stuffed, hammered all over the field, and as in the semi-final defeat to Biarritz the year before, we underperformed in several key areas. Aside from everything else that flows from the scrums, that hands a massive psychological advantage to the dominant team.

To a degree a great team had grown old together but our confidence was affected too, and Leinster winning three Heineken Cups in four years added to that. We were the old story and Leinster were the new story, which is fair enough, and the only way you change that is by doing something worthwhile on the pitch. Many of our players are only learning that now. Why would the media talk about us? We hadn't even been playing well. I told the lads, 'It's up to us to turn this around. You have a massive opportunity.'

There was possibly an over-reaction in the response to our win over Harlequins this year. We hadn't become a great team overnight. Sixth place in the Rabo doesn't lie, and furthermore had we performed better in the Rabo I genuinely think we would have beaten Clermont. It was too low a base, doubts were lingering in a few players, and that kills you. Yet fellas grew inches after beating Harlequins, and the performance against Clermont backed that up to a degree. These games have generated a feelgood factor and I think the respect is back among the supporters – and they determine the mood around here.

A favourite Munster game? I've loads of them. In January 2001 we beat Newport in Rodney Parade 39–24 and I scored twenty-four points. I enjoyed Wasps in Thomond Park, when I first introduced the banana kick. They're the kind of things I get a buzz off. When you practise skills, you want them to come good in a game, and it was against Lawrence Dallaglio. I like Lawrence because he took me under his wing on the 2001 Lions tour. He's an impressive person. And I didn't miss a kick in either of the two Heineken Cup-winning finals, which is important when your team is relying on you.

Unfortunately the bad days stand out more than the good ones, because losing is such a horrible feeling. It's more relief when you win, which is strange, but it means so much because you invest so much in it; when you lose you genuinely feel like it's the end of the world. That's tempered when you have a family. You have less time to think about a defeat or a bad day at work because you've other bodies in the house and other entertainment to take care of.

There have been countless unsung heroes too, like Aki Mullins, the ex-Garryowen hooker who cleans the changing-rooms. Fellas like him are key elements of Munster's success. He's a Limerick man. He's so passionate about it. If we lose, he's nearly still in tears on a Monday. He's been around all my career. Despite the advent of professionalism his core values haven't changed. He's sharp in his analysis about players and can detect the dynamics of the coaching team from afar, and spot trouble.

Jack Kiely is the bag man for the senior team and Aki for the A team. When we arrive at the University of Limerick for training, Aki is directing the car parking. In Thomond Park he used to make the soup and the stew after games before losing the contract when the new Thomond Park opted for fancier catering. But it was great that he was brought back in at the rugby level.

You can be sure that if there was a fella having pints giving out about one of the Munster players somewhere, Aki would jump in and put manners on him. He'd stick up for us if he knew the player was putting it in, although he wouldn't be shy about telling a player if he didn't think he was pulling his weight.

I'm not walking away from all this as worried about the future as I might have been a year or two ago. I think we need a few backs coming through, but there are some really good young players who have matured nicely. Admittedly there'll be a shift now that I'm not in the backs, but when Paulie goes that will be huge. His intellectual ability and game understanding, let alone the levels of passion and emotion he brings to the table, are irreplaceable.

I've played a few games with Ian Nagle, Paulie's potential replacement, and he looks impressive. He just needs to present himself fit and willing to train hard every day. Some of the younger fellas seem to think that you can jump from here to there as Conor Murray has done, but he's an exception to the rule. Usually it's a case of little solid building blocks and continual improvements, as Tommy O'Donnell has done. Especially in Munster, because the standard is so high you don't want average players getting games on the first team. That is the harsh reality.

Dougie Howlett has also confirmed his retirement, yet I believe Munster will win another Heineken Cup. I see enough ability there for a coaching team to make them one of the best teams in Europe again. I can't say they'll definitely win one, but I believe Munster, with the players they have, will be challenging within a few seasons. They are going to need a 10 who gets some big-game experience over the next eighteen months, but Earlsy, Zebo and Felix will be huge players for Munster, and there are all kinds of opportunities for Andrew Conway, coming from Leinster. Most importantly, though, the pack is strong. Essentially you could win a Heineken Cup, believe me, playing cup rugby with a strong 1 to 10.

Many of them have some learning to do and some maturing to go through, but I think in two years they'll be different animals altogether. Maybe I'll be back to coach them one day. If I like it and I'm good at it. If I don't and I'm not, I won't.

CHAPTER 3

The Balance of Power

Leinster were hanging on for dear life at one stage. We nearly scored twice in the first ten minutes alone. But as Brian has since confirmed to me, after years of pain at the hands of Munster, they'd suffered so much before that 2009 Heineken Cup semi-final that they'd simply had enough. I admire that.

From that day, Leinster have been dominant, even if it doesn't feel like they're ahead in some ways (in part because, as I said, I am convinced Munster will win another Heineken Cup). Since our two Heineken Cup wins they have claimed three, yet it's still only been four years. They had double that amount of hurt, from 2000 to 2008, and I now have some idea how they felt.

When we met in our first semi-final in '06 they were threatening to reach the mountain top before us. We were expecting Toulouse to beat them in France but Leinster produced an unbelievable quarter-final. That Croke Park semi-final was the biggest pressure game I've probably ever played. The build-up took over the airwaves and there was real uncertainty going into that match. But we did a job on them, even if that wasn't reflected until the last ten minutes.

Leinster always had cracking players, and by 2009 they'd also had nearly a decade of listening to us. That's a long time. In '09 we thought we could simply turn up and beat them, and they hockeyed us. Unless your attitude is spot on in this game you get hammered, which is what happened to us that day. We had eight Lions, strength in depth from 1 to 15, we were all playing really good rugby and we were all excited, which just underlines how the game is full of ups and downs. Leinster duly went on to become European champions.

They'd simply had enough of us being successful. As well as having seriously good players, they're proud. But it took them a long time to get their organization right, and given the quality of their players it should have happened much sooner. However, once they all bought into it they were always going to be a lethal province, and that's exactly what they are.

We had monopolized events for so long that when they beat us in Croke Park I suppose it shattered us. This was the start of their era under Michael Cheika, and Joe Schmidt turned out to be the ideal man to build on Cheika's foundations. They ensured Leinster never took their feet off our throats. Leinster's win that day kick-started a run of five successive wins over Munster during which we didn't even score a try. They not only went on to win their first Heineken Cup, defeating Leicester, but regained it two years later with a phenomenal comeback in the final against Northampton at the Millennium Stadium. When we hosted them in the Magners League final a week later *we'd* had enough of *them*, and it was a final in Thomond Park. If we were to retain any credibility, we had to win.

We'd watched Leinster the previous week. They were immense. Northampton's first-half performance was quite stunning, leaving Leinster 22–6 behind at half-time. We were thinking 'Northampton have this', but once Leinster came back into the game, you knew they would do it. They won 33–22. Had there been another ten minutes they could have reached 50.

Johnny Sexton has rarely played better, but out-halves depend on those around them and the systems in place. He is obviously a very good player but, as I know well, when all the systems and details are working, and everyone knows their role, and the game flows and the 10 is on the front foot, it's just a great game to play. That was exactly what he did, scoring two tries himself as well as having the character to speak up at half-time to convince them they could win. That's the sign of a mature player.

Watching that particular game – or any one of the three Leinster final wins we have been forced to watch in the five years since Munster last won the cup – always provokes mixed emotions. Brian is one of my best friends in the game, and I'd always be happy for certain individuals because all the lads in the Ireland squad are mates. I wouldn't be happy for Leinster though, because they are our intense rivals.

If I am to take any pride in what I do, I have to . . . not hate them, because that is too strong a word, but I have to outperform them, be prepared to do whatever that takes. Players are lying if they say they wish rival provinces well. I'd like to see certain people do well. I'd have fierce time for most of them and I consider a lot of them great fellas. But it's like Liverpool/Man United.

The rivalry with Leinster never soured relationships within the Irish squad, but has become poisonous between the supporters and perhaps also some of the non- or ex-internationals in both camps. The respect among the international players has remained, but for some individuals who don't play Test rugby things have become venomous. They are the drivers of the provinces in many ways, whose passion is total and admirable.

As professional players, you can't afford to care about what the supporters do or how they feel. We have to do the best we can for our team and be competitive but then put that aside when we come together for Ireland. What was really important, despite the state of affairs between Leinster and Munster – and indeed all the provinces – was how tight we became for the 2011 World Cup. That is the measure of the people within the national set-up. They would look to kill each other playing for Munster or Leinster, but when we come into Irish camp our bond has to be strong if we are to do well. In 2011 it was Team Ireland. Fellas treated each other like brothers, akin to a provincial set-up, and that wouldn't usually happen, to be honest. When the younger Leinster fellas came into camp and remained quiet at squad meetings, sometimes you'd wonder what they contributed in Leinster meetings. You can be sure they talked up more there, but if you want the Irish team to go forward you've got to share your ideas.

Before that World Cup, a week after watching Leinster's brilliant Heineken Cup final win against Northampton we had to do it for ourselves and for our fans: we knew how much they would suffer if we lost a League final at home to our main rivals. That would also mean Leinster completing a double – a huge achievement, and frankly one we had to ensure didn't happen.

They were operating at a really high level and it panned out like the 2009 game at Croke Park when we threw everything at them and they didn't break, except this time the roles were reversed: they threw everything at us and we didn't break. In another role reversal, we'd been huge favourites in '09 and they were probably favourites in this game.

Our main motivation that year, however, summed up what Munster is all about, for it's not only about the players but every single person within the organization. We've always had really good strength and conditioning coaches, and Paul Darbyshire was one of them. A terrific person, so positive, so energetic, a man who enjoyed life to the full. It always seems to be those people who are struck down early.

Only the good die young, as they say.

When Darbs first moved over he left his family in England, which was hard on him. He lived down the road from me with Brian Carney, who Munster signed from English rugby league – an extra special person as well. They were great company. We had them over for dinner once or twice a week and we'd also have breakfast after training and lunch together. Coming from rugby league they were so professional. Animal trainers, so we slagged them – some of it aided, and some unaided!

I can remember the day in Douglas, in June 2010, when Darbs rang me. He was crying and saying, 'I'm fucked, I'm fucked, I'm fucked. I got it, I got it.' He knew, from a twitch in his arm, that he had contracted the same disease his dad had passed away from, Motor Neurone Disease, so it was very raw with him. The confirmation came in September when we were in Glasgow for a Magners League game. As we walked through the city centre, he told me he definitely had it. It was a horrible,

horrible journey in the cold and rain. I'll never forget those dark and dreary streets of Glasgow. We just kept walking along the footpaths and talking because I don't think we could look at each other.

I knew he knew from his first consultation in the 'Bons' hospital in Cork. From just a twitch in his bicep, it accelerated aggressively to essentially leave him powerless. Many great people looked after him and he made it to that Magners League final in May 2011. At that stage his neck muscles were gone and he was in bad shape. To see such a big, strong, powerful man wiped out was horrible but he still had his sense of humour, and his iPad for communicating with us. He had his young boy Jack with him as well, so while it was great to win, the moment I put my hands on the wheelchair I felt that I wasn't at a game, which is strange, but these things put rugby in its place. It's sad that it usually takes a tragedy to do this. Alternatively it can be the birth of a child, as I realized when my kids were born. The game's important, but it's not nearly as important as life.

Darbs passed the following month at the age of thirty-nine.

As for the game itself, I recall making a good cross-kick for Earlsy, right to left, from which he scored. I had to work the ball out to him quickly so it was a bit of a rushed hack of a cross-kick but he caught it and stepped inside Shane Horgan and Isa Nacewa to score. (Not quite the quality of cross-kick for Shaggy's try at Croker against England in '07 – that was *the* cross-kick.) Dougie then scored a cracking try, and the pack had the satisfaction of signing off the game and the season with a penalty try off a scrum, which was a real feather in the cap for Hayes. As it was the last game of the season we had an almighty session, and as we'd finished it by winning a trophy, the next day we had another almighty session.

Axel always says that when you win, you have to celebrate for two or three days; you have to make it memorable. I agree with him, as this provides much of the motivation for staying off drink during the season – that you have a big one at the end of it, and all the more so if you win a trophy. Our mindset is like a child's, immature, but I don't make apologies to anyone. That's how we live our lives. That's our release. We don't get out much.

Winning the Magners League, or RaboDirect Pro12 as it's now labelled, certainly matters when you're out of Europe, and it becomes a serious salvage plan for the coaches! You only have to look at the 2013 Lions selection and note the number of Rabo players in the squad to appreciate it is a serious league. It's also very difficult to win outright. Winning it reflects as much as anything the strength of your squad.

The League provides ideal opportunities for mixing and matching players, and that's why they really need to see it as a massive opportunity to earn selection for Heineken Cup games. Playing in the Heineken Cup is more special – there's no point in saying otherwise – but, at the same time, if a club reaches a Rabo final and a European final, as Leinster have done for three years, they have to be in an unbelievably healthy state.

The League is the best breeding ground for the Heineken Cup. Tommy O'Donnell had forty or fifty Rabo games behind him when he made his Heineken Cup breakthrough last season, and then from there it can be a smaller step into the Test arena – as his Irish debut in America in June 2013 showed.

You have to have the Italians in the League. They're part of the Six Nations, and Treviso are a very good team. True, Zebre have struggled, although they're showing signs of moving forward, beating Cardiff Blues in Wales this year, but there are always teams at the bottom of any league table whom the leading sides are expected to beat but occasionally stumble against. Qualification for the Heineken Cup is a different issue, and the English and French have valid complaints, but there's no need to change the cup's pool structure or to tear the whole thing down.

Although we topped the table and won the final to claim that 2011 League title, Leinster remained top dogs by retaining the Heineken Cup in 2012, beating Ulster in the first ever all-Ireland final. To make matters worse, Ulster had beaten us en route at Thomond Park in the quarter-finals. They smashed us at the breakdown, and Ruan Pienaar's kicking was exemplary. He landed three outstanding kicks from inside the Ulster half. Two weeks later, out of the Heineken Cup, I watched Ulster against Connacht and he couldn't kick snow off a rope. 'You b******! Typical! Another big-game player. Why didn't you do that two weeks ago?'

Craig Gilroy scored that brilliant try to give them a 16–0 lead, and they are a dangerous team with a lead. He should never have been allowed to score; it was poor defence by us. The defeat didn't feel as bad as the Croke Park semi-final against Leinster in '09, but only because the first cut is the deepest. When it happens again the emotion isn't as raw.

Ulster were coming of age, and that win defined them as a good team, yet even though everything went for them and they led all the way, we still could have won. I kicked an important penalty at half-time and we went in thinking 'this can be done'. They're the games that define you, and what a comeback it would have been.

With half an hour to go we scored a good try in the corner through Zeebs, and my conversion from the touchline made it 16–10. One score. We were thinking 'this is it'.

Myself and Pienaar traded a couple more penalties but they kept us at arm's length and won 22–16. Some big calls went against us, and while 'playing the referee' has become a recurring theme, Romain Poite went through a sticky period with us for a good few months. Still, they were the better team on the day, so no excuses.

Jess was at the game with her mother and had brought Rua and Molly, and I asked them to wait for me in the car. I remember walking out of Thomond Park and the Ulster fans gave me the old 'Cheerio, cheerio, cheerio!' It was some low. I felt bad enough after the game. 'Oh, that's a new one. I must remember that one.' But sure if you give it you've got to take it.

There hadn't been as much of a rivalry with Ulster over the years because we used to beat them most of the time. Now that I'm finished I can appreciate their win was good in one way: you had a respect for them that wasn't there before. Up until then I suppose the general view of the Ulster players was that they were very cliquey, but actually they're really good fellas on their own. I'd like to think I have a strong relationship with Tom Court, Rory Best, Stephen Ferris, Paddy Wallace, Johnny Bell, David Humphreys, Andrew Trimble, Tommy Bowe and Paddy Wallace. Great fellas, all of them, and I really enjoyed training with Craig Gilroy and the freshness he brought to the Irish set-up.

Paddy Wallace, who has been in virtually every Irish camp since I started, is a very likeable fella. He's often misrepresented because certain journalists don't rate him, and that's become the general opinion, which is complete rubbish. Paddy learned early on from watching Munster players. He admitted he wasn't fit enough or strong enough, and didn't have the work rate. I think he reinvented himself and worked hard, which I admire in a professional. He wanted it badly. I think 12 suited him, although he needed a strong 10, and I personally enjoyed playing along-side him. You have to pump him up, but once you have him fired up he is brilliant. I'd like to think our dynamic worked very well. I would always have respected him as a player. A team could do things with him at 12 that mightn't be possible with other players, but he could be too quiet as a 10. This reflected his personality off the pitch, although he has a wicked sense of humour. He's a deep, very respectful individual, and I have huge time for him.

This mutual respect between Ulster fellas and myself may be contrary to the perception out there, partly owing to the incident with the Queen in 2009.

The Ireland squad had been invited to Stormont for an official congratulations ceremony with Her Majesty in recognition of the Grand Slam. I wouldn't have much knowledge about the royal family, though I admired Princess Diana. I met Prince William on Lions tours and after we beat Wales in Cardiff. He was approachable and friendly in the changing-rooms, and himself and Jessica got on well when they chatted. He told her that he hadn't understood a word I'd said. I've sometimes been slagged by Munster and Irish mates that I look a little like him too. I'd also enjoyed a good 'session' in a group including Mike Tindall and Zara Phillips after an Ireland–England game in Dublin when we slipped out the side door of the Shelbourne and were driven to Krystle nightclub. That was the extent of my knowledge of the royal family.

It was optional for players to attend the reception in Stormont but as a senior player I felt I should do so. This involved a flight from Cork and a train, so it was a big commitment. If I didn't like the Queen, or if I'd strong feelings about the monarchy, I wouldn't have travelled to Belfast.

We were in a private function for two and a half hours. We drank tea out of china, chatted with various people, and the atmosphere was very relaxed. We were advised about the protocol when meeting the Queen – how you stand and what you do. I can still picture the moments before meeting her. I had sweaty palms. I like to think I present myself well, so I put them in my pockets to keep them dry. That's also a habit of mine.

I was next in line to be introduced when an opportunistic photograph was taken a moment before I took my hands out of my pockets to greet her. If there is one thing I'd most like to clarify from my playing career, it is this incident. You don't disrespect the Queen, and the way this image was presented to the world was appalling. I was portrayed as a difficult Corkman. I received supportive letters, from rabid republicans! I am a very proud Irishman and a Catholic but I am not a republican. I don't have any strong political feelings either way; I am not politically aligned. Ninety per cent of the Ulster team are Protestant and many of them are my friends. But irrespective of how strongly you feel, be it the Queen or the Pope or anyone in a powerful position, and especially a lady, I don't believe you should be rude or treat them discourteously.

It is an amazing photo. Brian's face suggests something is happening. It couldn't have been staged any better. We'd been informed that it was a private function, in which case the photo was a breach of confidence. There were a few things that didn't add up.

Some people are so stupid for thinking it was a statement, that I was trying to insult the Queen. The fallout was disturbing, and I'm glad to have an opportunity to explain what truly happened. It bothered me, and I wouldn't be bothered by much. I'm thick-skinned, but I'd like to think as time has passed people would appreciate that I am respectful. Critics can slate the arse off me all they want, but this was about manners and respect. This reflected on my upbringing, my parents, stuff that means something to me. I was described in the *Irish Independent* as a lout; Kevin Myers said it was 'loutish behaviour'. I understand it was largely my own fault, but it was never my intention to offend anyone. I wish I had taken my hands out of my pockets sooner. I was in a relaxed environment and I was looking forward to meeting the Queen, but it turned into a bit of a horror show.

I rang Rory Best, because it had become big news, and I'd be sensitive about things like that. The Ulster lads still slag me about it. As I was away for his wedding as well, Bestie still says to me, 'You've snubbed the Queen, you've snubbed my wedding. What is your problem with us?' But that's a sign of friendship, because as they say 'you're not allowed to slag if it's true'. I buy into that theory. Slag away.

Like Leinster before them, perhaps even more so, Ulster had suffered years of looking enviously at Munster, and then Leinster themselves. Like Leinster they brought in some quality signings such as Pienaar, Johann Muller and then John Afoa to replace BJ Botha. They beat us in that one-off game, and that's the beauty of the Heineken Cup: you get one shot at it.

Everyone thinks now there's been a massive swing, but if we had played them the following Saturday who knows how it would have gone. I don't think beating us once necessarily puts them ahead of us. They haven't reached the knockout stages or won two or three Heineken Cups in a short period of time, so things need to be kept in perspective.

I've never been on a losing side against Connacht, and nor would most of the Munster players, yet it's an interesting province. More can definitely be done, but the IRFU have to decide if Connacht are a development province, because if they're in the Heineken Cup that status loses all credibility. Connacht people would hate being viewed as a development province, and they're dead right. For the first time that I can recall, in the last two years they've been viewed as a full-on professional outfit.

On a bad night the Sportsground is very tough, but we've had some nice days up there. We've had a few close struggles but there's a big difference between close struggles and getting over the line. I had my best kicking performance there, five out of five off the ground, all shunted, with no tee, into a wicked wind. It was a skill I'd been practising, like a three-iron. I dug into the ground, placed the ball and did a run-through kick.

Coincidentally, I actually tried one in Musgrave Park this year against Connacht. Some people don't even notice! It's good to actually try something you're working on and be rewarded. It was a sunny day in Galway, but there was a strong wind and we were playing up the hill in the first half. The first kick was from the touchline, so I hadn't a hope of even reaching it if I opted for the tee. I could hear gasps from the crowd. I'd say they were wondering 'What is this fella doing?' If I'd placed the ball on the tee it would have been blown away. I also needed the ball to carry straight, and with this method the flight is much lower. I can picture it vividly to this day, and I remember running back smiling to myself. It's weird, the little memories that stick with you.

My dad played for UCG and Connacht, and it could have come to pass that we were reared in Galway, sent to 'Bish' – the Jesuit secondary school Coláiste Iognáid – and so on from there. I certainly wouldn't have wanted my province to be pigeon-holed as a development province. In that scenario, a team develops backs aged nineteen to twenty-two who have really good skills and they are then filtered into the other three provinces. That would be very hard for Connacht players and supporters to take. There's no heart in that, and Irish rugby is based on heart and passion. Judging by the eight thousand who turned up for the Toulouse game in their first season in the Heineken Cup, the Galway and Connacht public are dying to support them.

To a large degree, the only people who can help them are themselves. But it doesn't help when players leave for other provinces. I can understand Mick McCarthy's ambition to win a Heineken Cup, but what message does it send to the other players when he leaves for Leinster? In the last year or two, players like Kieran Marmion, Tiernan O'Halloran and Robbie Henshaw have looked really promising, and Connacht have got their act together big time.

At interprovincial level, Irish rugby is rocking. At the start of each season, Ulster, Leinster and Munster will set a goal of winning the Heineken Cup, with legitimate reason. That is so far removed from where we were a decade and a half ago. It's a different world now. People have short memories and are fickle, but the infrastructure of the Irish provincial game is fairly solid.

I'm a little too removed to comment accurately, but while I see plenty of good work in the Munster set-up, I wonder what's the best step after school. It's a pity the AIL isn't more relevant, although I think it is a more important stepping stone than it's given credit for. I saw the Clontarf–Lansdowne final and it was a bloody good game, but just as important as the availability of provincial players is the attitude they bring back to the club game. They cannot sulk and throw the toys out of the pram because they're playing for their club on any weekend. As I've mentioned to a few fellas who are trying to break into Munster, you have to be at least 20 to 30 per cent better than every other player on that pitch so people will talk about you after the game. You can be sure that will filter back to the Munster management. You do that three or four times and you'll be given a crack. You do that once and then have an average or poor game and you'll actually drop back to the bottom of the ladder.

However, Munster are going through something of a transition, with so many players retiring, hence there are plenty of players in the senior squad or on the provincial A team at about the same level. The A games are mostly against English Division 1 teams, against hardy fellas and often on open pitches exposed to the winds, as opposed to a Test match on a surface like a carpet surrounded by stands. Nevertheless, in the eyes of provincial managements these A games have superseded the AIL, and so the same is true for the players. But if a player has a good AIL game and a good British & Irish Cup game, a decent coach will say, 'Yeah, this fella is making progress, I'm going to give him a crack.' And if not, then the management are at fault.

There has to be an avenue for young players. There cannot be a great divide. The club game remains highly competitive, the next step is the B&I Cup, and then the provincial team. The club game is the first rung. Climb the ladder, and you'll get there.

About twice a season I bring the kids to Temple Hill on a Saturday afternoon for a Cork Constitution game. I'll always owe a debt to Con. They were as important as Pres and Munster in my formative years. The AIL was a serious league, a high standard. The big difference back then was that you played for both Munster and Con.

It's a very mixed bag. There are club stalwarts with no interest in the professional game who are playing for the club they love and the buzz they get from the game. Then you have the ambitious wannabe professionals and you can immediately identify them at the early stages of their career and by physical comparison – some of them are freaks. The semi-pros and the academy kids have to play regularly in the AIL otherwise it becomes junior rugby, and there has to be an avenue through the club game, be it youth rugby or the AIL. It can't be just through academies and provincial A games.

Furthermore, we get late developers in Ireland. We're not all the finished products at eighteen, particularly props, although not only props. James Coughlan persisted with Dolphin for years, made his Heineken Cup debut and is getting better. It fascinates me the power some people have when selecting academies. They're probably looking at a player's power output, speed output and strength output, yet where are the decision-making drills, the passing drills, the kicking drills? What are the criteria for selection?

Evan Ryan used to play for Con and was very effective playing at centre for Clontarf against Lansdowne. He was never exceptional in the gym but I always thought he had a brain for the game, and he makes me wonder if players are being picked as athletes first and rugby players second. Yes, rugby is a game of power and strength and speed in most positions, but in the decision-making positions it isn't. There's still a role for calling the right play at the right time, doing what needs to be done at 9 and 10, and even 12.

I watch Leinster Schools rugby and it's incredible compared to Munster Schools rugby. I can scarcely believe the level of detail in their game plans. I saw Belvedere and Blackrock in the final at the RDS and it was frightening. Schools Cup rugby teams are treated as seriously and professionally as the Munster or Leinster full-time set-ups! The only problem is where to go from there. Ideally these boys go on to college, which should be enjoyed, but it seems to me there's no balance to life for these kids. It's extremely difficult, because if you want to make it as a rugby player you have to make huge sacrifices. I think everyone of my era appreciates that we came into the game at a very good time, because the standard was lower and you could enjoy yourself and enjoy your career. Nowadays an ambitious schools player is virtually semi-professional from around the age of fifteen onwards.

Munster Schools rugby was always behind – due to numbers, facilities and so forth – but it has fallen further behind. It's big business in Leinster. Salaries attract coaches. In Munster, schools rugby is more outcome-based than performance-based. It's win at all costs, which stands to you in cup rugby, but there has to be some aspiration from the coaching staff to play the game for enjoyment. You want young players getting touches and expressing themselves while also making good decisions, but in the games I've seen it's a case of getting out of your half and anything else is a bonus.

Even so, despite all this I think there's a swing back towards Munster because of the players coming through. Leinster aren't experiencing the same wave of retirements which hit Munster two or three years ago, but Johnny Sexton and Isa Nacewa are gone and Brian has only one more year. Matt O'Connor also has to step into some big shoes. Losing Joe Schmidt is going to have an impact on a daily basis because, judging from my experience, there aren't many coaches of his calibre out there. They're like the very best players; it's not as if there are sixty of them in the world. It's a very select group, and people whose judgement I trust put him in that bracket.

So change is in the air. And the IRFU have built a very solid base, although the game could be improved in Ireland with more influence from businessmen in the management structures. There are some really intelligent people out there who can make improvements to any organization and who care sufficiently about the national game or their province to offer their services voluntarily. However, it takes secure people, and a secure organization, to offer such an opportunity to business-men, and I wonder if the powerful people within the union and the provinces are willing to do so. Some of the best businesses in the world are based in Ireland, and all the successful businessmen have been challenged in every regard. I would like to see, for example, a SWOT (Strengths, Weaknesses, Opportunities and Threats) analysis of the Munster module, to ascertain how it could be improved.

If there was more outside investment it could be the difference between the provinces signing one or two quality foreign players. You've got to speculate to accumulate, as Leinster have been doing. By spending, they're driving their fan base. I always hear the argument that Leinster are based in the capital city, but Brand Munster is worldwide. Leinster overtook Munster by virtue of signing Rocky Elsom, CJ van der Linde and Isa Nacewa; Ulster reached a Heineken Cup final after signing Ruan Pienaar, Johann Muller and replacing BJ Botha with John Afoa. With benefactors driving recruitment in French club rugby, the provinces need to attract the best-quality foreign players among their five imports if they are to stay at the top of the European mountain.

Believe me, the climb is worth it.

CHAPTER 4

Centurion

Negotiations regarding new contracts with the IRFU were always very simple. I never had an agent. I did it myself and signed long contracts of three or four years. If you do the business, they'll reward you. I possibly made it a little easier for them by walking into the negotiating room and giving them a figure. They generally accepted the first offer, which perhaps shows I should have aimed higher!

For the last deal, two years ago, I did sound out John Baker, the agent I believe knows the scene the best. While that deal understandably saw a decrease, his advice was spot on. The previous contract had been for four years, the first three of which were very good before an average last year. At the time though, in 2007, I wanted to buy a family home and needed some security.

As a one-club man who had the same employers for sixteen years, it would be a little rich of me to complain unduly about the IRFU. Nor would I want to – I really admire what they're doing. They deserve credit both for being well organized and for being ahead of the game in managing their players. If anything, we're managed too well and suffer from not playing enough rugby. This is the only downside to having a national contract, but I can't recall ever being tired during a season. I can honestly say I looked forward to playing every game as opposed to thinking 'Oh Jesus, I've another game now next week'. Instead, at times I wondered 'When am I going to get some bloody rugby?'

Players need to trust the system, and I did, because for me the system worked. Even with a twenty-two-game League and play-offs, very few players in Ireland play over thirty games. Sometimes we kid ourselves about the dangers of playing too much and end up not playing enough. I feel that ideally we should be playing three out of every four weeks. If you factor in four weeks' holiday and a good eight weeks' pre-season, you're left with forty weeks, and playing three out of every four equates to thirty matches per season.

Four weeks' holiday is plenty. At Munster in recent years I've noticed players take only one or two weeks, and train on the sly. That's the competitive level in our rugby culture for you. On holiday a few years ago you ate what you wanted, you drank and you had late nights. You switched off completely and felt refreshed, but then you were behind when you returned to training. Now the directors of fitness expect you to hit the ground running and make improvements in the first week. It's almost a vicious circle now.

I've also been lucky in never having suffered a serious injury. As well as playing every season, since the Americas in 2000 I've been on every single tour: the Lions in 2001, New Zealand in 2002, Australia, Tonga and Samoa in 2003, South Africa in

2004, the Lions in 2005, the tours to New Zealand and Australia in 2006, 2008 and 2010, the Lions in 2009 and the three-Test tour to New Zealand in 2012. The only exceptions were the World Cup years of 2007, when fifteen of us were rested from the tour to Argentina, and 2011, when we came back earlier for extensive pre-seasons. My seasons have been long and have taken as much out of me mentally as physically, so you need a three-month window away from playing.

I recently heard one pundit saying on the radio that I could have worked harder. I worked my arse off in the gym. Anyone I've worked with would verify that. I am not, by nature, the strongest, but I wouldn't be a weak link either. I take pride in my gym work. You have to do whatever it takes, even extra sessions – but I am a rugby player, not a weightlifter.

I can look back on sixteen unbroken seasons, covering three Lions tours, three World Cups and eight Irish summer tours, 128 games for Ireland and 240 games for Munster, missing only a handful for either my province or my country. I have to admit that wouldn't have been possible if I hadn't spent my entire career in Ireland. I believe the most important thing is that I've always maintained my appetite for the game. We were given enough time off to stay hungry and to produce performances – otherwise, no matter who you are, you'll be chucked off the team.

Another key factor is having good relationships with the strength and conditioners, and I place a huge value on massage. In Munster we've had Dave Mahedy and Mark McManus, then Damien Mednis, Paul Darbyshire and Bryce Cavanagh as our S and Cs, while my main link, as I said, has always been Aidan O'Connell. He's been there as long as I've been there. He's local and he understands the Munster mentality. He watched me progress and knew what worked for me, so was flexible about what I did. I never sought to have my own programme though and always did what everyone else was doing, because I think going your own route can be a soft option. For the first ten years I thought 'more is better' but gradually I realized that sometimes 'less is more'. Aidan was good to talk to about that because, in this business, getting your head right and believing in what you're doing is three-quarters of the battle.

If there are flaws in the Irish system, the biggest one is probably the relationship between the Irish head coach and the four provincial head coaches. I think there needs to be more trusting communication between the provinces because Team Ireland isn't representative of the four provinces. In the last four years I think we've operated at around 40 per cent of our potential. For example, if there's a good skills coach in Ulster, why not bring him into the Irish camp occasionally? I've always believed insecure people don't share ideas; secure people are willing to educate and learn. Some coaches feel challenged and threatened and become insular, and in that scenario a team will not grow. I appreciate there will be times when, say, Munster won't want the international management near their training, or vice versa, but there are other times when everything is a little more low-key, and it would be beneficial.

In New Zealand, the Super Rugby sides play in a very recognizable style which mirrors the All Blacks. You cannot say that's the case in Ireland, although the Heineken Cup's prestige makes it difficult to fuse the provinces with the national team. The Heineken Cup is a stand-alone competition. In New Zealand the emphasis is on Test rugby and the All Blacks. Here it's obviously every young boy's dream to play for his country as well, but thirty fellas can also live the dream of lifting a Heineken Cup. From the perspective of Team Ireland, there's a danger of the Heineken Cup becoming a monster, although given recent events, who knows what tournament is going to represent European rugby in the future? But people should look at how the Champions League and all the TV money has changed soccer.

I know full well how rewarding it is to win a Heineken Cup with the mates you've been training with for ten months, and it's crucial that the bulk of any provincial squad remains driven by young, home-grown, ambitious players, and that this filters through to the Ireland team. I want to bring my kids to the Aviva one day as a supporter, and when I do I want to see fifteen Irishmen on the team. I don't want to see seven overseas players who have qualified by residency. I was born in the United States, but that was merely my place of birth. I'm Irish. I was reared in Ireland, and in Munster and Irish rugby. Something has to be done about this issue or else our game is going to be diluted. The strength of the GAA is its parochialism, which is why people buy into it. The Irish team has always been based on passion, and players representing where they come from, but, for example, Ireland could have two front-rowers who are not Irish-born, Richardt Strauss and Michael Bent, with Jared Payne qualifying next season, and more to come. Everyone is doing it, so why shouldn't we? This is, however, something the IRB should change.

Commitment doesn't come into it. I don't question the commitment of overseas players for one minute. I'm sure they are every bit as committed. But to play for a country and stand for its national anthem you should have lived there for ten years. Three years is way too little. Even five is too little. Seven isn't enough either. It has to be ten. Non-negotiable. Deal or no deal. You can't deny someone the right to represent a country where they've lived since they were a kid. Manu Tuilagi's brothers played for Samoa and he plays for England, but he arrived in England in his early teens. He was reared there, made his home there, and he's bought into everything English. This isn't a fella who landed at the age of nineteen as a career opportunity.

Take CJ Stander. He's South African, and he's 100 per cent proud to be South African. But if he's not good enough to play for South Africa he's got to keep trying. Since when has Ireland become second best?

Richardt Strauss came here as a South African and used the three-year residency rule to qualify for Ireland; to his credit he even learned the words of the national anthem for his debut against South Africa in November 2012. I was there. He's a great fella, very proud and very passionate. But where does it stop? You could have eight or more players in a national team that arrived in the country only three years previously, and I could go to Lansdowne Road with my kids to watch them, but they're not Irish. It's a dangerous road to go down. We run the risk of losing our identity.

There is another way of expanding our playing base. We're not the biggest of countries but we're sports mad. We're mad for a ball. Given the chance, we'll have a go at most games, although in much of rural Ireland the only option is Gaelic games. Every county in Gaelic football has a panel of thirty or more footballers/athletes, some of whom might like to have a try at a professional set-up if the IRFU held open trials and actively scouted talented young GAA players.

Rugby schools have been the lifeblood of Irish rugby but remain relatively elite and don't reach out to these rural communities. They provide an established pathway to professional rugby – very often players' dads attended the same school and played rugby. But these schools don't tap into the GAA talent pool. I spend much of the summer watching GAA games, and all of them feature hugely talented athletes. Aussie Rules isn't shy about tapping into this. Tadgh Kennelly, the former Sydney Swans player and Kerry footballer, essentially tries to poach the pick of the talent to set them up in Australia. The Sydney Swans have held open camps to select players for trials in Australia, so if they can do it I don't see why the IRFU and the provinces can't organize talent identification weekends.

For example, Darren Sweetman, who has played inter-county hurling for Cork and under-age hockey for Ireland, has joined the Munster academy. He's very talented and is, I think, attracted by a professional lifestyle. I've spoken to Seán Óg Ó hAilpín about this, and he would have loved it. His brother Setanta is making a good living as an Aussie Rules player, and if GAA players are prepared to try Aussie Rules they'd be willing to try rugby in Ireland as well. They would clearly prefer not to train from six a.m. to eight a.m., and from seven until nine at night, while working nine to five during the day.

Of course, the vast majority of Gaelic footballers would have no interest in playing rugby and I respect that completely. I'll always be thankful to my parents for giving me the opportunity to play soccer, hurling, football, pitch and putt, and tennis, as well as rugby, from a young age. I bring Rua to Under-5 Gaelic football in Douglas on Saturday mornings and it is so well organized. They're barely able to kick but they do ball skills and passing. Generally, kids won't start playing rugby until Under-6 or 8.

In any case, like Tadgh Kennelly, dual sportsmen such as Eric Miller in Leinster, Alan Quinlan in Munster and Gavin Duffy in Connacht could be employed by the IRFU to scout Gaelic footballers as possible recruits. It only requires one or two recruits to add significantly to the strength of a provincial squad.

Ideally, players would need to be identified by the age of seventeen or eighteen, because if you have aspirations to be a back in Ireland you'd want to be well on the road to making it by twenty. The younger the better, really. The younger you are the easier it is to learn a skill, so if they were given the option of dual status, even from twelve to sixteen, I'd say they'd embrace it. So much of rural Ireland offers only Gaelic games, and it's the same as anything else: if it's on your doorstep you'll be interested; if it's not, you won't be too bothered.

Things have changed of course, and the union, through branches and regional development officers, have broadened rugby's base. Rugby is big in Kerry and Tipperary now, which would have been unthinkable before professionalism. This shows that rugby has plenty to offer – the attraction of playing in World Cups and travelling the globe to a range of rugby-playing countries as well as a professional way of life. Rugby is an appealing product, more so now than ever before.

The IRFU have been rewarded for their player management. Six Heineken Cups by three of the provinces and a Grand Slam would have been unthinkable in the late nineties, and players' careers have lasted longer, with John Hayes, Brian O'Driscoll and myself all reaching 100 caps.

My 100th game for Ireland should have been one of the best days of my life. It was the first international at the Aviva Stadium, against South Africa on 6 November 2010. I presumed I would get the start for that. It was a tight selection between me and Johnny Sexton, and it was the first of four Tests that month – Samoa, New Zealand and Argentina were all also due in the Aviva – so there would be game time for both of us. As I was only the third Irish player to become a centurion, I thought it would have been fitting to start me. My plan was to bring Jess, Rua and Molly, my brothers, parents and friends up to Dublin for the game and for them to see me run on to the pitch first. It would have been very special, a massive occasion.

Deccie was asked about it by the media but he didn't want to give me a start. That's the brutal reality of it. It was one of the biggest disappointments of my career. It can be brushed under the carpet as a small thing, but when you are the one involved, it hurts like hell. If you're lucky enough to reach a hundred, you want it to be a memorable occasion. Earlier that year I'd been picked to start in two Six Nations games and came out with a 100 per cent kicking record, so it's not as if I was off the pace.

When Deccie began changing the team after the 2009 Grand Slam, and particularly making the change at 10, I began to think I mightn't reach the century. Both Malcolm O'Kelly and Peter Stringer fell just short. Momentum is everything in life, and when you have it you've got to keep your foot on the throttle. But, whereas normally I'd be itching to get on to the pitch, initially I was almost hoping I wouldn't be called on. I'd have preferred to start the following week against Samoa.

I can remember Juan Smith picking off Eoin Reddan's pass and showing serious wheels to score at the other end. The South Africans took their chances and we were 13–6 down at half-time. We were 23–9 down when I came on. By then I was motivated and pumped up for it. I was thinking, 'This is going to be beautiful. My hundredth cap wasn't from the start, but it will be remembered in the right way. I can pull this one out of the fire.'

When your team is that far behind you've no choice but to go for it. Tommy Bowe scored off a cross-kick by me, but I had seen from the bench that there were acres of space out wide – it was a soft try for them to concede. Watching from the bench can be an advantage, and I suppose that's also the benefit of having experience there, especially at out-half, as a 10 can change a game around.

I landed the conversion and then helped work the ball to Rob Kearney for another try soon after – which I have to admit was a lucky score. Initially I thought that conversion would go over as well. It was a sweet kick. I clobbered it too. It wasn't a dead duck. But the ball stayed in line with the post all the way. That was our last chance, and we lost 23–21. Even a draw would have salvaged something from the day. It would have felt like a win.

There had been no announcement over the public address system of my 100th cap when I came on, although the crowd applauded me warmly, as they always did. Through all of the 'sub days', as I call them, the crowd always helped to keep me motivated. Even though I'm a Munster player and a higher pro-portion of the crowd at the Aviva for Ireland games nowadays is Dublin-based as fewer supporters travel up from the country, they were always very generous to me and it's something I'll never forget. A big regret is that I never had the chance to say goodbye and thank you to the Irish fans.

I'd use the memory of the crowd's support when I came off the bench the previous Saturday to fuel my desire at Monday morning training sessions. I cannot put into words how much that support meant to me – the thought that people became excited at the sight of me coming on. I'd have hated it if there had been silence. It helped me stay positive. You're appreciated and they want you there as opposed to 'Jaysus, will this fella ever feck off?'

That said, the camera focusing on me whenever Johnny missed a kick was pathetic. We used to joke about it on the bench!

I love it that John Hayes reached 100 first, on 27 February 2010 against England. We are still great buddies. We played all our careers together and won our first caps together, at Lansdowne Road on 19 February 2000. We shook hands as a ritual before every game, and to get the Bull's hand is a nice gesture. He's a proper, proper man. He's quiet and proud, and I like that. I also like the way he transformed himself from a second row to a world-class tight-head in his twenties, and both his province and his country became totally reliant on him for a decade. He demolished all the other potential candidates at tight-head over such a long period. As well as being so valuable, he was a good man to have a coffee with, even if he usually had a cup of milk. He has a great sense of humour and was always in the right frame of mind.

There will, of course, be centurions in the future. The show goes on. Donncha O'Callaghan is within touching distance of

100 caps and Paul O'Connell will be there soon. I think Jamie Heaslip could easily make it; Rory Best too; Rob Kearney could, and Tommy Bowe, although it's harder for outside backs, who are more reliant on speed.

I think the future is hugely exciting. The players are there. Take the backs. Even in the short term there will be Murray and Sexton at half-back, Tommy will be there another four years, Kearns and Zeebs for even longer, and Luke Marshall looks exciting. We've young loose-heads, we've loads of good hookers, and although we need cover for Mike Ross, he's still doing a good job. There are three veteran locks in Munster and Leo Cullen in Leinster, so we need Ian Nagle and others coming through, but Tommy O'Donnell is adding to a good mix in the back row.

I also believe Joe Schmidt will bring the best out of Keith Earls. I know he's a fan of his and Earlsy thrives in a positive environment where a coach believes in him. Schmidt himself comes highly recommended, more so than anyone else I can remember. It's the standards he sets, the culture he builds and the level of detail he brings. In fairness to Deccie he ran a really happy and united ship, and tapped into how important it is to play for your country and what it means to the public. That's vital, but if you can add a little game detail, that's what gets results at Test level.

For example, when Leinster beat Stade Français in the Amlin final at the RDS in May 2013, two of their three first-half tries were created off the pitch, which is a rare achievement. For one of the tries, they dragged Stade into the middle, having identified that their inside defensive pillar wasn't 'tagging', and for another they detected that Stade had no sweeper in the line, that the small scrum-half tracked back – and so Andrew Conway beat him to the jump and set up Sean Cronin for the score. I think the detail which has gone into the Leinster coaching is at a different level, and only rugby nerds understand.

No matter how experienced you are or how good a player people think you are, you still seek an awful lot of direction from your head coach. It's a hard enough game at Test level when you're competing against your opposite man, who is usually as good as you. Sometimes you might be better than he is and other times he might be better than you, so you need twenty-three people buying into the game plan and a coach transmitting his message effectively to the whole squad. Video sessions are Schmidt's forte, and he conveys his game plan coherently.

Some coaches, even at international level, can dilute the effectiveness of their message because they aren't 100 per cent clear. You're left wondering 'Is it ball carrier plus three in this ruck?' or 'Who's clearing this ruck if we hit here?' But it's second nature to some coaches, clarifying the numbers at breakdowns and the shape to put on a team. That can be very technical and only a few people understand. Plenty of players have no interest in understanding; all they want to know is their role. The skill of the coach is in piecing the whole thing together.

When people look back on Irish rugby in the 2000s and the so-called Golden Generation, I don't believe it will be seen as a peak. A Grand Slam and three Triple Crowns are bloody good, but when you consider Wales have won three Slams and a Six Nations title in the same era it could have been more, especially as we won four out of five games in five of those years and in '04, '06 and '07 we only lost to France.

We've been nowhere near a Triple Crown in recent years, and we have to walk before we can run again. Look at the results. This team has struggled in the last four years. In fact it has gone backwards. You can talk about injuries, but we should have a squad that can cope with that. We should never be losing to Italy in a Six Nations game, even in Rome. The mood in the camp wasn't right for that game last March. I know because I was involved in that Six Nations and when you leave your head clears. You've been immersed in a bubble and you're listening to the same voices all the time, but sometimes you need to take a week away to clear your head and come back at it from a different angle.

It was like the 2007 World Cup. When you care about it so much your solution is to work harder. We probably needed to stop training as hard as we did, but that was the natural competitive edge in us, and so we tried to fix it on the training pitch. But come game time, we were worn out.

Calling us the Golden Generation is a compliment which may or may not be justified with regard to the quality of our players. I'd like to think the Bull, Brian, Paulie, myself and others will be remembered both for what we have contributed to our provinces and to the national team, but the brutal reality is that it's backed up more by what we achieved with our provinces – multiple Heineken Cups – than with our country and just that one Six Nations championship.

Results always speak for themselves though, and over the course of a career, the numbers back them up. I was interested to read that in my 128 appearances for Ireland from my debut in February 2000, we won seventy-three times, a winning percentage of 57 per cent. When I started – in eighty-seven of those

128 caps – we won fifty-three times, a winning percentage of 61 per cent. But when I only came on as a replacement, we won less than half the time. Up to and including the Grand Slam in 2009, before Deccie started to make changes, Ireland won 64 per cent of the games I started. Since then we've won only 42 per cent of the games I've been involved in. It's a significant fall-off.

Still, the stock is so low now for the national team that there has to be a 'bounce back' from Schmidt taking over. Then it will be a question of sustaining it.

Whereas rugby is the national game in Wales, a young Irish lad's sporting memories are more of winning All-Irelands in the seventies and eighties. But rugby has been transformed in this country in the last fifteen years. Internationals always used to draw big crowds, but that was only a handful of times a year; now people are attending rugby matches in bigger numbers than ever before.

Young Irish fellas will have vivid memories of Cardiff in 2009, and that day remains the pinnacle for Irish rugby. The World Cup two years later was a missed opportunity, but with the quality of players we have and a good draw in 2015 in England, Ireland can go very well in the next tournament. I'm sure that's the plan Schmidt is hatching.

CHAPTER 5

The Sub Game

At the end of the updated edition of my autobiography in 2009, following the Grand Slam win, I wrote: 'People might be afraid now that this is the end of us. We've reached the top of the mountain with nowhere left to go. Don't believe it for a second. We're only getting going.'

Unfortunately, it hasn't turned out that way. Ireland had been at or near the top of our game throughout the 2000s. If you win 80 per cent of your Six Nations games, as we did more often than not, I think you've had a good season. Not ideal, but it was so much more consistent than Ireland had ever been before. We won seven out of eight games under Eddie O'Sullivan in 2006/07, and that's probably the best Irish team there has been. Some people won't like that claim, but we were very unlucky against France in Croke Park after going four points up near the end when Vincent Clerc scored from the restart. That cost us a Grand Slam. We had a change of management and coaches in 2009, but we had the same players.

After the 2009 Grand Slam, we began the 2009/10 season with a draw at home to Australia before Johnny was brought into the team for the wins over Fiji and South Africa. I got an almighty shock when Johnny was chosen to start against South Africa ahead of me. He did well against Fiji when we hammered them, but I didn't think he would be picked for the South Africa game. I was keen to play in that match. After the disappointment of the Lions Tour, and what had happened in the second Test, I had unfinished business.

The Lions were one down in the series and the scores were level with less than a minute to go in that second Test at Loftus Versfeld. Stephen Jones had just made it 25–25 when I ran back to retrieve the ball inside our 22, with most of my team-mates in front of me. I ran outside our 22 and launched an up-and-under to the middle of the pitch in order to contest the ball and maybe give us one more shot at winning the match. The alternative was to kick to touch and sacrifice any chance of victory, and maybe hand them one last chance from a line-out around halfway. Many people have argued that a drawn series is better than a lost one – which is what happened, because I ran into Fourie du Preez as he caught the ball and conceded that fateful penalty. Morne Steyn duly won the match and clinched a series win with the last kick of the game, a penalty from inside his own half. But I wouldn't change my decision.

Not starting the first Test had been painful. I was playing well, Munster had won the Heineken Cup in '06 and '08, and Ireland had won the Grand Slam in '09. If there had been more Irish coaches with the Lions that year I think I would have been picked. That was the way I reasoned it and I thought that was an accurate way of doing so. I had kicked seven from seven and scored a try – twenty-two points in total – in the opening win over the Royal XV in Rustenburg, and then kicked another twelve points in the 39–3 win over the Natal Sharks in Durban. Stephen Jones and the Lions hadn't started well in the first Test, so when the team for the second Test was announced to the squad I remember sitting there expecting my name to be called out – but instead I was named on the bench. It showed that the management were simply keener on Jones.

The way that second Test then panned out was particularly disappointing. I came on for Jamie Roberts with twelve minutes to go, after Shane Williams had replaced Brian three minutes earlier in a makeshift midfield. I had a massive shiner after being busted by Pierre Spies, and then missed a tackle on Jaque Fourie for the try which briefly put them in front. To this day I still have no feeling where I had that black eye. It's killed all the nerves in that area. Apart from that I've come out of the game in reasonably good shape.

Before I kicked the up-and-under to halfway I signalled to Tommy Bowe to chase the ball, but for some reason he ran towards the left of the pitch. I've seen his comments on that moment since and he admitted he didn't do me any favours. If I had enough time to get under the kick, then certainly Tommy had enough time to do so as well. If we'd won that ball, we were on the front foot. 'Give me a drop goal and I'll get it for you' – that was my thinking. Some will think 'this fella is delusional, crazy', but there wasn't an opening two years later at Thomond Park against Northampton either for forty-odd phases. We'll come back to that later.

I'm not trying to be unrealistic and dishonest. I'm not a stepper. I can't beat people from back there, and I'm not going to get tackled thirty yards from my line and give away a penalty by not releasing the ball. I have an accurate kicking game and it was at altitude, where you get an extra second of hang time, and I was counting on one of the best aerial wingers to win the ball (as it turned out) against their number 9. There was actually a bit of logic to what I was trying to do, even if what transpired was horrific. But that's sport. What disappoints me most, to this day, is that Paulie was captain and I think he was scapegoated for the whole tour by some of the English media. He was popular within the squad and it would have been a really special moment in both our careers if I had landed a drop goal at the other end and the following week he could have been captain for a Lions series win.

I remember sitting around the pool after that game with Jess and the kids – Rua and Molly were eight months old then. To suffer something like that in your career is a horrible experience. Many people still maintain – I've read plenty of comments about it since – that I would have been better off kicking the ball out of play and settling for a draw. But that genuinely never came into my head. Now, of course, I can understand such a viewpoint. Draw the second Test, win the last Test, and secure a drawn series. But I've had a winner-takes-all attitude through-out my career and I wouldn't change that.

I presume the coaches were disgusted, and I wouldn't blame them, although like any other moment in a match, one decision doesn't cost a team the game. And for Morne Steyn to land the penalty from fifty-three metres, under that pressure and in only his second Test, was admirable.

For such a big sporting event, with such a high profile, there was inevitably a huge reaction, some of which was particularly disappointing. A few former players were quite severe in saying I'd never play a game for the Lions again. I remember being tipped off about an article in the papers the next day by Jeremy Guscott. 'O'Gara missed a tackle on Jaque Fourie and then gave away the penalty at the end. He is going to be hanging his head in shame in the dressing-room,' he wrote. 'Those guys gave absolutely everything and must have been on top of the world at half-time.' Guscott wasn't alone in thinking it had all been my fault and I should hang my head in shame.

Like everything in life, you deal with it head-on, try and learn as much from it as you can, and move on.

Because of those memories, I desperately wanted to play against South Africa in Croke Park the following November. Instead, Johnny kicked five penalties and played well as Ireland beat the Springboks 15–10. So it was game on between us.

In the 2010 Six Nations, although we were hammered in Paris, we beat England in Twickenham and Wales at home, with Johnny starting both games, and had a Triple Crown at stake when Scotland came to Croke Park for Ireland's last game there.

That defeat was probably the beginning of the rot. A year after winning a Grand Slam, it was a huge setback. Great teams kick on from a Grand Slam. As in any sport, it is hard to back up a title, and it is very difficult to win back-to-back Grand Slams or Six Nations. My gut feeling was that we had a team good enough to win the Grand Slam but not a great squad, and in trying to create a great squad, in my view, Deccie disrupted the team.

There's no disputing Johnny Sexton is a good player and Deccie was fully justified in bringing him into the squad and giving him game time, but I definitely felt he was picked probably a year too early and I don't think the best was brought out of him as a result. In fact the best of him in a green jersey is yet to come; I think he'll dominate games more now that I'm gone. It's hard for a young player coming into international rugby for the first time to compete with a big name in that position, even subconsciously. I remember exactly what it was like when I was first brought in ahead of David Humphreys, but after a few years you forget about it and you kick on. I accept that Declan did ultimately develop a more competitive squad, but in the process, I maintain, he took away from the team.

I watched the first fifty-two minutes of that Scotland game from the bench. We played a very adventurous brand of running, offloading rugby and the Scots did well living off our mistakes, but we were unlucky at times, a few passes not sticking.

I was waiting on the sidelines to replace Johnny just as he lined up a penalty which, to his credit, he nailed to reduce Scotland's lead from 17–7 to 17–10.

After Tommy Bowe scored in the corner, I landed a conversion from the touchline, and drew the sides level again after a penalty by Dan Parks, but they closed out the game with another penalty by Parks. They'd seen a big lead wiped away by Wales a few weeks before and were determined not to be mugged again.

That summer we played two Tests in New Zealand and Australia. I played in the first, in Yarrow Stadium in New Plymouth, where we would subsequently play the USA in the World Cup, but on this wet and windy night we lost 66–28. We actually started well, but they scored off a turnover and then Jamie Heaslip was sent off by Wayne Barnes in the 16th minute.

Later in the first half I pulled back Cory Jane after he burned me and I was sin-binned for the second and last time in my Irish career, leaving us with thirteen men. I watched the next ten minutes from the sidelines as the All Blacks ran in three tries, all of which Dan Carter converted, to put them 38–0 ahead before half-time.

Dan Tuohy scored a try for us on his debut soon after I came back on, and I converted three more in the second half. Our attack game was actually very good that night, and at one stage it looked as if we were going to lose by an awful lot more. None the less, it was an embarrassing defeat, and it was my ninety-ninth cap for Ireland. Still, I suppose I should be grateful that it wasn't my 100th.

I stayed on the bench for the full eighty minutes a week later when we lost 22–15 in Perth.

The following season I came on as a sub in three of the four November games, only starting against Samoa, and it was the same against Italy in Rome and France at home. The Italians are always fired up on the opening weekend, especially at home. We made enough handling errors to lose two matches yet still butchered enough chances to win two games.

We were 10–6 up when I was brought on for Johnny in the 66th minute, but Romain Poite began penalizing us heavily at the scrums and in the breakdown, and after Denis Leamy was binned Luke McLean finished off the kind of try that was usually beyond them to put them 11–10 ahead. It would have been worse too if Mirco Bergamasco's conversion hadn't tailed off.

Down to fourteen men, we had five minutes to avoid a first Six Nations defeat to Italy. But we stayed calm, Brian put us on

Left: Where it all started – my international debut against Scotland on 19 February 2000.

Below: With Axel after the Miracle Match against Gloucester in 2003. It was a magical night, but at the time I didn't realize how important my final kick was.

Below: Alan Gaffney maybe doesn't get the credit he deserves for his time as Munster coach. This was after we won the Celtic Cup in 2005.

Above: The Triple Crown in 2006 was immense, with Shaggy's last-minute try at Twickenham. He's on my left here, with Wally on my right.

Right and below: There were even bigger celebrations to come that year, after my third penalty sealed the Heineken Cup win over Biarritz. Shaun Payne and Quinny share the joy at the final whistle.

I'd like to think I learned valuable lessons from all of the coaches I played under. Eddie O'Sullivan (**above**) was in charge when we had great success in the green jersey, while Tony McGahan (**left**) gave me great confidence both as an assistant then as head coach at Munster. As for Deccie (**below**), It may not have ended the way we wanted, but he was there throughout my career.

Above: The rapturous reception in Limerick as we are crowned European champions again in 2008.

Right: I have to give due credit to Dave Revins, whose skills as a masseur with Munster and Ireland kept me going through the years.

Below: With Leams, Denis Fogarty, Earlsy and the Magners League trophy in 2009. It's an essential tournament for young players to learn how to perform on the biggest stages.

2 May 2009: The day the tide turned in favour of Drico and Leinster. That Heineken Cup semi-final defeat at Croke Park was hard to take, especially with Johnny Sexton (**below**) getting right in my face following Gordon D'Arcy's opening try. We're good friends now!

Above and below: The drop goal. If you look carefully, you can see Paulie on his knees after the ball sailed between the posts.

Celebrating Ireland's 2009 Grand Slam at the Millennium Stadium with Drico and then (**below**) in the dressing-room with Jamie Heaslip, Tomas O'Leary and Prince William. I used to get slagged that I looked like him!

Above: A proud moment for Jess and me at the post-match dinner after our Grand Slam victory in Cardiff.

Below: I'm happy in this book to clarify that in no way was I disrespecting the Queen at the official congratulations ceremony at Stormont. You can read all about it on page 57.

the front foot, and from Eoin Reddan's lovely pass I dropped a goal to get us out of jail. I felt I'd made a point, but more to the point we'd saved ourselves from a shocking defeat.

By the time I came on at home to France in the 63rd minute we were 25–15 behind, but although I landed a difficult conversion to Jamie Heaslip's try we kept going for the win rather than the draw and came up short.

I was then picked to start away to Scotland. To be honest, I wasn't expecting that. The pressure was on me and the team. If we lost, we were out of the title race, and if I messed up, no doubt loads of people would have been quick to say I was past it.

Tommy Bowe was back from injury, and with Tomas O'Leary ruled out, the other change saw Reddser return. We got most of our basics right, played most of the rugby, led from early on and scored three tries to nil, before the usual inaccuracy and ill discipline nearly cost us. We were hanging on for a 21–18 win at the end.

My kicking game went well, and Jamie and Reddser each scored tries which I converted before I scored my sixteenth and final try for Ireland. Seanie put us on the front foot with a couple of big bursts and I handed off Ross Ford to reach the line. For some reason I was so pumped up that I even stepped Chris Paterson in the in-goal area as I rounded the posts. I shouldn't have done it, and I've no idea why I did do it. That put us 21–9 ahead, but Paterson kicked a couple of penalties and I wasn't happy about being replaced. There was little Johnny could have done in the last twelve minutes and, as I said, we were hanging on at the end. We were developing an annoying habit of letting games get completely away from us.

I started again away to Wales, and the pattern repeated itself. Again we scored early through Brian in the third minute after plenty of phases and good work by Tommy Bowe. Again we had enough chances to win two games. Again we began making lots of handling errors and conceding penalties, and the game slipped away from us. But that day will always be remembered for the Mike Phillips try off a quick line-out which won the match. The referee, Jonathan Kaplan, and the touch judge, Peter Allan, should have ruled it out for any of three reasons – from where it was taken, with the wrong ball, and because their hooker, Matthew Rees, had his foot in play. Apart from that it was fine.

I wasn't happy to be replaced immediately after Phillips' try, and we still should have saved the game. Johnny was restored for the final match, when the prospect of England completing a Grand Slam in the Aviva seemed to concentrate the minds of the players and the supporters. Finally we stopped making errors and conceding penalties, Johnny played his best game for Ireland so far, kicking five out of six, and by the time I came on in the 70th minute we led 24–8 and the game was over.

After the World Cup in 2011, I won my last twelve caps off the bench. I don't have a major problem with that. For starters, I genuinely didn't think I would play on after that tournament. I enjoyed it so much and I also felt there was such a gap to the other 10s that I'd be crazy not to play second fiddle to Johnny. The World Cup had given me every reason to keep going because I fought and got my place back, and that meant every-thing to me. But then I realized that for the team to progress Deccie needed to give the young fella his time. Until then I wouldn't accept that because the World Cup should feature the best players, whether they're thirty-eight or eighteen, and that's what Deccie did, so fair play to him. But afterwards I had to be realistic. The team had to move forward and I wasn't going to be much good to them unless they needed a get-out-of-jail card, somebody with a bit of experience. I could offer them that. It was discussed with Deccie and we agreed that I should stay involved, that I could bring value to the squad as an experienced player and an impact sub. I would have done exactly the same as Deccie for the last season and a half.

In the latter years of your career, the one downside is that the warm-up becomes a killer, because you don't have as much adrenalin. You warm up, you sit down, you stiffen up again. I couldn't prepare for that. It was very difficult.

Over the years I'd developed a routine that worked for me, and my Munster routine was so much easier, because I was starting games. When I was younger I would go out on the pitch an hour before kick-off. In later years I only needed thirty-five to forty minutes, because I generally had to play eighty minutes for Munster. That equated to 115 to 120 minutes on your feet with maximum effort.

You learn these things, and how to adapt, with experience, although another problem with warming the bench as you get older is the Irish weather, especially over the course of a rugby season. It's usually cold and damp, which makes you stiffer. It sounds bad, but I wouldn't have been the best sub in terms of professionalism. I always preferred playing and training on tightly cropped football pitches under clear blue skies with a hot sun on my back. I loved that. So much easier.

Although solely confined to bench duty, during the 2012 Six Nations I became the competition's highest points scorer and most-capped player of all time. I was aware of these landmarks, though at the time you don't care about them too much. But it's true what they say: when you're retired you're able to enjoy some moments of reflection. Those records are there for somebody else to break now. The same with being Ireland's record points scorer and most-capped player – although that's why I was half hoping Brian would retire!

These are other reasons why I'm so content with finishing. First and foremost, rugby is a team game; no matter how hard I or any of us work as individuals, we couldn't achieve anything without our team-mates. Even so, I can remember well my first cap against Scotland and genuinely wondering beforehand if that would be it. Would I get a second? Then you count them in fives, and after a while you forget about them. You reach fifty, then suddenly you realize you're nearing the century. If I'd been told the night of my first cap I would go on to win 128, grateful wouldn't have been the word.

It's been an incredible journey, and it's also been very strange since retirement. Until then I was permanently in 'match mode', but now I've finished I've been stopped in the street so much more.

Aside from my Munster and Ireland team-mates, I have a close network of family and friends. I wouldn't have embraced people outside those circles. I'd imagine there is a perception of me as insular, difficult, maybe even rude, even though people who know me wouldn't use those words.

The Irish dressing-room wasn't much different from the Munster dressing-room. We had so little turnover in my first 100 caps we were virtually a club side as well. I won most of my caps with Gordon D'Arcy outside me, and virtually all of them with Drico outside me. Denis was there for ages, as were Shaggy and Simon Easterby as well as the Bull and Strings, with all of whom I won my first cap. And there were so many more: Girvan Dempsey and Geordan Murphy, Tommy Bowe and Andrew Trimble, all the Munster lads, Rory Best, Paddy Wallace, and so on. We had some great craic, and it was a very tight-knit squad. It wasn't in any way inferior to the Munster dressing-room. Munster is more parochial obviously, you're spending more time with people, but during the 2011 World Cup there was every bit as great a club feel to the Irish squad, in part because the more time you spend together, the more you're drawn closer.

Over the years, Guy Easterby and Kevin Maggs were out-standing characters – the jokers in the dressing-room – as was Simon Easterby. All of them had special traits. Geordan is a deep man, but hilarious in his own right. Keith Gleeson is another deep man, and a fascinating bloke. Brian was probably my closest mate. As well as all the Six Nations and November series, we toured together with Ireland and the Lions or went on World Cups every year from 2001. We went through each stage together, from being the kids in the squad to the last two stand-ing, sharing the same interests on and off the pitch. He deserves to become Ireland's most-capped player.

It's an honour to hold the record for a little while before him, and individual records are absolutely tremendous. I won the Heineken Cup Player of the first fifteen years. I have the Irish and Heineken Cup points records and, for the moment, the Irish caps record, so I can look myself in the mirror. But overall we, as Team Ireland, didn't fulfil our full potential. At least we did leave some kind of legacy with the Grand Slam. I was seven years old when Michael Kiernan's drop goal beat England to win the Triple Crown and the championship in 1985 and I can vividly remember watching it.

But, as I said, the Heineken Cup has become such a monster in Ireland that there's a danger of it devouring the national team. The supporters from Munster, Ulster and Leinster need to chill out, get real and appreciate the value of the national side, and certain players need to stop using the Heineken Cup as a safety net for underperforming. The Heineken Cup is a club competition. The majority of the teams you face still have three or four average players, whereas at international level you very rarely encounter average players. Until that mental issue is addressed, the Ireland team is never going to achieve what it is capable of achieving.

Ireland needs to be placed on a pedestal. In this country we're afraid of putting our necks out, and I can understand that at times. We are not, by nature, a brash nation. All the more reason therefore to restore some confidence in the national side. We need another Grand Slam, or a Six Nations title, or a Triple Crown far more than we need another Heineken Cup.

CHAPTER 6

So Near Yet So Far

For many of us – it was certainly true for me – there was a desire in 2011 to exorcize the ghosts of four years earlier. It had to be addressed. The 2007 World Cup had been an absolute disaster and we felt like we'd let the country down, because when it comes to World Cups we seem to take particular pride in being Irish. We also knew that even though we were playing on the other side of the world and the matches kicked off at breakfast time back home, if we gave them any reason to do so, this time the Irish public would row in behind us.

Our form had been patchy in 2011, losing at home to France and away to Wales in the Six Nations and only redeeming ourselves in the final game at home to England to deny them a Grand Slam. When England returned to the Aviva in August to inflict our fourth warm-up defeat, and both David Wallace's World Cup hopes and career were finished by a bad knee injury, the public and the media hadn't bought into us. We simply hadn't kicked on in the two Six Nations since the 2009 Grand Slam.

In that last warm-up game, Tuilagi beat Earlsy on the outside early on for a try and the criticism of Earlsy was scathing. Anyone can miss a tackle but plenty of pundits cited his physique. He was simply in the wrong position. Earlsy is actually the most powerful back in Irish rugby in Tests. He'd have the highest 'clean' lifting weights and highest CMJ (counter movement jumps).

Paulie was captain against England, so you can be sure we were prepared and well up for it. Losing to them at home is always a disaster, and so was losing Wally. All the players appreciated what a freak he had been; the things you virtually took for granted when playing with him, such as his speed to recover after a misread. Defending at 10, as I did, is challenging enough, because with the game as it is now the out-half defends the second man. It was only after Wally retired from Munster that I realized something needed to be discussed with my sevens. I'd taken it for granted for ten years. It all depended on where the blindside winger came, and therefore who was the second man. If the opposition blindside wing hit the line outside their number 10, I was on that blindside winger, and the inside men were marked by our 9 and 7. If the blindside wing wasn't involved I was on their 12, so essentially I had to look at three men. With Wally there it was so easy. I just had one man to take.

Where's Wally? He was my 'go to' man in attack too. They say it's hard to score in the green zone, but Wally usually got there just by dint of his freakish power, and in the process he made our decisions look good.

The first of our four warm-up defeats was in Scotland, with a very mixed team, and being the first game after an extended pre-season the standard wasn't great. Scotland were beatable and good teams, certainly the great teams, would have managed a victory there. Ireland seem to have lost that ability to win not playing well, and losing subconsciously tightened the pressure for the back-to-back games with France.

Ironically, I think France in Bordeaux was probably our best performance in the warm-up games. It was a humid, hot and sweaty Saturday evening, but I remember it being a good match. Maybe I'm biased – I didn't play against Scotland – but in Bordeaux I did well, kicking four penalties. I love the weather in France, the pitches, the passion of the fans. It's like Munster in reverse, when you have massive home support; it's good to be on the receiving end of that too. Lots of players can do it at home, but the real test of a player is his ability to perform when all the odds are against him and when the crowd are on his back. That's why you are challenged in France. They boo and go mental when you're taking a kick, which is great. You'd be aware of it, and my warped mind enjoys it!

They pummelled us at the start, but we hung in there and we were going strong at the end. Conor Murray came on in place of Reddser for his debut with twenty minutes to go, and he played well, but there's no comparison between Conor then and Conor now. He's very calm and composed, and that's a big thing about him; while as an athlete he's on a different level to most scrum-halves, and with experience his game understanding will improve.

A week later we were 8–0 up with a Cian Healy try, but France were so completely on top that day and went 26–8 ahead when François Trinh-Duc picked off a pass by Tomas O'Leary for an intercept try. The environment had been shaped by then, and some people were going after Tomas, which happens. A big deal was made of that intercept.

I came on for Darce, with Johnny moving to 12, and Johnny and Sean O'Brien scored late tries which I converted to bring some respectability to the scoreline. We'd trained very well for that game. In fairness to Philip Morrow, who was moving on to Saracens after the World Cup, training was brilliant, and despite the defeats there was as good a bond in the squad as I've experienced.

All the provincial barriers were addressed. What creates barriers are the hard-core provincial players. I can admire their viewpoints. The Shane Jennings and Leo Cullens are proud, staunch Leinstermen who will do anything for Leinster and anything to keep Munster down; fellas like Axel, Quinny and an awful lot of Munster players would have been the exact same in reverse. Some players are different in the Ireland set-up from their provinces, which is a bit disappointing, but I think players like Donncha O'Callaghan, Paulie, Hayes, Flannery, Marcus Horan, David Wallace, myself, Strings, Brian, Sean O'Brien, Luke Fitzgerald, Rob Kearney, Johnny Sexton, Cian Healy and Jamie Heaslip are the same players for Ireland as they are for their provinces.

In international camp the Leinster lads were really good trainers, in the gym and in terms of their standards. You get pushed. It's a different stimulus. There's nothing like being pushed to your limit to extract the best out of you. That's what happens in Irish camps now. Brian would readily admit that for years Munster fellas set the standards – bossing the fitness, bossing the strength, bossing the speed, bossing the skills and setting the trend. Now Leinster have jumped us and the likes of Fergus

McFadden, Kearney, Sexton, O'Brien and Sean Cronin have all been strong men who push you and set the pattern.

The thirty-man squad for the World Cup was announced after the second defeat to France. Fellas were surprised that Tomas was left out, effectively going from first- to fourth-choice scrum-half. He was lambasted on TV after the defeat at home to France, and I don't know how much influence the pundits have, but at the time some of us thought the management were listening too much to outside influences. But maybe that was just us.

The core of the squad were all four years older, and more of us were in our thirties, but our strength in depth was better. For example, Jamie Heaslip, Rob Kearney, Tommy Bowe and Luke Fitzgerald had all been left out in 2007, and they were now seasoned internationals, along with Sean O'Brien, Cian Healy and Mike Ross.

I think too many Irish fellas have been scarred by New Zealand. They don't enjoy going there. Whether for Ireland or the Lions, we were regularly beaten down there, and that has an effect. To Deccie and the management's credit, however, they put serious thought into the preparation and the itinerary. Starting off in Queenstown for a week was a masterstroke. We had a good piss-up the night we arrived, which has to be done. There was no dwarf-throwing, although it's as well there weren't any cameras on us, because stories can be created out of absolutely nothing. Everyone was relaxed and giving it holly, and there was a day to recover before getting back into it.

It's important to have a contrast between social activities and good training. We went hard at it for the two hours' training in the morning, and the hour-long review in the evenings, and did all the various activities in the afternoon or just chilled out. In France in 2007, in that glorified industrial estate outside Bordeaux, inner turmoil was eating away at you, killing you. As Bryce Cavanagh in Munster repeatedly says: 'Rugby is all about the other twenty-two hours.' It's easy to do something for two hours, it's what you do for the rest of the day that determines how you are as a pro. And that's why Queenstown was really good. Brian and the senior players, and the management, set up good committees. There was good craic on the coach to and from training, and that is vital.

It was a really happy camp, despite those warm-up games. Deccie and Ger Carmody, the team operations manager, had obviously been planning it for a long while. We had some laughs on the speedboats and the shooters, and go-karting. They were lethal. How we were allowed on them I will never know. There could have been horrific injuries. I nearly broke my arm. It was like slalom-tobogganing on a four-wheel scooter. Some of the boys even did bungee jumping. Not for me.

After a week in Queenstown, and three days before playing the USA Eagles in our first pool match, we travelled to New Plymouth on the North Island, in good spirits. Match night was wet and horrible, and Eddie O'Sullivan had them fired up. We started slowly. We lacked a little confidence and we made a few errors. I was given a nice bit of game time, thirty minutes, and given the way the warm-up games had gone I was pushing hard to be selected from the start. Johnny played average but missed a few kicks.

We were leading 10–3 when I came on, and soon after Rory Best scored off a maul. I missed the touchline conversion. I was freezing on the bench and it was a brutal kick. Barely made the posts. So much for being the attentive sub! I got into it when I'd limbered up a bit. I hit a good conversion after Tommy Bowe scored his second try. We were pushing for a bonus point try when Darce threw an intercept which allowed the Americans to score with the final play. We should have had a bonus point in the bag by then. It was an unconvincing start and not the launching pad we were looking for, but shit conditions can be a great leveller in rugby. When you have a dry ball you don't think about passing or catching, you just play.

The next day, a Monday, we moved on to Auckland for our game against Australia the following Saturday. We were in a lakeside hotel on the outskirts of Auckland, a long way from the city and in a place with nowhere to go for a coffee nearby. It brought back a few memories of the lakeside hotel on the out-skirts of Bordeaux in 2007. I was also annoyed when I wasn't picked to start. Rob Kearney, Sean O'Brien and Cian Healy were all fit again and Eoin Reddan also started.

Match night was again dirty, wet and cold. By the time our coach arrived at Eden Park it was already dark, but there was a cracking atmosphere. That was the start of the World Cup proper. The Aussies didn't really rate us and thought they'd take us handy, but we were superior to them in every aspect. The forwards played really well. Stephen Ferris was immense. Our scrum was huge, and Cian Healy set the tone with a dump tackle on Quade Cooper. Ferris frogmarched Will Genia back into his own 22. Big moments from big players. It was a power-ful performance.

Johnny missed a few kicks before I was brought on with half an hour remaining, again for Darce, with Johnny moving to 12. He missed another one and I was told I probably should have taken it, but you always give the benefit of the doubt to the nominated kicker. Johnny hit the post with that one. I then kicked a couple of penalties which weren't particularly difficult but were high-pressure – exactly what I needed to kick-start the competition from my point of view. More importantly, it sealed a massive win over Australia. Ireland hadn't beaten a Tri-Nations team in the southern hemisphere since winning both Tests in Australia in 1979.

The final score was 15–6, but we should have won by more. We were defending hard on our line when we broke away and Tommy nearly scored but was tackled into touch. Conor Murray had a lovely try disallowed. It could easily have been 22–6 and no one would have complained.

David Pocock being ruled out had definitely been a bonus. We were well prepped for them that week and had identified Pocock and Genia as major threats. With Cooper sometimes defending at 15 we felt that was an area to exploit with our kicking game. I wouldn't have been the strongest defensive 10 by any means but you cannot really shirk your responsibility. I know some defensive coaches position out-halves differently, but you're mentally conceding when you hide your out-half. Ian Humphreys has been moved to the wing or full-back, and the same with Cooper, but I think this gives the opposition the upper hand from the start. Unless you've played there, full-back is a nightmare of a position. Kearns did well, and both he and Kurtley Beale were brilliant in the air that night, but that was part of our strategy, to kick and get Kearns competing in the air against Cooper. And there's only one winner there. Cooper had a bad night, and we were hoping to rattle him. He's a fascinating player, perfect for exhibition games, but the pressure can get to him and that was always in the back of my mind.

I'd been having a tussle with Johnny since 2010, but I was confident that when the pressure came on I would give them no choice. They would have to pick me. The competition brought out the best in both of us, as with me and Humphs, and the Irish team benefited because whoever was playing at out-half was a player in form. Conor came on eight minutes after me for Reddser and had a big impact too. When you have half an hour to influence things it's almost as good as starting. It shows the coach has the conviction to bring you on, and you feel so much more a part of it. It was a big-pressure game and Johnny is a great kicker but something made him miss which is very unusual. My experience probably helped me nail the pressure kicks. This will happen for him the more he matures.

The next week was broken up cleverly. We spent four nights in Lake Taupo, where we had a nice hotel, a good gym and a small island on the lake with a pin and a green for some hole-in-one golf. From there, four days before we played Russia, we took a coach to Rotorua. The highlight of that trip was a visit to one of the natural springs and spa for relaxation therapy. Included in the package was a massage, which had some of the boys very excited. So we had some laughs coming out of the place as it transpired that the masseuses were Maori versions of John Hayes. How shall I put this? It was a major disappointment! It was funny though. Anything to break the monotony for forty fellas in camp.

Some of us were now, for the first time, beginning to enjoy New Zealand. It helped that at last we'd won there against good opposition, even if it wasn't the All Blacks. As it was later in the year than our customary June tours, the weather was nicer and the evenings were longer. We'd never enjoyed so much support either: because of the economic crisis at home, thousands of expats were on hand in New Zealand and followed us around, many of them in camper vans. We also suddenly found we were very popular with the locals after beating Australia. For a while it seemed like we were New Zealand's second favourite team. It was a snowball effect.

As I said to Declan at the time, the scheduling was great. We moved on, attacked a place, got the job done, moved on again, reassessed, embraced the local people there, and went again. It was like a road trip, and very well organized. Deccie and Ger had reccied the entire thing.

We beat Russia 62–12, which sounds like a thrashing, but we played well. It was a good-quality performance. Nine players were brought in, and everybody who hadn't yet played was given a game. It was nice to see Paddy Wallace make his World Cup debut in his third World Cup. It's been easy for me because I was a regular starter for ten years, but for somebody like Paddy, you can imagine his and his family's relief. That might have been the only day when he felt he belonged. Unlike in 2007, it also meant everybody in the squad felt they were a part of this World Cup.

Fergus McFadden got a crack and scored the first of our nine tries from a cross-kick by me – a simple one, more a kick-pass – and Earlsy secured our bonus point by the 38th minute with the first of his two tries. Tony Buckley scored our ninth and last try.

I was given my first start, and after the Australia game I knew what was at stake. It was obviously close between me and

Johnny. When Johnny missed a conversion, after he and Reddser had come on for Isaac Boss and me, Bossy smiled and kind of nudged me as if to say 'you're in'. Unfortunately the cameras were on the bench and it's become a YouTube moment, but it was nothing. I wasn't thinking like that at all and I'm sure Bossy wasn't either. I'd felt really good, but I wouldn't wish Johnny to miss his kick. Ever. That's serious loser territory.

We flew on to Dunedin the next day with a great buzz in the camp, although we were a little worried about Italy, because they were fighting for their lives. If they lost, they were out, but we also had to win to make sure we qualified for the quarter-finals, and as group winners, otherwise the win over Australia mightn't count for anything.

There was huge competition for places, and the players who'd been given their chance against Russia had grabbed it. The match was being held in the newly built enclosed Otago Stadium so we trained in Carisbrook all week before we were told the team on Thursday night. I had gone well against the USA and Australia, had a very good game against Russia, and got the nod, with eight other players recalled, including Brian and Paulie.

It was so satisfying to be picked, especially when so many pundits had heralded a new dawn – a new dawn which didn't feature me. I'd done exactly what I'd set out to do.

We kicked well, we created well and we scored four good tries. Darce was big in the centre for us that night. I kicked my third penalty to give us a 9–6 lead at half-time and the Italians were hanging on, but the pressure told in the second half. After I had kicked a fourth penalty Brian scored a lovely try off something the management had identified. Tommy went around

Mirco Bergamasco and Brian cut back to support on the inside from a dummy loop and touched down under the posts. They hadn't filled that hole, and we'd also targeted Luciano Orquera's defence at out-half with Darce and Tommy. Italy defended the way we thought they would. It's great when you identify plays and they work. It gives all the analysis team and all the staff a massive boost, knowing they are on the right track and that players buy into it as well.

The atmosphere was quality. It was a thirty thousand sell-out and virtually everybody wore green. Irish rugby was on the road to its own Italia '90 moment. Beating Australia had been the biggest victory in the World Cup. The global media highlighted that win and all the Paddies in New Zealand, Australia and beyond rowed in behind us. Winning that night set up a quarter-final against Wales in Wellington, with Australia having to face South Africa, and in the same half of the draw as New Zealand.

Did that lure us into a bit of a comfort zone? I'd definitely say so, even if a few of my team-mates would disagree. I can only speak for myself, but it is very hard to achieve the kind of emotional and mental pitch we reached against Italy once again a week later. Wales hadn't broken sweat in beating Fiji 66–0 a week before our quarter-final.

The preparation was good in Wellington that week and we were excited. Maybe a few of us thought we were already in the semi-final. We were dreaming, and you couldn't blame us. There was so much at stake. This was our chance to reach a first ever World Cup semi-final.

The Welsh seem to have a different mentality at Test level, as they've shown with three Grand Slams in the last nine years.

Once they achieve some momentum they think they're God's gift, but they back it up, to their credit. They took that momentum into the game and hit us with an early try by Shane Williams, which they seemed to score at will. We dominated the possession then, but struggled to get over the gain line.

We turned down a couple of kicks at goal, from a difficult angle to the right, to go instead for the corner. At 7–0 down with the wind behind you, you're thinking that even with three penalties you're only 9–7 ahead. We felt on the pitch that we needed to make a statement, to make our territory count. These are the decisions you make, but I don't think the defeat was down to any one incident. It was quite calm. The chat between Brian, Paulie and myself was good. It just felt like we needed to score a try.

I kicked a penalty, but then so did Leigh Halfpenny to leave us 10–3 down at half-time. There was no panic. We knew that with one score we were all right. Fez and Tommy set up Earlsy, who dotted down well in the corner for a good finish. I converted from wide out on the left and we were 10–10 after fifty minutes. We should have kicked on. Running back to our half I was thinking, 'We're going to fucking steamroll these fellas. This is it now.' But I didn't kick particularly well from hand. I went for a few ambitious kicks that went the wrong side of the corner flag by small margins. That's the difference between absolutely beautiful and horrific.

Within six minutes of Earlsy's score, Mike Phillips scored the killer try on the blind side of a ruck, beating Darce and Tommy. It was too soft a try to concede at that level. For some inexplicable reason one of our players left the short side and all week we'd identified the threat posed by Phillips. I think there was disbelief in our team when we saw him scampering in. It was a fucking hammer blow.

Myself and Conor were subbed a few minutes later and watched the team push and push, but another try by Jonathan Davies left us 22–10 adrift. Too much ground to make up. I was disappointed with my performance, which was probably a reflection of how we all played. I didn't dominate the game but it felt that they had momentum up front and that's the difference between kicking off the front or the back foot. I erred a few times by forcing the kick. I had no problem being substituted. The other half-backs are entitled to their chance as well.

Shaun Edwards and Warren Gatland did some expert analysis for that quarter-final, particularly on Sean O'Brien and Stephen Ferris. Wales's chop tackle was so effective and up to then that tackle had gone out of fashion. Now it's off-the-cuff lingo, modern vocab in the world of rugby, and it was reinvented that night by Dan Lydiate, Sam Warburton, Toby Faletau and the Welsh pack.

It was a big downer. We'd had a good tournament and we'd enjoyed every moment until then. When you have momentum in sport the easy thing is to keep it going. If you get knocked overboard it's a disaster. You come crashing down and it's a horrible feeling. It's happened plenty of times and usually the reaction is to hit the bottle for a day or two. Avoid reality. That's not joking. You can't think straight. I had met up with Christian Cullen during the week for lunch, and we went to his bar after the game, but it was a hollow night. No amount of drink could dull the pain.

If we'd won that game we'd have had another two matches.

We would have been there until the end of the tournament, for the first time ever. Even if you are beaten in a semi you can at least compete for a bronze medal. That would have been something, something to give you pride in your work. And that was the annoying part. We're not bottlers. There are enough winners in the team.

The family were ready to come out for the last two weeks if we'd won the quarter-final. My dad, my mum and my brothers were looking to book flights and I'd have flown out Jess and the kids. That was the deal, because I was missing them all, particularly the night we beat Australia.

In my mind I was finishing after the World Cup because of the way things had gone since the Grand Slam. I was targeting the World Cup, and I wasn't thinking beyond that. When I spoke on television after the Australia game saying as much, that was genuinely how I felt. I never have anything prepared, least of all straight after a game. I speak what comes into my head, and this was five or ten minutes after a game which I hadn't started, but then I had a big impact and helped us to a famous win. In that moment it felt like it could be the biggest and last victory of my Irish career, even if we were trying to get to the semi-final at least, or even win the bloody thing. In my head I was stopping after the World Cup.

Several of us have now been to three World Cups, Brian has been to four, yet none of us has ever reached one semi-final. But we can solve it. When the emphasis which has been placed on the provinces is given to the national team, the outcome will be different. I think it's possible Ireland will win a World Cup one day. Certainly a semi-final is within reach, and then anything is possible. Breaking the quarter-final barrier is the challenge, because it's a mental barrier, like England in football World Cups with penalty shoot-outs. They never win, and every time I watch the sport it drives me mental when they say the penalty shoot-out is a lottery. It is far from a lottery. It's a challenge, and it separates the men from the boys; it tests the ability to stand up, pick a spot and deliver. There's nothing 'lottery' about it. If anything it's a mental weakness.

I've thought about this long and hard. Penalty shoot-outs fascinate me because one of the regrets of my career is I never experienced a penalty shoot-out in rugby. Against Clermont when we were six points down I was envisioning kicking a penalty, then having two and a half minutes to work a drop goal and force the game into extra time. I was thinking 'a draw at the end of extra time and then a penalty shoot-out'. The lads slag Johnny Murphy for missing in the Leicester–Cardiff shoot-out at the end of the Heineken Cup semi in 2009, but imagine how good it would feel to be involved in one.

Back home I stayed engrossed in the rest of the World Cup. I couldn't help thinking about what might have been. It felt so far away, so different, yet I was thinking, 'I was playing in that.' Watching Wales play France off the park, yet lose, in the semi-final it was hard not to think that it could have been Ireland in a World Cup final. Alain Rolland's red card against Sam Warburton had a big bearing on that result. I can appreciate the directives which referees receive from the IRB, but in the heat of the moment I don't think there was any intention on Warburton's part. That dump tackle didn't justify a red card. And look at France: with a different ref in the final I think you've a different result. I stand by that, but it was probably better for everyone's mental health that New Zealand won.

Still, they had the rub of the green, and as we know the ref has a big influence and can be the determining factor.

I've no doubt we could have beaten France, because not only would we have had momentum, we would have been in bonus territory. And when you're in bonus territory the shackles can come off. There would have been a huge emotional release, we had a strong game, a load of players in form, and we could have got Seanie and Fez and Jamie offloading.

We all wanted to stay on in New Zealand for another two weeks. That would have been a first. You also felt you'd let so many other people down, both the people back home and the expats. That World Cup was massive for them, and our departure must have left a little void. The 2007 and 2011 World Cups were poles apart. The latter was a huge anticlimax. We won 80 per cent of our games, four out of five, yet we went home; France and Wales each lost three games, and finished second and fourth. We were aware it was knockout rugby by the time we played Wales, but I believe subconsciously we thought the knockout rugby would start in the semi-final.

It was Ireland's best ever World Cup yet it was the most dis- appointing in the end because of that. As players and as managers, that's the way you analyse it. We won four pool games out of four, then came one devastating result. It would have been great to have another crack, but them's the rules.

The tournament reaffirmed to me the importance of getting the process right, and the consistency of performance, after which results look after themselves. If you become result- dependent you neglect the process and what is required to achieve results – skill levels, accuracy and intensity. I think Joe Schmidt is big on all of that, and as a venue England should suit us in 2015. A familiar country, familiar conditions, and accessible to Irish supporters.

And at least the Irish squad will travel to England without the mental baggage we took to New Zealand from all previous World Cups, but especially France 2007. That 2007 tournament left a deep scar, but 2011 demonstrated we can perform on that world stage. Maybe we will stick around for the last two weeks next time.

CHAPTER 7

Attention to Detail

One of the most influential people in my career never played or coached rugby. He's actually a dyed-in-the-wool GAA man and was project manager on our house.

I was introduced to Michael O'Flynn for the first time one day in 2004 in Fota Island golf club, and we clicked straight away. We kept in contact and developed an unbelievable relationship. He is a hugely successful developer – the O'Flynn Group – and is one of the sharpest people I've ever met in my life. Michael's ability to identify what is required for each game and express it with the right words was invaluable for me and is the main reason why I place such store in people outside the rugby bubble.

It is important for players to trust in intelligent people outside the game as it gives them another perspective on the sport which coaches and other players often cannot provide. I think this ties in with why I enjoyed popping up in the last minute to try and win games. I'd almost been broken on so many occasions but something inside kept me going. There is probably some genetic reason for it, along with how we were nurtured and shaped, but in addition to this I found Michael's ability to read situations uncanny. Especially for a fella who has no upbringing in, and no knowledge, of the game. His feeling for it was incredible.

I have been blessed really. From when I first picked up a rugby ball I've had my dad to advise me. Unlike some parents of other players I've witnessed over the years, my dad could always remain detached. Unless he's been hiding it from me, I have rarely, if ever, seen him cry or even become emotional when singing an anthem. He'd normally just wink at me from the crowd. That would mean a lot, and he also influenced me like no one else. He has always underlined the value of hard work, such as the importance of doing my homework early in the week to free up time for rugby. That's probably the professor in him, and with my mum being a teacher this was constantly reinforced.

Michael's words of advice never conflicted with those of my dad, they added to them. They both emailed or texted bullet points to me prior to every game and I'd compare and contrast them before adding my own slant. As it was at school, your homework had to be done for each game too. It's particularly important for young out-halves to be sure of what they are doing off, say, scrums on the right-hand side, or plays off line-outs in different areas of the pitch. As Roy Keane always says, 'Fail to prepare, prepare to fail.' I know it's a cliché, yet it is so true. If you don't have your homework done you get punished.

Michael is steeped in GAA and Éire Óg, with whom he won

three Cork county championship titles in his day. But for some-body who isn't in rugby's inner circle his ability to read a game is amazing. I can't reveal the content of his texts to me because I promised him I never would, but at times I have been astounded by his ability to transfer his business acumen and life skills to rugby.

In terms of preparation and influence, my dad and Michael effectively became my coaches in the last four or five years of my career. A player can become insular in his thinking on the game when he is living in Carton House for seven days without much contact with the outside world. Declan Kidney bringing in Enda McNulty as a sports psychologist to the Irish squad last year was a good move, but I never really got to appreciate Enda as others will do. I'd say we were about to engage. He's a deep person and I'd enjoy a deep conversation too, but he was only there for my last three games. Enda came on to the scene too late for me.

Like Keane's dictum, 'attention to detail' has also become a cliché, but it's what sets the good coaches apart. Not just in ensuring that sessions and game plans are meticulously well pre-pared, but also to make the game simple, and all the while improving little aspects of each player's skills set. If a coach can achieve all of that he's most of the way there. And, of course, it helps if his team wins matches.

Over the years I've realized more and more how the simple little details can mean so much. For example, if the ball is passed to the player's hip, the move is finished; if the ball is passed in front, there is every chance of something happening. But it's amazing how many times moves in both training and matches break down due to balls being passed to hips, above the head or at the feet. These basics were what Joe Schmidt concentrated on with Leinster and they became the best passing team around. That was no coincidence.

Without a shadow of a doubt, Declan is the coach I know the best. I've spent so much time under him and with him, from Pres through two spells with Munster and two spells with Ireland, as an assistant coach and a head coach. Indeed, I've probably experienced him more than any other player, hence I've lived through every possible emotion with the man.

I don't take any joy from picking out his weaknesses or strengths, or anything like that. What I can say is that Deccie was probably learning his trade as a coach as I was learning mine as a player. Irish rugby itself was learning how to shape up in the professional era at the same time. We were all on a journey together.

It would have been interesting if we'd been under the direction of a different coach at that time but then I don't think anyone tapped into 'Munsterness' better than Deccie. It's easy to criticize in hindsight. We are all experts in hindsight. But some of his ideas were fantastic. Many of the quirkier ones are out there by now, like the coaches starting a team meeting looking like eejits wearing fez hats, a remote-control car carrying the kicking tee, and having the speakers blaring at Musgrave Park during training in the build-up to the Saracens game at Vicarage Road in 2000. This is a long time ago and it took a fair bit of organizing. It's all very well talking about it but you've got to demonstrate it, and he did.

I believe he was hugely beneficial to me, all the way through to becoming and then surviving as an international, but then I probably relied more on technical expertise at that stage because, partly with his help, I was mentally strong and able to motivate myself. Hence, over time his role became less influential for me.

There is no doubt he is a very clever head coach in ensuring a happy and united camp. I think he gets the best out of people emotionally, and I genuinely think he's a good person, although at times I became severely tested by the way he tapped into people emotionally. Now that I'm out of the bubble I can appreciate his ability more, whereas it was more difficult towards the end because I felt – and I've since showed – that I had more to give. Unfortunately, Deccie effectively made the call that finished my international career. Some might find it hard to believe, but I am genuinely not bitter about his decision. Everything happens for a reason and that was the way my career was to end. There's nothing worse than a slow death, and I got shot nicely in front of everybody.

When you're the player concerned, your family think you are the only one it has happened to. No, it happens to everyone, so you accept it and you get on with it. I've had setbacks throughout my whole career, but you come back from them and show what you're made of. To have the conviction to then play two of my better games in Europe, against Harlequins and Clermont, also made me happier with my decision to retire.

Admittedly, Deccie's decision made me angry, and gave me the jolt that inspired me to play as I did in those two games. I'd be lying if I said otherwise. Players derive motivation from anything and everything.

I've often been asked what I look for in a coach. Is it his experience or technical or motivational abilities? I look for everything. The way we are in Munster especially, where for years we revelled in being the underdogs, you look for any bit of motivation. So, if I had any pride in myself, I had to come back fighting.

There were days when I wondered, 'Am I still as good as I used to be?' It's only natural to have those doubts, and it didn't help that, with the passing of the years, I no longer felt that I was regarded by the Munster management as an irreplaceable part of the team. I'm convinced of that. I could have had a harder decision to make under different circumstances. But I think it was only after the Harlequins and Clermont games that the penny dropped, as it were.

I definitely think there could be a good role for Deccie in Irish rugby. He would be invaluable to the under-age set-up, perhaps in the fifteen-to-twenty age bracket. He is big into a balanced lifestyle too, and that's important. You can't be all rugby, and nowadays there are one-dimensional gym monkeys coming out of the schools. When he advised players to, say, do a course, it often annoyed them, but you can be sure that when they reached twenty-seven or twenty-eight they said, 'Jesus, that was a great idea. Fair play to him.'

He genuinely cares about a player's life outside of rugby, which as I said severely tested me at times, but in all his decisions I am sure he was doing what he felt was best for the team. So it was that John Hayes wasn't brought to the 2011 World Cup, and I was dropped before the France game in March 2013. We had our disagreements before then, and I wasn't always shy about speaking my mind. Some might like to think that because there's been friction between Rog and Deccie over the years, he enjoyed dropping me. I genuinely don't believe he did.

You can also have too much of a good thing, or too much of listening to one voice. It wasn't his or my fault that he coached me as much as he did. Hence there were times when I had to switch off because what he was saying didn't stimulate me, and I needed to concentrate on my preparation for the weekend. That probably happens in any job when you have too much of one person.

There were plenty of good times along the way. Having been with him for so much of my career, I had mixed feelings about Deccie coming back to Munster for a second spell in 2005. When you look back, however, in his last six seasons as Munster's head coach, from 1999/2000 to 2001/02 and from 2005/06 to 2007/08, we reached four Heineken Cup finals and won two of them. For teams to win two Heineken Cups and a Grand Slam the 10 has to believe in his coach, otherwise the system breaks down. They are two of the most important people in the set-up.

Eddie O'Sullivan was also influential in my career. He coached me with the Irish Under-21s and the Ireland team, and I was a big fan. At the time I needed detail in my game, and in this I thought he was way ahead of other coaches. After we lost to England in '02 and '03, we beat them four times in a row, and often that was due to Eddie's game plan; he also had the cop on to realize it didn't work against other teams. He identified weaknesses in England, and that is skilled coaching.

When we beat England at Twickenham in 2004 – their first defeat since winning the World Cup – Girvan Dempsey's try was straight off the training ground. By going wide right and wide left, we exploited a softness outside. There were other times you had no choice but to take them on up the middle before picking the moment to go wide-wide; as they were too soft in the 13 channel you would always get the outside against them, and if you got on the front foot on the wide channel then you could just play.

I appreciate he used expressions that some used to laugh at, but as well as having a great game plan to beat England I thought his general attention to detail was very good. Obviously a lot of players struggled with his man management – some an awful lot – but I think that's a two-way street. He wasn't very approachable, but many may not know he is deaf in one ear. Some players felt they couldn't communicate with him easily, but while I found it difficult to approach him the first or second time, thereafter I couldn't say a bad word about him. I really enjoyed my time under him playing for my country.

Admittedly, we couldn't beat France under Eddie, or at any rate after beating them in the Six Nations in 2003 we lost to them seven times in a row, including two World Cup defeats. But for those defeats to France, another two or three Grand Slams were potentially ours. France were our nemesis. It was hugely frustrating. We could have beaten them once or twice but we were tonked by them a few times too. Today they are a shadow of what they were back then, but quite why they were our nemesis I don't know.

Niall O'Donovan was Eddie's assistant and forwards coach, as he had been for Munster alongside Deccie. He is now back as Munster's manager, and I think he has an awful lot to offer. I like Niallo and I think he has great knowledge of the Irish game. He's an extremely diligent, hard worker. He transformed one of the rooms in his house into a video library a long time ago, which would typify his attention to detail. He's probably suffered for not speaking with a southern hemisphere accent, but himself, Anthony Foley and Brian O'Brien were three Shannon stalwarts with strong beliefs, and I admire fellas with strong beliefs because they ultimately care about Munster. They want only the best for Munster, and that's why they're there and that's why they should be listened to. Munster tapped into that Shannon mentality and Ireland tapped into Munster, because Shannon were the best and Munster became the best simply as a result of playing cup rugby.

Tony McGahan came to Munster halfway through the 2005/06 season as defence/assistant coach and was a big part of our two Heineken Cup wins before becoming head coach for four years. As assistant coach he did much more than defence, running our back play as well in training.

Dumper gave me confidence. He genuinely believed in me and that I could bring out the best in people around me, and how people respond to you is invaluable in rugby. I suppose he'd seen me deliver for Munster, and before games he used to call me 'The King'. No matter how experienced you are, to hear that from your coach just makes you feel ten feet tall. There were days I felt I had the ball on a string in Thomond Park.

Now I need to learn how to transmit this to younger players, because how a player feels internally will drive so much of his performance. Not everyone will tell you truthfully and exactly how they feel, and only you know how you feel. I find that fascinating, because it is the unknown grey area between two ears that decides, either consciously or subconsciously, whether a player will get up off the ground a second earlier.

Tony brought out the best in me. He publicly backed me too,

and that may seem unimportant, but a coach publicly backing his players is crucial.

He brought in Laurie Fisher as forwards coach, and Laurie was brilliant. I wouldn't be best placed to comment on the intricacies of forward play, but his attention to detail, work rate and knowledge are incredible. Munster's maul and scrum became less potent in his time, but we improved significantly in terms of our breakdown work, which had 'Australian' written all over it. The Brumbies appear to have come on hugely under Jake White and Laurie.

One of Laurie's theories, which I believe holds true, is that the subconscious requires three weeks to learn a new skill, and the older you are, the more you have to de-train the mind to eradicate poor technique. This is even more pertinent from a coaching perspective, as the younger you are and the earlier you start playing, the easier it is to learn a skill. It actually takes three weeks of repetition days to embed a new skill. Tony and Laurie improved our skills by constant repetition. In passing drills, Tony reinforced the need to keep your elbow up and point your hands to the target when running, what foot to have up when you're starting your run, and keeping square. I think back then the Aussies were ahead of most of the world because they all came out of the Australian Institute of Sport, where attention to detail like this seemed to be excellent.

Dumper could be very harsh on the younger players. Myself and Paulie had several meetings with him and made this point, and he'd take it on board, but when he got cranky, by God did he get cranky. His view was that he had been chopped as a promising rugby player in league and, as whoever was coaching him was harsh on him, he felt by being especially harsh on the younger players they'd come through stronger. But this approach doesn't work on all youngsters, because at a younger age I think you break easier. Murray, Earlsy and Mike Sherry certainly prospered under him, but other young players struggled.

In between Deccie's two spells at Munster, Alan Gaffney was head coach for three years and was also the backs coach under Deccie with Ireland. He was really good in one-on-one video sessions with players, although as head coach your time becomes so precious that this dilutes one-on-ones.

There would have been a split in the Munster camp over the Gaffney years. The non-internationals suffered an awful beasting from him. They trained really hard and had tough video sessions with him, yet he used to say that there would be a ray of sunshine over his head when we came back into town. He'd lighten up and be in great form.

I liked Alan, or Riff, as he's better known. I thought he was good for Munster. In the latter stages of his time as Ireland's backs coach I think he became bogged down and a little confused in what he wanted to achieve. He was dealing with a lot of young, ambitious and temperamental internationals, which demands highly organized and detailed coaching. It seemed to me at times as if he wasn't prepared enough for sessions. Players have to take responsibility, but no matter how experienced you are you like some structure to your sessions and some guidance.

Warren Gatland gave me my Irish debut in 2000, and he was also on the Lions coaching ticket in 2009. Gatty was a young coach when he got the Ireland job and I was a young player. I was only too delighted – no experience, no knowledge, but mad keen to impress. It had been a blessing in disguise that I collided with Eric Elwood at a training session in the ALSAA complex by Dublin Airport. I picked up a knee injury as a result, which ruled me out of a possible debut in Twickenham when Ireland were beaten 50–18. Instead, two weeks later I was one of five new caps against Scotland in Lansdowne Road, we won 44–22, and I was embarking on my international journey. Gatty deserves some credit for the changes that day. He had the vision to pick the five of us, and all of us now have sixty-five or more caps: Hayes (105), Strings (98), Horgan (65), Easterby (65) and myself (128). That's 461 caps between us. There are no duds there.

Gatty was usually up for a bit of fun. There was a glint in his eye, shall I say. He kept you in your place, but that was good. I got on well with Gaillimh, Claw and Woody back then, and there would have been a bit of mischief in me as well. I'd try to impress a few senior lads by joining in a few jokes with Gatty, but he would kind of look at you as if to say 'know your place young fella'. Which was good: you have to learn your place.

He was a young coach who would become a great coach, but even then he had a good insight into the mentality and emotions of the game, as well as that hard-nosed Kiwi edge. Having said that, if I'm being totally honest, I never really got to know him properly. At the time things were very simple: 'We're going to smash around the corner and then we're going to kick to the corners.' But that was the game back then. Ireland were only starting out. Before that we hadn't managed more than one or two wins in a season in the Five Nations since the 1980s.

Brian McLaughlin was another coach whom I worked with at both under-age and Irish senior level. We won the Under-21

Triple Crown with him when he succeeded Eddie, and I keep in contact with him to this day. We had great times under Laughs with the Under-21s. I used to hook up with the squad after playing for Con, have an almighty session on the Saturday and then train, dying, on the Sunday. Brian was an unbelievable man for the breakdown; we had horrible drills that killed us as he hammered home the correct height at ruck time. But he is a very nice man and I enjoyed playing for him. I think it always reflects well on someone that after it all you stay in contact, and I always appreciated his complimentary texts after big wins. With Ireland, as a skills coach, he was again very effective at the one-on-ones, and always applied himself with massive attention to detail and work rate.

Graham Henry was my first head coach with the Lions but I was like a fish out of water on the 2001 tour. I can still go through the team selection for the second Test. Jonny Wilkinson was the automatic first-choice 10, but Neil Jenkins was crippled with his knees. He could barely walk. However, Graham told me, 'If there's a penalty in the last minute, forty-five metres out, I want Neil Jenkins to kick it.' At the time I was gutted – I was thinking, 'Am I going to be involved here?' – but with experience I can appreciate that was the right call.

The Lions is so pressurized to get a result in such a short space of time that I don't think you can get a true reflection of the tour's head coach. You're only getting a snapshot. You don't get to know them. Only working with a coach on a day-to-day basis over a longer period of time allows you to gain an accurate assessment. In 2001 I was there to learn as much as I could with a great bunch of players, and without that experience I wouldn't have the knowledge I now have. I would have accepted every single word from a coach as gospel. It was such a good place and such a happy time, I was just appreciative of the opportunity.

Donal Lenihan was manager of that Lions tour, and he was an influential figure at Con as well as being my first Irish manager. I have always been hugely respectful towards him because he has presence and authority, and it's important to respect people who've done it all. As he was a lock and I was a 10 we didn't have too many rugby chats, but I respect his opinion and he's a 'go to' person in Cork. A few others would fall into that category, like Jerry Murray, Jerry Holland, Michael Bradley, Ralphie Keyes, Squeaks (Brian Walsh), Ian Murray, Tommy Kiernan, Anthony Horgan and Kenny Murphy (Noel's son) – and that family have been very good to me.

Tommy Kiernan has probably given more to Irish rugby than anyone I know. He broke his arse attending voluntary meetings and he created both the European Cup and the Irish provincial system. He almost single-handedly revolutionized the Irish game and much of European rugby, and that's some statement.

Les Kiss came in under Deccie and he's a really good defence coach who was then given attack as well. This is hard to do as attack is the least black-and-white area of the game. It's about decision-making, and it's open to interpretation. He had some very good ideas, but when you're essentially viewed as a defence coach it's difficult to change your spots and fully convince the whole group. It probably would have been easier for a coach coming from a different background, but I think he's a good man. He's knowledgeable, organized, detailed, and understands that playing isn't that easy. As a coach it's important to be realistic and have patience when dealing with players, and cut them some slack.

Some ex-players, when they turn to coaching (or indeed punditry), apparently think the game has become quite simple. Almost overnight they completely forget that when they were out there a few times themselves they actually weren't able to run through everyone.

CHAPTER 8

The Perfect 10

I'm a traditionalist who believes the number 10 has to have the ability to change a game if something isn't going well. I'd be very big on game management and I'd look upon that as the 10's job, although I see that becoming less important in the sport, which is disturbing. Some 10s nowadays have just become a pawn on the chessboard, but in my view he's the king and he's got to be prepared to put his neck on the line. Some days he's going to get it wrong, but there will be days when it goes right, when he does what he believes in and trusts his instincts. That's what separates the great from the good.

A trend is developing in which the newer breed of out-half is content to be just another piece in the jigsaw, whereas the way I was brought up, the way I learned rugby, the 10 was the boss and should generally exert the most influence on the game. If a match wasn't going your way, you had to dig deep mentally to come up with a play that might change the game. Where are you playing the game? Are you playing it in the right zones? Are you rewarding your forwards? Nowadays there's little or no appreciation of the massive return to be gained from putting the ball in front of your forwards. Forwards are big tired boys and when they get up from a ruck, ideally they want to see the ball in front of them. That can come from a passing move, but the way I was raised, there's nothing better than seeing the ball trickle over the touchline. You can see the forwards increase their jog into a semi-sprint. It does wonders for body language, the crowd and the mood, and those mental games within the game.

The 10 definitely was the most dominant figure, even though the 9 now has a bigger role due to the rule changes I will talk about later, primarily in terms of kicking from defensive zones. They also have plenty of responsibility when it comes to bossing the forwards and controlling the game, so the most important team-mate for any out-half is the scrum-half. After all, he supplies us with about 90 per cent of the ball we receive in any given match. And I've been lucky. I've played with some great 9s. All vastly different too.

Peter Stringer is an unbelievable passer and has a serious ability to marshal forwards. The fact that the 9's burden of responsibility has increased has probably pushed Strings out quicker than he should have been. More than ever now a scrum-half has to box-kick and challenge defences and go on his own. But I think he still has a huge role in terms of his ability to slow down or pick up the speed of a game, and given his unparalleled knowledge of forward play. That's the big thing Conor Murray has to learn – watch more rugby, play more rugby, and when he does he'll have it all. Conor has some pass too, but Strings has a unique way of passing. It's like a spinning top through the air which arrives lengthways instead of sideways. It's perfect to catch because it means you don't have to adjust it in your hands.

The 12 is important for the 10 too. He is vital in terms of 'keep it' or 'hit me' or 'miss me'. Rua Tipoki was definitely the best communicator I played with. I loved playing with him. I loved everything about him. He was an inspiration, someone I am very proud to have been alongside. A serious team man and a great guy. There was Trevor Halstead too, and I'd have serious time for Darce. I thought Paddy Wallace was under-appreciated, under-respected. I enjoyed Rob Henderson's company immensely, both on and off the pitch, and he doesn't get the recognition he deserves either. Kevin Maggs was another great team man, a great guy, just so proud to play for Ireland. He always got over the gain line for you.

But there's no doubt that 9 and 10 are where it's at. That wasn't what drew me to the position, although I did receive plenty of ball at 10 and as a young fella that's what you want. I never really played anywhere else since starting fifteen-a-side at Under-12s. It suited my physique. Grant Fox was my first boyhood hero, followed by Michael Lynagh, who I thought was very graceful. I suppose I could see a bit of myself in Fox. He was small and slight but could give the ball a fair thump when he needed to.

At Pres we robbed a senior cup medal from David Wallace and Crescent Comprehensive, and when I made the Probables for the Irish Schools trial in 1994 I had one of the games of my life. Yet I ended up third choice behind Emmet Farrell, now the Leinster video analyst, and Richard Ormond from St Mary's, on the B side to play the Australian Schools teams that were touring Ireland before Christmas. This made me ask myself if they truly valued the concept of 'Probables' and 'Possibles' after I'd started for the Probables, scored two tries and kicked everything.

Moving into the Munster set-up, I'd say my first rival at out-half was Barry Everitt. Killian Keane and Aidan O'Halloran from the Cookies – Young Munster – were also on the scene when I first subbed for Munster in 1997 against Connacht in Temple Hill. Aidan was always a threat on the pitch. He was lively, sparky and a good kicker, and back then, if your club did well you had a chance of making the Munster squad.

The following season I was brought on the pre-season tour of Scotland with Killian. I was his apprentice for that season before I did my hamstring at the start of the campaign. Barry Everitt was playing really well and for most of 1998/99 was ahead of me. I thought he was very good. He was a nice footballer and quite exciting as a player. He started out as a running out-half and had issues at the beginning with his goal-kicking, but went the full circle, became a kicking out-half and enjoyed a long professional career in England.

Killian was very helpful to me. Although he could play 12 we were going for the same position then, but as competitive as he was, he always had time for a chat or some advice. As a player, he was solid, calm, influential, had good basics, would do the right thing at the right time, and made the game plan look simple. He had a good brain for the game, he was good at tactical appreciation, and I think you're shaped in that way before you're twenty. I think it's very hard to 'make' an out-half, but if you get the right advice then it stands to you for a long time. For the last sixteen years the longest I'd have gone without contact with him would be three months. He's been a constant, be it in a big or a small way. He's always been there.

At the end of the 1998/99 season, Con beat Garryowen in the All-Ireland League final (my only AIL winners' medal) but Jeremy Staunton was picked for the tour to Australia ahead of me by Gatland, along with David Humphreys and Eric Elwood. As with Barry Everitt, there was an edge to my rivalry with Jeremy, but I still got on with them both. We were going for the same position but it never entered my head to cold-shoulder either of them. How would that give you an advantage?

Jeremy was hugely exciting. You never knew what he'd do next. He was a very instinctive player, fast and a bit of a dare-devil. A bit like Barry, Jeremy went on to have a long professional career in England, and along the way he also changed from a running into a kicking out-half.

By the start of 1999/2000 I had risen to third in the Irish pecking order due to becoming Munster's first-choice out-half and then the impression I must have made when we beat Ireland in a World Cup warm-up match in Musgrave Park. The World Cup came too soon for me, however, and they only took Humphreys and Elwood.

Eric Elwood was the main man in Irish rugby when I came on the scene, before Humphs put pressure on him and took the 10 jersey in the 1999 Five Nations under Gatty. I admired Eric as a player, and for his passion and his love for Ireland. As a young out-half, you'd be inspired by this. As I've said before, it was a completely different game then – there were fewer rucks and more scrums and line-outs – but his qualities were still evident. I also learned close-up how good he was at barking and organizing the defence. He was a great man to talk, and that's important too, as long as you're saying the right things. There's nothing worse than a fella talking for the sake of it, but he certainly wasn't quiet. You always knew Eric was on the pitch. He's also a very nice individual and I've stayed in contact with him to this day.

Humphs was probably the most talented of them all. He was cheeky, he was inventive, he was bright, he just did things and made them look very easy. He was a master of the quick 22s. He was rapid for a 10, and he scored some unbelievable individual tries. He was just a lovely footballer.

If you recall Elwood playing in Lansdowne Road, the weather was usually wet or windy, or both, and he put the ball into the air more. Rugby became more the game I now know when Humphs came on the scene. I watched other out-halves more than any other player, and I probably watched Humphs more than any of them. For years Ulster would play on a Friday night. Whereas a lot of the Munster lads' rivals were Leinster players, my competition was in Ulster. So I watched Humphs and Ulster avidly. I'd be lying if I said otherwise.

I remember one night in October 2001, a couple of weeks after we'd played badly and lost the rearranged Foot and Mouth game in Murrayfield. It was a few days before the team to play Wales was due to be announced. I watched Ulster play Wasps at Ravenhill in the Heineken Cup, and Humphs scored thirty-seven points: six penalties, four drop goals, a try and a conversion. Ridiculous! The next day we were away to Harlequins, with me thinking, 'I have my work cut out here!' I did my best, four out of four and a try for sixteen points, but Humphs started against Wales the next week, kicked seven out of seven, and I was on the bench for the rest of the season.

When Humphs was hot, he was very hot. Watching him

motivated me to become a better player. There were definitely things you could pick up from his attack game. In the early days of my European and even international career I made way more line breaks than I did in the latter stages. The game was easier, you were less known and not as marked; there wouldn't have been as much analysis. I scored four tries in the 2007 Six Nations. But out-halves generally make fewer line breaks nowadays.

Ultimately I got to know Humphs better than any other out-half, through being in so many squads and kicking sessions together. He has a great sense of humour too, which probably wouldn't be so well known. He's mischievous and he's good craic. We used to have some laughs driving Rala's van – Rala being the Irish bag manager, Paddy O'Reilly. Humphs would take the wheel and lose the run of himself, and Rala would nearly lose his life. He's the kind of fella you'd like to get to know more and more; his company was so enjoyable.

I suppose I had more doubts than most out-halves, but didn't cave into them. I came back for more, but there were days when I didn't want to come back. I practised an awful lot on tackle technique and general defensive work, as well as kicking and passing. I tried to do as much as possible, especially from 2001 onwards. That Lions tour was the biggest learning curve ever. Not only was Jonny Wilkinson devoted to his kicking, I watched him work on his side-stepping skills with Jason Robinson. Jonny opened my eyes.

Gregor Townsend was the opposition 10 when I made my Ireland debut against Scotland, and he was a major rival in terms of selection for that 2001 Lions tour. He was a cracking player. He could have played in any era, especially nowadays. He was so talented and so superior to other Scottish 10s that perhaps he needed someone to tell him to work on his kicking game because he didn't really have a sufficiently consistent one for international rugby. If he'd had that, he would have been nearly the best in the world. On the 1997 Lions tour he was unbelievable. A good running game, good hands, a great man for a break – and there aren't many out-halves with an X factor.

But it was Wilkinson who made the biggest impression on me, without a shadow of a doubt, due to his work rate, his attention to detail, the way he carried himself, what it meant to him, the preparation and the sacrifices. I was lucky to be around in the same era and I've lovely memories of playing against him. He's obviously an iconic figure in world rugby so it was always good to play against the best and measure yourself against him.

I first played against him in Lansdowne Road in October 2001, when I came on as a sub and kicked a couple of penalties – the first was a dead duck. Prior to the Lions tour earlier that year I hadn't known much about him. I still don't know that much about him, to be honest. He keeps most people at a distance, but I was lucky to have come across him at such an early age, because if it had been later it would have been too late. I was twenty-four on that tour whereas he was twenty-two, yet it felt as though I was younger. I've rarely come across a more driven professional. Paulie would be driven too, but in a different way. Jonny is driven individually, whereas Paul drives the team. I did a fair amount of kicking on that tour. From then on, that Lions trip was the benchmark because I didn't have anyone in Ireland making me aware of what was required. It's always good to work up close and personal with your opposition. You're dining at the top table.

In 2003, England hockeyed us in the Grand Slam shoot-out at Lansdowne Road, and I think that Jonny was then at his best. He nailed a drop goal with his right foot into a swirling wind from about forty yards. It was exquisite.

I suppose my most enduring rival in international rugby would be Stephen Jones. Before that I played Neil Jenkins a few times, and he was just a machine. When Wales beat England at Wembley, Jenkins kicked everything. He was another player who as a youngster you could look up to. I admired him hugely. The Welsh could always churn them out. Jonathan Davies was a bit special too, but he didn't play for Wales enough really. Gavin Henson had talent when he was young, and still has talent, no question; unbelievable physique too, all the more so after Gatland grabbed hold of him. But he never came close to fulfilling his talent. Just goes to show the power of the mind.

When Wales were very good, Stephen Jones was very good. He was probably under-appreciated outside of Wales. To the layman he looked awkward, so he probably didn't get the recognition he deserved. He was bright though, he worked hard, he was always fully prepared, and I think you could build a team around him. He was reliable, brave, had presence, and with Llanelli he was a competitor. Partly as a result, they were consistently the best side in Wales in my time. He could play a running game or a kicking game – he mixed it up well. He's another very nice fella too. Likeable, humble not cocky. There have always been good Welsh out-halves around. Dan Biggar and Rhys Priestland are good players, and with Stephen gone, one of them is going to kick on over the next five years and make that red 10 their own.

Compared with Wales, and other countries, French out-halves

seem to come and go. My first Heineken Cup game in the Stoop was against Thierry Lacroix. He was typically French, but a bit like Humphs in style. He was majestic, but then, unlike Humphs, he could be terrible. No consistency. French out-halves tend not to last the test of time. They have had an awful lot more to choose from, but they need some consistency of selection if they want to get results, because as I said, 10 is key.

Some French coaches seem to lack a full appreciation of the importance of patience with their 10s. If coaches give players confidence, especially out-halves, they get a huge return. In France it seems they change for change's sake. They also have 10s who play at 9, like Freddie Michalak and Jean-Baptiste Elissalde. Michalak did some damage over the years with his variety of pass and the pace he could inject into the game. He could do the unexpected, but I didn't think he controlled or managed the game well.

I've played against François Trinh-Duc a few times and I think he's very good. It's a bit of a mystery to me why the French don't have more faith in him. He's a lovely running out-half with flair and an X factor, and he has a big accurate boot. Again, though, his career has suffered due to the French impatience with their 10s.

Andrew Mehrtens was the first All Blacks out-half I came up against, and I thought he was class. I would have watched his game inside out; studied everything he did. His all-round game was brilliant. He was a really good kicker, an excellent long passer, and just a lovely all-round out-half. I thought he was phenomenal, and was a massive fan. I wasn't as big a fan of Carlos Spencer, I suppose because I could see a bit of myself in Mehrtens; I couldn't see any of myself in Spencer. There was plenty of Jeremy Staunton in Carlos Spencer, and I suppose a young player is more likely to be drawn towards a player he resembles. They say never meet your heroes, but I was glad I met Mehrts. He lived up to all my expectations. He is great craic. I think 10s need to be strong personalities, big characters in the team room, and that was exactly what I saw in him.

I first came across Dan Carter on the Lions tour in 2005, and his performance in the second Test in Wellington was as good a game by an out-half as I've ever seen. He was exceptional. Yeah, a beautiful player, although I might put Wilkinson ahead of him for a last-minute penalty, and definitely for a last-minute drop goal.

Because New Zealand are so good, so dominant, and they play in a team where everyone trusts each other, the 10 obviously looks better. When there's adversity, sometimes you need your 10 to come up trumps, but New Zealand very rarely need a last-minute penalty or drop goal – certainly not against us! The one time a 10 had to against Ireland, in the second Test in Christchurch in 2012, Carter's drop goal barely made it. I came on in the 51st minute for Darce in that match. It was a really enjoyable game – I loved every second of it. That was a big chance for us. Near the end, with the scores level and Israel Dagg sin-binned, Nigel Owens penalized us instead of them at a scrum. I could see some fellas were disappointed, like Sean O'Brien, but several weren't that gutted because they don't understand that with the All Blacks, chances like that come along very rarely. It was hugely disheartening. That sort of pain doesn't go away.

But that night in Wellington in 2005, when he scored thirty-three points against the Lyons, Carter was brilliant. He is a beautiful running out-half, and dangerous. I'd say of all the out-halves I've come up against he was the strongest. He's recognized as the best out-half in the world and I agree, because he's done it consistently year in, year out.

I was nowhere near as good as Carter, but if there was one trait I could have taken from any out-half it would have been his ability to 'ghost'. He always seems to pop up in the right place at the right time to glide through gaps. And when you've an appreciation of the position, it's nowhere near as easy as he makes it look.

Carter was the opposition out-half who put me most on edge, because he was such a threat. Not that you'd be marking the 10. In latter years, of course, there would be more analysis and you'd be more aware that he had a very good step off his left foot, but an out-half in defence would watch the 12 more. Usually there was no monster at 10 anywhere, bar perhaps Henry Honiball, but against the All Blacks I used to think 'for us to win the game I need to exert more influence on it than him'.

Perhaps that was indicative of the way we over-respected the All Blacks. Still, Dan Carter's an incredible player. If you don't think he is an incredible player then there is no such thing. I wouldn't know him as well as Mehrtens, but he seems like a decent fella, not big-headed or cocky but respectful. I have both of their jerseys, and I think I have one of Wilkinson's, and a Stephen Jones as well.

I played against Stephen Larkham more than any other Australian out-half and he was a typical Aussie. He had a lovely running game, was a beautiful passer and was superb at moving his backline, but he had no kicking game. George Gregan did a lot of tactical kicking from scrum-half even then. He was ahead of his time, but the longer you're around the more you are criticized; then you retire and you're great. He's the world's most-capped player yet the Aussie media slaughtered him beyond belief for the last few years of his career.

I like and admire Matt Giteau as a player, I just don't know if he's a 10. He's brave for a small lad, very talented; he has a great skills set, and I like the way he's kept going. He's been written off plenty of times and is under-appreciated, yet Australia want him back now for the 2015 World Cup.

Similarly, I felt Butch James was more of a centre. South Africa were also one of the first to react to the law changes by entrusting more of the kicking to a great 9 like Fourie du Preez, who also took more responsibility defensively.

As for Felipe Contepomi, let's just say that we had an edgy rivalry. Given that he played with Leinster and Argentina, and I played with Munster and Ireland, it was never going to be any other way. There is no doubt we brought the best out in each other.

I thought he was over-appreciated in Leinster, and in my view the best thing that happened to Leinster in the 2009 Heineken Cup semi-final was that the man with balls came in to get them over the winning line. More on Johnny Sexton shortly. So I think Contepomi is a serious player for the Baa-baas or for exhibition rugby, but I don't think his mentality is suited to winning cup rugby. He is really skilful, but I think you had to see what kind of mood he was in to know how his team would go. If his first contribution went well, great, he could beat a team on his own; but if things didn't go well, it wasn't going to be good for his team. That's no way to build a team.

Physically he was very brave. He was powerfully built and

carried the ball really vigorously. I don't know if I've seen a better half in terms of converting tries within five or ten metres of the opposition line. He had a serious 'chop' step. There is no doubt he had true individual brilliance. He would try things – quick taps, chips, reverse passes, anything. Maybe he was more suited to 12 than 10, and that can happen to talented players. Keith Earls is another example. He's a really good rugby player, but what's his position? If you want to be the best in a position you have to be allowed to nail your colours to the mast.

When Contepomi was inspired, he was unstoppable. He scored twenty-five points against Munster at the RDS in December 2005 and after scoring his second try jumped on to the perimeter fence to soak up the crowd's applause. When I scored a late intercept try at the Heineken Cup semi-final the following April in Lansdowne Road and did the same, it was not in response to that. They were both heat-of-the-moment reactions.

There was a bit of sledging between us. As well as our provincial and international rivalries, he was fiery and I was fiery on the pitch. It was a perfect storm. He wasn't shy about giving his opinion – whether it was accurate or not, as the case turned out. He stirred it up by going after a few of the Munster forwards as well. His claim that we sledged him during a Musgrave Park encounter was a figment of his imagination. We did target him tactically, and there were plenty of verbals on other occasions. It's probably a good thing that it has gone out of the game as back then you could have eight players abusing the 10s on both sides. That was part of the game's culture. I think it possibly reached a peak in Australia on the 2001 Lions tour, but after being highlighted then it was gradually phased out.

I was sledged plenty myself, and gave plenty of lip back, before team-mates I respected told me I had to stop it. It's a distraction from your game. It's exactly what the opposition are looking for. I became more aware of it and I tried to stop, but there were occasions when I couldn't. I'm not perfect by any means, and I try and learn from my mistakes, but one small little blond-haired fella from the Ospreys gave me some cheek one time in Musgrave Park and I just lost it.

I said, 'Who the fuck are you? You little fucking prick! The Under-12s are playing tomorrow.'

Mike Phillips heard it and erupted laughing.

Felipe and myself have since shaken hands. I can remember walking somewhere with him, having a chat and a laugh. I don't bear any grudge towards him. That was purely on-the-pitch stuff.

From playing against all these out-halves I learned that I was a competitor. I didn't think I had the individual brilliance to outshine any of them but I think the collective skills set, game management and the will to win could get me a percentage point ahead of my opposite man. Some days, of course, it didn't, but that was the way I had to think.

Johnny Sexton is almost worth a chapter in himself. Our relationship started badly. When he took to the pitch in that Munster–Leinster semi-final at Croke Park in 2009 I knew very little about him, if anything at all. He wasn't really a big name at Leinster even though he had been around the scene for a while. At the time I was delighted to see Contepomi going off because I thought it would weaken the team. We now know with the benefit of hindsight that it strengthened Leinster. I think it became the making of them, because it gave them a general with balls at 10.

I can still picture Johnny standing over me screaming when they scored a try – clearly a release of frustration. Aside from having to wait for his chance with Leinster, I'd most definitely said something to him as well. It's a pity I don't recall what I said to fire him up, but as we also now know, it doesn't take much. For the benefit of our relationship in the future – for the next two years anyway – I have to know what makes him tick. But certainly that scream was him announcing to the world 'I'm here, and I'm here to stay'. And fair play to him. That's what he's done.

For the next couple of years ours was the trickiest relationship I've ever experienced with any player. The good thing about it, looking back, is that while we mightn't have been pally-pally, the team was getting on. An out-half has to have a relationship with everyone in the squad, in different ways, from John Hayes to Brian Carney, with different jokes for different lads. But I would have avoided Johnny and he would have avoided me. I had my same spot on the bus all the time with the same fellas at the back – Brian, Paulie, Rob – and Johnny was nowhere to be seen, up at the front on the left. There was no possibility of his being drawn into even a general conversation among, say, ten of us. But over the years he eventually thawed out and came down our end!

Initially, even for kicking practice, it seemed as if he had to go to the dentist or the doctor a lot on those mornings. Typically, Deccie landed the two of us in a room together when the tension was at its height. I just said to myself, 'Oh my God, is this for real?' I'd imagine it was worse for Johnny because I was more senior. I never had such a distant relationship with Humphs. I think it's always trickier when the younger fella is laying down the law to the more established player. There were times when it became heated between me and Humphs in training, and heated for a few hours after training. He wanted to show the young fella who was the boss, and I wasn't prepared to let him think he was. There was a little bit of that in Johnny too, and we are also two very stubborn fellas. When we were forced to room-share I don't think he even stayed in the room. Maybe he did one night, but it was a two-night camp and he definitely wasn't there for the second night.

When we went for kicking practice, if there was another player around or, say, Taints – kicking coach Mark Tainton – was driving the van, everything was rosy, no problem. But neither myself nor Johnny was going to start a conversation to get the car chatting. It was worse if Rala was there, because Rala would be in the front, leaving the two of us in the back. At least if there were three of us one would sit in the front and we wouldn't even have to look at each other. Not even Rala could get us talking. Not even the Pope would have mended things at that stage.

I don't remember exactly when or how things thawed, but they certainly had by the time of the 2011 World Cup. Time is a healer in everything. Perhaps typically of the two of us, it was probably played out in print – one of us reading a complimentary comment made by one of us about the other, or something like that. I can recall seeing one or two remarks that were positive, so I probably returned the compliment – but I'm pretty sure I didn't instigate it. I suppose the more time you spend with a fella the more you appreciate what kind of person he is.

The relationship progressed to such an extent that Wednesdays became a great kicking day. He could have opted to stay at home, but he'd stay in camp, in Carton House, where we had breakfast, and he'd do a bit of stretching before we drove to the Aviva. The Aviva's facilities allowed us to do the kicking and recovery, as the IRFU made the hot and cold baths there available to us. Even if you drove back to the plush facilities of Carton House, it would have a big impact on the body. So we kicked for an hour to an hour and a quarter, and did our recovery there. Apart from matches, they're actually the things you miss the most when you stop playing, because we'd also have a game of soccer there with Majella, Stuart, Jimmy and Bobby, the groundsmen in the Aviva. We had some craic with them. After that, myself and Johnny would lunch together in Juniors across the road on Bath Avenue. They do a lovely sandwich and soup. Then he'd usually go away and do something, so I would meet the other non-Dublin players in the squad who stayed in camp in Bewleys on Grafton Street – typical culchies – for a three-hour chat to kill the afternoon.

Since the World Cup, both our friendship and the level of respect between us have grown. Johnny's clearly a very good player, and I think he's also becoming a very intelligent player, in pulling the right plays at the right time, which is a key attribute in becoming a great 10. That's the route he wants to go, and I think he will get there.

There are plenty of good players, but what separates the great from the good is often how driven they are. Johnny wants to become a great 10, and to that end he needs some silverware with Ireland. With Joe Schmidt in charge we are well placed to do so because we still have great players. It will be interesting, because himself and Schmidt are very tight, but I think Johnny has had way more influence on how Leinster play than on how Ireland play, and that's a two-way thing. That's a coach believing in his 10 and that's the 10 getting on with a coach who shares the same vision. I think Johnny has dominated games as a 10 for Leinster but this has yet to happen for Ireland. I'm going to try and instil some of that game management into him because occasionally I think he's happy to pick up positions on the periphery. I'd like to see him boss it and become the king on the pitch as opposed to just that piece on the chessboard. Then again, maybe it's something Schmidt or Leinster have designed, and I may appreciate this in time. Maybe it's another way of doing it which I'm not aware of.

I think Johnny has just found his best goal-kicking routine – his perfect rhythm. He's exactly where I was. He's not happy with kicking the ball over the bar. He wants to hit it over the black spot every time, and to that end he's been working with different coaches including Dave Alred. I've been there, working on power positions and everything, but I think Johnny has made a decision that works for Johnny. He's practising these things in sessions and getting the results, and we will see them with Ireland in the years to come.

He'd have loved to have been the Lions' kicker in Australia, to test himself in that environment. Not being chosen to do so will therefore be a huge motivation for him, and also because some will wonder, 'Well, does this fella goal-kick? He didn't on the Lions.' That would be typical of the fickleness of the Irish. Many will also compare him to Ian Madigan because he had the best stats last season in the Rabo Pro12. It doesn't make sense, but Johnny will be the one who decides what routine works for him, not any goal-kicking coach. He can be guided in a small way, but Johnny already has 95 per cent of it.

Dips or off-days happen in sport. No player can stay the exact same all the time, but it's important that you find what works for you. The one thing I've said to him is that your bad days are four successful kicks out of six or five out of seven, and the good days then are five out of six, six out of six, three out of three, two out of two, six out of eight. You can't go from six out of six to two out of seven, then four out of four back to two out of four and, say, three out of six. As a kicker you have to be consistent, you can't be hot and cold. Not only will inconsistency create uncertainty in your head, more importantly if a team knows they've a 10 who is going to nail a kick they're going to break their balls. If it's a one-score game with ten minutes to go, they know if they keep pushing, then from the moment the referee's arm goes out, they are probably safe.

The kicking coach has a small role in all of this, in delivering the right knowledge and technique at the right time, and couple that with hard work. A kicker can be out there all day but if he's not doing the right thing he's wasting his time. A kicking coach can help by devising sessions for him to get the best repetitions out of hand and from the ground. He can recreate game scenarios, because there is a huge variety of kicking involved nowadays, from restarts to slow ball, to having four or five seconds to shape yourself when a ball is kicked long into a 22.

With all of these, and cross-kicks too, Johnny's way down the road. He is one of the best players in Europe. He just needs to do it season in, season out, especially as he's now entered a new period of development in France and will be playing every weekend.

Opportunity knocks now for some young Irish out-halves, but I believe Johnny is on a different level altogether. Ian Madigan and Paddy Jackson are below that level, and I think Ian Keatley and JJ Hanrahan are chasing Jackson and Madigan. Those four are fighting so that one of them can put the heat on Johnny, and Madigan has made a really impressive step up to Leinster and European rugby. He's been phenomenal really. I have to give the fella credit for taking his chance, especially away to Wasps in the Amlin quarter-final.

The game doesn't wait for anyone; it was the same when Paulie was missing for Munster for eighteen months. Up to that point Johnny wasn't missed by Leinster, but then when he returned he brought a nice solidity to things. He brought his presence again. But Madigan has been impressive. He's hungry. He's sharp. He has a smashing attitude, which some supporters mightn't believe because of his Blackrock background, the flashy boots, the hairstyle and the way he prances. However, as with Simon Zebo, the game has to accommodate characters; it can't only have meat-and-two-veg players like me. I was chatting to my brother-in-law about this, and he views rugby as entertainment. He pointed out that supporters actually pay to be entertained. George Hook does that very well. He's an entertainer in his role as a pundit, and some players are more likely to be crowd-pleasers and entertainers as well.

Madigan is an exciting player, doing the right thing at the right time and playing winning rugby. I don't think he can do much more on the pitch, he's just got to back it up, because he's on a crest of a wave. When he has his first dip in form, people can't lose faith in him. Nor can they expect him to maintain his try ratio, although if he does he's going to be one of the top scorers in the League every year. It's an astonishing feat for a 10.

The 2013/14 campaign will be his most challenging. Not only is there Second Season Syndrome, but as a result of what he's done in the last six months opponents will be doing more analysis on him. They know he's been a threat with the ball, but that's partly because he was a little unknown. He does have really good feet, so you wouldn't be surprised if a few defensive coaches put a hit-on-suspicion target over his head – pick a defender who is not answerable to anybody else and tell him 'no matter what he does, you've just got to take this fella out'. Coaches do this, have someone tackle the targeted player and hold him down so he's not involved in the next phase. It's the same with good 9s. We 'hit on suspicion' with Morgan Parra in the Clermont games, without being stupid about it. If you could tackle him and lie on him then hopefully he wasn't available to direct the next ruck.

Paddy Jackson has been really impressive since he came into the Irish squad. He has lovely hands, and you forget how young he is. I think he has a huge future because he's humble, respectful and aware of where he is, and while he might find it a small bit daunting at the minute, I much prefer that to a fella who fools himself into thinking he has all the answers.

I know he was struggling with an ankle injury last season, and to play 10 at that level is very tough. It wasn't severe enough to make him put his hand up and say 'I have to stop', but I don't think he was jumping out of his skin either. He couldn't really kick properly in training, and that's probably the part of his game that requires two or three years of settling in. Because Ulster want results and Ulster have Pienaar, Paddy is always going to be number two, so give the fella a break. Be realistic about him.

It's hard in Ulster because most southern hemisphere kickers are end-over-end kickers naturally, whereas I think Paddy is a natural spiral kicker. I hope he is really diligent – and I'm sure he is – with his kicking routine. But who is he practising with? How much is he doing? Is he writing it down? That's the kind of stuff a young 10 has to do. After ten years you can leave down the diary – be it static kicks to the left-hand touchline or static kicks to the right-hand touchline. I'm sure people like Neil Doak and Humphs are providing him with plenty of inform-ation, but it's also important to have someone to do the routine with. Maybe Stuart Olding would be the perfect companion.

Paddy also has a beautiful tackle technique. He is an excellent defender, and brave, and you can definitely build a team around him. When he plays with Pienaar, however, the South African is the dominant half-back – and, as I've said elsewhere, the kicking game of the 9 has become so much more important. Pienaar assumes the role and Ulster clearly want him to help bring Paddy along, which is also how Conor Murray came more into his own as the dominant half-back alongside Paddy in the Six Nations.

Conor will have that role in Munster now as well, alongside Ian Keatley or JJ Hanrahan. JJ is much younger and the junior out-half, but he's a competitive little fella and he backs himself, and I love that in him. It's a genuine belief, and I'd say he pictures himself listening to the anthem in the Aviva already, and that's what a young player has to do. He has to want it, and if he wants it that badly he'll get there. He feels he belongs in international rugby, which is a great starting point, so it's all to play for in Munster. They've backed the two boys, it's a shoot-out between them, and next stop is Ireland green.

I haven't seen enough of JJ to know whether he has a consistent kicking game, and, after all, in Ireland it's wet, by and large, from September to March. It's bloody hard playing in such conditions all the time and usually it's not until Heineken Cup semi-final week that the weather picks up. Until then it's hard going, and the importance of a good kicking game – not only by a 10 but by all seven backs – is often under-appreciated.

I think Keats is a very good runner. He's fast, and I hope the one thing I've passed on to him is the benefit of hard work. He does work hard on his game now and realizes how much is required if you want to play out-half for a team like Munster. So much unseen work. He has to get himself right, but he also has to make sure that the team is right. Is he happy with the line-out plays, the scrum plays, the kick-off options? What are we doing off slow ball? A 10 has to be starting regularly to acquire all that knowledge, but when you play with Paulie these things are expected of a red 10. It will be a steep learning curve, but I think if he can survive the first season, his game could kick on.

The red 10 is a big jersey. Ralph Keyes, Barry McGann, Tony Ward . . . There's always been a certain mystique about the position, especially since Munster beat the All Blacks. When there's such a tradition associated with a specific jersey, you are aware of it, and you can either flourish or let it overpower you. I suppose it's very easy for me to sit back and say that now I'm finished, because as a young fella I admit I was extremely nervous, daunted by the whole thing. However, I always realized the importance of playing for Munster – that's something I never underestimated.

None the less, it's like any position, if you get on the Munster team you're one step away from the Ireland team – as Tommy O'Donnell showed last season when he was capped for Ireland on the summer tour. It can be hard for young fellas to believe they'll have an opportunity but they should realize that if they get on the Munster team consistently, they're very close to representing their country.

I may be over in France with Johnny now, but I'll stay hugely interested in all the Irish 10s. I'll be trying to think what they're thinking, what play they're playing, maybe find out the game plan for my own benefit and see if they are sticking with it. In every game I'll try to be inside their head, playing it through their eyes.

Maybe this will be another substitute for not actually playing any more.

CHAPTER 9

Nothing is Impossible

French club rugby is booming. The Top 14 is the biggest domestic league in the world, and with a new, more lucrative television deal looming due to the emergence of the Qatar-owned beIN Sport as a rival to Canal+, there is no sign of this coming to a halt any time soon. The leading French clubs have been luring big-name players from all over the world, and the threat to Irish rugby has never been greater. Johnny Sexton is the first truly big-name Irish player to come to France, and he may not be the last.

As with everything else, the rugby world is becoming smaller, and clever businesspeople and agents have virtually monopolized clients. They have so many on their books they're able to offer players to both hemispheres, and it's hard to know how the increased threat to Irish rugby will pan out.

I would hope that the likes of Peter O'Mahony will remain with Munster for his whole career. I think this is something that the game needs. An Irish player in Peter's position might earn

€50,000 more in France but his ability to earn off the pitch in Ireland should counteract that. Remaining in Ireland would also suit his lifestyle and underline his loyalty to Munster – and it's important that the core of a provincial team is made up of home players. We have all had options to go to France or somewhere else in our time but, by and large, no one went. That was our mindset in Munster, and you'd hate younger players coming through nowadays in Munster, Leinster, Connacht or Ulster to lose that. I think that love for your home team is much stronger in Ireland than it is here in France.

But I've seen the facilities in Racing Metro now, I've witnessed the investment by Jacky Lorenzetti in this club and by others in their French clubs. A handful of French clubs have four or five times the budget of the Irish provinces. So the challenge facing the provinces in terms of keeping their best players is massive, and the prospects are grim, due to the economic picture in Ireland. Everywhere you go there seems to be cost-cutting and negativity, and players have only a short time to earn decent money so they have to do what's right for themselves.

Dublin has just hosted an all-French final of the Heineken Cup, which could be interpreted as a sign of things to come, but I still think the provinces will remain contenders. If the French teams gave the Heineken Cup the same emphasis as the Irish teams then it might be a little different. But the Top 14 is what's king over here and in one-off games the Irish provinces are always capable of winning.

The competitiveness of the Irish provinces has helped make the Heineken Cup what it is. There are also very few dead rubbers because the scrap for the final two quarter-final places offers a lifeline to almost everyone, and in the quarter-finals the eighth-ranked team is often capable of beating the top seeds away.

Winning the Heineken Cup is almost as good a feeling as winning the Grand Slam. I made my debut for Ireland in 2000, and six years elapsed before Munster eventually won a final, after being beaten in two of them. We'd been knocking on the door, but you have to get over the line if you want to be taken seriously.

I don't believe it's any harder to win now for the Irish provinces. As difficult as Munster's season was last year we could very easily have won a Heineken Cup. With all the doom and gloom around it would have been a lift for the country to have had Munster in Dublin in a Heineken Cup final against Toulon. At worst it would have been a fifty-fifty game. As good as Toulon are, and as effective as their game is, support does wonders for a team. This is the big challenge confronting Racing, because all the big teams have the best supporters: Leicester, Toulouse, Clermont, Munster, Leinster. Even Glasgow are getting their act together, and they're playing better rugby as a result.

It's no coincidence that Leicester are consistently England's strongest team in Europe, because they have the support base and the Welford Road factor. Tradition demands respect and earns opportunities. A player is expected to perform to a certain level when he is in the Leicester jersey. That's the culture they've created and that's the culture within Munster, which has to be sustained, and in this the role of the supporters is critical. The adrenalin and support on match day cannot be created on the training pitch. That's partly why there is the Tarzan/Jane effect – why players train like the latter and play like the former.

Some opposition players are still spooked by Thomond Park. I know it's losing a small bit of its X factor but that can be revived very quickly. It's been a rocky few years, but the one thing that remains loyal in Munster is the support. You never, ever, take that for granted because it's crucial that the supporters keep their patience. They understand there are a lot of younger players in the team now, but they are still expected to win, and that should never change.

Without the crowd, we would never have pulled through against Northampton with that forty-one-phase drive and drop goal, or on countless other occasions. Often when our heads were down or we were on the back foot, the crowd pulled us through. Whenever we were in a hole, they'd always stay with us.

Against Clermont in December 2008, a week after we had lost over there, we were under fierce pressure when Benoit Baby broke through and looked certain to score. Tomas smashed Baby, and himself, under our posts to save the try. We were hanging on for dear life but managed to hoof the ball up the pitch, and the place lifted.

That was in the new Thomond Park, which showed it can still find its old roar, although it is a different stadium now. There's definitely more of a commercial aspect to the place today, which for most of my career wasn't the case. Even so, if ever there was a ground with knowledgeable supporters, it's Thomond. The Aviva is different, as Quinny highlighted in the *Irish Times* a while back. The international games attract a lot of social fans on a weekend in Dublin. On the other hand that's the great thing about club rugby – most of the supporters care passionately about their team.

This is also truer of Irish fans abroad. Whether they are expats or supporters who pay the cost of travelling, they'll make a bigger effort to wear the colours and sing. Something special was building at the 2011 World Cup in New Zealand and that's what made the disappointment of going out in the quarter-finals so cutting. A lovely bond had developed between the team and the supporters and the team fed off the supporters' belief. That night in Dunedin against Italy was better than a home game in the Aviva. This is partly to do with the Aviva's design. It's very hard to create an atmosphere when the stand behind one goal is only ten seats deep, and a lot of them are rent-a-crowd on drums and waving flags. Playing the other way at the Aviva is cracking. For a kicker, it's like Croke Park with three different levels to aim at. It had a Stade de France or Millennium Stadium feel about it.

The old Lansdowne Road was incomparable to anywhere else. It was a great ground for generating support. Unbelievable passion came down from the stands and the terracing – and a standing area does give an extra buzz. Nowadays spectators don't like standing, but I'm sure plenty of rugby fans would like to stand, and that's the difference: they're there to work for the team, to roar and jump. It takes more effort and work on the terraces.

The art of kicking a rugby ball under pressure in great grounds like these is both simple and complex, but the key to it is repetition. Practice makes perfect, as the saying goes, and I have to say I did practise drop goals more as my career advanced. On Thursdays and Fridays I'd hit ten or twenty off a pass every time. But a drop goal in a match scenario, particularly when the match is on the line, hinges on how rushed you are. A drop goal in practice is very easy; a drop goal under pressure is very different. The kicker is also dependent upon the quality of ruck ball, the speed of the pass, where it is delivered to him, how many players are charging at him, and how hard they're charging.

When Munster lost by a point in Ravenhill in 2012, pundits questioned why I didn't attempt a late drop goal. It would have been pointless even attempting one because Ulster had done a serious job on me and we couldn't get front-foot ball. What really annoyed me that night was not actually having the time or the space to drop the ball on my foot. As much as I was criticized for not taking it on, I could still go to bed that night thinking 'I gave it my best shot'.

Not that it wasn't very frustrating. I absolutely loved the pressure of taking on those last-minute drop goals or conversions or penalties. It came from a refuse-to-lose attitude. 'Whatever it takes, I have to get us over the line today. These are the boys who break their arse for me, and I need to do my job.' Essentially it is my job, or part of my job; I don't see it as a bonus. The number 10 is one of those positions on a team where you're a big player, and it is the responsibility of the 10 for Ireland and for Munster to put up his hand and do it.

As the years passed I enjoyed all of it more in a perverse kind of way. I always needed to put myself under pressure to perform, which I didn't particularly enjoy in the build-up to games, but I don't think I could have performed if I hadn't continually done that. When I had children I realized 'you're going to have to start enjoying this – this is what you do'. I suppose for ten years I hadn't really enjoyed it. I'd just put myself under too much pressure. But we all operate differently. It's also one of those things where the more you do it, the more confident you become in your ability to repeat it, all the more so in high-pressure situations such as, say, when a Grand Slam is at stake. It's akin to finally winning one Heineken Cup. After that you think you can win ten, but until you actually do it it's very hard to convince others that you can. That's why a goal-kicker, especially, has to learn himself. As the saying goes, 'You can bring a horse to water . . .' After doing something once, the body will go where the mind takes it. Subconsciously you derive massive confidence from having done it before.

Also, maybe there's an element of when you've done something once, like winning a Heineken Cup or nailing a drop goal to clinch a Grand Slam, thereafter subconsciously you're in credit. At least you have one to your name. You've moved on to a different threshold.

Then again, good players shouldn't make the same mistake twice. Anyone can miss once, but what you want to establish is a recurring theme, and hopefully this is what I achieved. The flipside of the coin is that in the home game against England last season the crowd were pissed off with me because I didn't get Ireland over the line. I came on before half-time after Johnny did his hamstring, when we were 6–0 down, and nailed two kicks out of three to bring us level in the second half. If you watch that game again I missed one kick at goal in horrific conditions, and Owen Farrell missed two out of six. If we had won that game I'd have been proclaimed the hero, and it was very close. With a bit more self-belief, that game could have gone our way, I'm convinced of it. But our body language wasn't great that day. However, because I had done it in the past, I was expected to steer us over the line. You could sense the crowd thinking, 'Well, dammit, Rog is on for Sexton, but maybe we've the right man in the driving rain. He'll get us over the line here.' I was thinking 'this is exactly what I need now at this stage of my career', and as we got back into the game I was actually loving it. But I got slated, and I think the criticism was more severe because it was me. 'Ah, this fella doesn't have it any more.' But that day we were playing against a bloody good England team who won the collisions, and collisions win everything.

Friends and family said to me afterwards, 'Jesus, you got absolutely slated.' But I pointed out, 'You know, it's actually an inverted compliment, because close game, driving rain, this fella here, game manager, come on, do the business and get out of town.' England laid down the law in the first twenty or thirty minutes, and I think they just had the jump on us all day. Pundits and supporters wouldn't have had the same expect-ations of Johnny if the positions had been reversed, and certainly not of a younger, less experienced player like Paddy Jackson or Ian Madigan or Ian Keatley. Michael O'Flynn had warned me that this might be the case. I had done it before and it was just presumed that it would happen again, and the first time you fail to do it there's an over-reaction.

Ultimately, all careers return to the same common denominators. If you're good enough, you're old enough and you'll get your opportunity, and then it's a case of trying to stay at the top for as long as you can.

After missing four kicks out of four in the Heineken Cup final in 2000 and then suffering with the Adidas ball that Andrew Mehrtens called 'the pig' in New Zealand in 2002, I needed help. At that stage I had to acknowledge that was exactly where I was. I didn't have the answer. I didn't know what to do. I was broken and I needed help.

Kicking is so complex because the mind is so complex. The mechanical part of the kicking isn't complex really. It's proven that with more practice and proper technique goal-kicking ratios have improved dramatically over the years. If you look at the stats of goal-kickers in the Celtic League, many of them are higher than 70 per cent, whereas five years ago there might have been only one kicker over that figure.

After the 2002 tour, through Eddie O'Sullivan I met PJ Smith, a Limerick-based sports psychologist. I went back to him three or four times, and he helped me exorcize many of the demons in my mind and embrace the concept of visualization, which entailed picturing a small target behind the posts. I worked bloody hard all that summer, and at the beginning of the 2002/03 season I started for Ireland against Romania, Russia, Georgia and Australia, against whom I kicked six penalties out of six in an 18–9 victory. That was the turning point. Until then I hadn't been anywhere near consistent enough.

After that there were different stages in my kicking development. I worked with Dave Alred, who re-energized me mentally and got me thinking completely differently. I tried some of the stuff Alred talked about, such as kicking with your core, kicking with your body and power positions. It was all hugely interesting, but maximizing the benefits of working with him wasn't possible solely by email. There was no such thing as Skype then. I felt I needed to make a decision and work with Mark Tainton, and he was very good. Taints said, 'Rog, trust your technique, you have great rhythm. You're a timing kicker.' And I just went with that. It was always a work in progress though. The day you think you have it made, you're in trouble.

My technique has been essentially the same for the last few years. I have a few cues, but primarily it's about staying tall with a big follow-through. The myth about Jonny Wilkinson is that he's crouched, but that is his preparatory pose; on addressing the ball he's tall through the kick. I have two cue words, 'tall' and 'through'. I might exaggerate staying tall with my chest out. Fergus McFadden rips the piss out of me. At every kicking session he does an Elwood; he does Matt Jarvis at Connacht with one step; he does a Sexto. He's absolutely hilarious, and he mimics my chest-out stance beyond belief. I pick out my black dot between the posts, the middle of my chest in line with the black spot, two and a half steps back to the side, happy with technique and then visualization.

Visualization for kicking out of hand is crucial too. If I want the ball to go through at about fifteen metres off the ground, I'd aim for a point ten feet higher. I don't know what it is about the mind but I guarantee that if you aim at the point where you want the ball to travel it will never go that high.

That applies to goal-kicking as well. The further you are from the posts, the higher your target has to be. The ball travels way further, and that's why the timing has to be perfect, as opposed to lashing the ball. Your eyes are so important in goal-kicking.

Following through prevents you from stopping on the kick. I had a tendency to do that occasionally earlier in my career, and that would make the ball shoot off to the right. By going through the kick I keep a nice slow leg all the way up.

Sometimes messages can be sent down to a kicker if a glitch is spotted from the sidelines or the stands, but that happens very rarely. I was crying out for some sort of message after missing the first two kicks against Harlequins this year, for someone to give me some guidance, because it was the quarter-final of the Heineken Cup. My kicking had been good but I'd been dumped out of the Irish squad. It even crossed my mind that Rob Penney could whip me off at half-time for not landing three-pointers. That's where I was, but I'm glad he stuck with me and I think he and the team are glad too.

The first kick was bloody great. I hit it well, very well, and then at the last moment it took a serious whip to the left of the posts. There are no excuses for missing those, because of what I've done previously. It's three points. Not only is it a massive blow for me, it's a massive blow for a developing young team away from home. I'm very conscious of that. The next one was fifteen metres in from the left and I blew it left and wide. You've got to reward forwards. The third one was five metres in from the left touchline. Every kick is the same really, as stupid as that may sound, but I think I was just a little bit slower on it maybe, and I exaggerated my technique, and I nailed it. Nailing one gives you confidence, and then you just keep going with it. After missing the first two I was telling myself that I was playing well and directing the team well. You have to convince yourself you are doing all of this, and that the supporters appreciate it as well, but they want points on the board for the team. This is why the goal-kicker is so important.

As for kicking out of hand, the key to this is 'left shoulder forward'. The left shoulder does everything for me really, and thereafter I try to make it as natural as possible. When you're kicking to touch it's about targets, timing, ball release and ball placement. It's a skill you learn at a young age and I kept practising it throughout my career – and that should be a lesson to all emerging players.

Virtually all my kicking sessions were with another out-half, so in latter years I did an awful lot of work with Scott Deasy. He's finished with Munster now but we used to kick to each other, doing end-over-end and spirals, one drop end-over-end and one drop spirals. 'One drop' means the ball is only allowed to bounce once in front of the other kicker before it lands in his hands, so we'd work thirty to forty yards apart, just pinging it to each other. We also worked in the five-metre channel alongside the touchline to put pressure on ourselves.

You can't kick on your own, believe me. You can goal-kick on your own, although you'd want to have a lot of rugby balls – the most annoying thing about kicking is having to retrieve fifteen or twenty balls. That is one of the great things about Rala: he organizes fetchers. On average I practised twice as much out of hand as at goal, although there are days when a 10 will do two-hour goal-kicking sessions. It is hugely frustrating and at times mind-boggling, and Leigh Halfpenny deserves so much credit. Pundits wax lyrically about Neil Jenkins' influence, and if anyone knows all there is to know about kicking it's probably him, but he doesn't actually kick the ball. Jenkins can do everything he can to make it as easy as possible but the responsibility – and it's a lonely, isolated position – lies with the kicker.

When I went into Irish camps with Humphs and Taints, we had loads of sessions and options, and with Johnny we did our own thing. When you work with another 10 for a long while you get a feel for it and after a while it virtually runs itself. You don't say anything, and when you get one thing right you move on. The number of sessions and the length of them would vary. I put in some serious hours over the years but in latter years I reined it in because I was happier with where I was at.

I worked on my left-footed kicking as well, although it's funny how a left-footer seems to have to use his right foot more often than a right-footer uses his left. I think some kickers like to show they have a left foot if they are a right-footer and they position themselves accordingly, but this is usually detrimental to the team. In my opinion, if you have a stronger foot, use it, unless you have no choice, and then if you have to use your weaker foot you have to be equipped to do so.

When forced on to my left foot, I usually went for a spiral, but I had to put in a fair bit of practice for the few occasions this happened. I remember hitting one nice left-footed drop goal aqainst Perpignan in Thomond. I just went off the right foot and bang. Mind you, I've had some horrible attempts in training. In most games I didn't use my left foot at all.

Then there were the long raking kicks that rolled into the corners and over the touchline. The Roggies! They gave me huge satisfaction because they gave my team-mates satisfaction, but I hope it's not a dying skill. I'm going to be on Johnny's case hard about spiralling the ball. I think it's such an important kick, such an easy kick, such a valuable kick. Especially if the pitch is wet and the ball lands on a spiral – it skids off the surface and keeps rolling. If it's kicked end-over-end the surface usually kills it. It can even backspin. Admittedly, with a rugby ball it's very hard for anyone to be 100 per cent sure what is going to happen when it lands, but there is a better chance of it skidding and rolling on with a spiral kick.

Players don't do it any more because they don't back their technique. That's exactly it, and they can say what they want.

It's so easy to kick end-over-end. Johnny Sexton is well able to spiral. Wilkinson, for a player who practises his kicking so much, is all end-over-end now. He's not transferring into matches what he has in his repertoire. He is undoubtedly the best two-footed out-half I've ever seen. No question. That said, I wouldn't rate him as the game's best tactical kicker. Over a dead ball, very effective, but Jonny is bounce, step, step, kick. I rarely see him pinging the ball in behind the wingers. Dan Carter is a far better tactical kicker. I think Wilkinson is a lovely restarter, and obviously an incredible goal-kicker, although for a few years his stats weren't as impressive as would generally have been thought. I looked into it once and I was shocked. The perception sometimes isn't the truth.

Another huge weapon in any out-half's armoury is the grubber in behind the opposition's defensive line, all the more so if it stops in, or just short of, the in-goal area for an outside back to score. That's a five- or seven-point kick. Yet for all the tries the grubber created for Christian Cullen, Doug Howlett, Denis Hurley or whoever, we never once practised them. That was instinct. That was playing. I have practised cross-kicks with wingers in sessions but I've never practised grubbers, which is weird, because it was only when I was sent a DVD of my Munster highlights that I realized there were so many of them. I'd have thought there were more cross-kicks but there were actually more 'worms', and, as I've said, I never once practised them. What is particularly satisfying about them is simply doing the right thing at the right time, which may sound cocky but isn't meant to be.

Next to the Grand Slam drop goal, my favourite throughout my whole career was the one to beat Northampton on 12

November 2011 at Thomond Park. Even I still feel disbelief watching it. I'd like to think people regard me as respectful and humble, but that was as good a buzz as I've ever had in my life. To keep the ball for as long as we did and for it to happen in a game with a crowd watching is special. If you tried to tell someone that you did that in training, they wouldn't believe you. It never happens in training. Ever. It's one of those freakish events that, in terms of execution and kicking skill, would give you massive satisfaction for a long, long time, and for a team to execute such a match-winning drive provides enormous pleasure.

Without that drop goal we would have lost our first pool game at home. Instead, it ignited our season. It was a different mood going into work on Monday for everyone, whereas losing your first game at home puts serious pressure on the team. You almost feel like you're in bonus territory.

I have to admit I thought the game was up. We were going nowhere for the first twenty phases. There was no great plan or pre-ordained move. The most important commodity was patience. Northampton couldn't afford to give away a penalty, as hopefully I would have kicked it, so we just had to keep the ball and get into range.

The following week we played the same get-out-of-jail card in Castres when with the scores level I landed a drop goal after the eighty-minute mark. But for that drop goal against Northampton we might have been zero out of two. Instead, perhaps because of what happened a week before, we had the ability to hang in away from home a week later.

I love to replay what happened against the Saints. Seventy-seven minutes and fifty-five seconds, Munster scrum. It buckles, but Leams gets the ball away to Tomas, whose carry sets up a ruck five metres inside their ten-metre line. Tomas is brilliant at that. Although there is probably more space on the outside, I want to keep us near the posts. Varls makes a couple of great carries. We could move it on another pass but we're conscious of keeping it in and around the posts and become a bit narrow. We almost cross at one point, but Hayes does brilliantly to step out of Mafi's path and then come back for the clean-out. Hayes and Leams are brilliant off the bench for us that day.

The crowd are getting more into it, although they're clearly wondering what we're doing. We're just keeping ball and going through phases.

Tomas is patient. Forty seconds to go. Twenty seconds to go. Good carry from Niall Ronan – a completely under-appreciated player. Peter O'Mahony, good footwork in the 80th minute. We're still going nowhere though. Keep the ball. Leams backing up again. He's isolated, so I go into the ruck, thinking I've got to stay on my feet. Ten seconds left. It's hard to see where we're going to go. There's nothing on my side. And we don't seem to be going anywhere.

Time's up. Nigel Owens calls last play. We're just trying to get a soft spot but Northampton aren't giving us anything. We're back in our own half, fifteen metres back from where we started, after twenty-one phases. Will Chambers makes a positive carry and puts us on the front foot. You can see the difference it makes. They have to be onside. No point in going wide, even though we easily could go wide.

Niall Ronan beats the first man again. Leams makes a great carry, Mafs a great clean. A good carry by Tomas after clearing out slow ball. He can't do anything else with it. Leams shows up again. Great carry, Donncha. Now it's on outside, so I give it. Will Chambers, good carry, gives us front-foot ball. Now we can play. Mafs could have a go but I don't think there's any need. Leams, brilliant. The drop goal is potentially on, but it's on the right-hand side, so it's very hard. Now I'm just conscious of keeping it around the posts. We could easily go outside at this stage but again we're just keeping ball. At one point we're in a good position but I'm not on my feet. Leams and Paulie, great clear-out.

We're guilty of hoof passes. We've had the ball for four minutes and twenty seconds. They slow it down again but we're doing all right. Tomas carries again, brilliant clear-out by Varls and Wian du Preez. Over thirty phases now. I could probably step into the pocket at this stage but I feel we have numbers on the right. Johnny Murphy does well to keep the ball in contact. Now we're twenty-five yards from the line. Great hands, John Hayes. He is brilliant at this stage.

Paulie, a good clear-out. Well done Leams, carries and holds on to the ball. Paulie passes to me in the pocket, but the drop goal is not on. So I move it right, and Dougie breaks their defensive line. And he beats another man. Well done, Dougie!

Yeah, now it's on. Leams, another good carry. I take it flat going left and I'm isolated for a second but luckily Wian is inside. Tomas has to clear out along with Donncha and Dougie as I run back into the pocket, and Leams passes to me. Beautiful pass off his left hand. It's slow ruck ball but because we've worked them over so many phases they only have one player chasing me. I have time to fix the ball in my hands because Hayes fills the block channel and Donncha gets on to his feet to block their one chaser.

I nail it.

At the full-time whistle there is no reaction from Paulie. Typical. Johnny Murphy lifts me into the air. I try to be respectful to the opposition and have a few words with Chris Ashton. A bad reputation, but a good fella. Honestly. He's actually very respectful and professional, but because he does a swan-dive when he scores people think otherwise.

That drive and that score took five minutes and forty-five seconds – forty-one phases. It was the product of a sheer desire to play for each other. That epitomizes Munster. In the last sixteen years how often have we seen the ball being retained for over five minutes? Fantastic effort. Outstanding.

I'll miss that all right. When will we ever see anything like it again?

CHAPTER 10

Modern Rugby

Rugby is played by athletes now, whereas when I started it was played by rugby players. As a consequence, rugby today is less skilful and more reliant on power. That's the challenge facing academies and coaches, to find the balance between a really skilful player and a gym monkey.

I'm only beginning to realize what's required nowadays of young players who want to break into the professional ranks. In many cases they're doing weights from the age of fourteen. I began doing weights properly at twenty-two. I had dabbled for a few years after leaving school, but standards in the gym improved significantly when I was in my early twenties.

Where my era missed out was in not being properly coached in 'clean' or 'snatch' techniques, and that, essentially, is how you can become more powerful. The roles of the strength and conditioning coaches are therefore crucial in teaching younger kids correct technique.

One of the pitfalls of this focus on gym work, however, has

been the increase in the rate of pubic symphysis injuries, with more young players experiencing problems around the crotch area and more operations required as a consequence. There must be some correlation between the increase in squats and cleans and the resulting wear and tear. In Munster alone we saw this happen to Barry Murphy and Keith Matthews.

There were always bound to be huge changes in a contact sport which went from amateur and semi-pro to professional. When a sport becomes professional it swiftly learns to maximize its resources, whereas for an amateur game, players trained on Tuesday and Thursday nights, even if a few were ahead of the posse in doing weights. The game is more physical now. Players are packed stronger. The hits are harder, but players coming into the game who don't know where to place their head in the tackle make the game potentially more dangerous. In this and in much else, under-age coaching will help to safeguard the future of Irish rugby, for instance in learning how to fall – knees, hip, shoulder. If you stopped most supporters on the street they'd have limited knowledge of that kind of stuff, but that was drilled into us as kids. True, we were all told the harder they are the bigger they fall, but that's bull. The truth is the harder he is, the harder he is to get down! Seeing a big hit often makes some spectators squirm, although actually a great deal of technique is involved. Sometimes you have to be careless and put your head anywhere to try and stop a player, but nine times out of ten a player will remember the basics he learned as a six-, eight- or ten-year-old – 'cheek to cheek', as our first coaches always told us.

The changes in body shape have inevitably affected how the game is played. Take the role of centres. In the amateur era they were elusive and creative; now they are no longer the best passers and have more of a role in getting over the gain line. Wingers have also changed from skinny, quick finishers into bigger, physical players. The only two positions still reliant on skill are 9 and 10; for the other positions, any player with both football and athletic ability will shine.

I was lucky to have had plenty of football ability even if my athletic ability was very average, but fortunately when I started there were probably only one or two monsters in each team, bar the English team of the early 2000s. Hence less physical out-halves like myself, Neil Jenkins, Paul Grayson and others, even the slightly built Arwell Thomas, could cope.

It's not all lost though, as transferring that greater physical power on to the pitch is another matter. Some players are very strong in the gym but don't bring it to the pitch, so it still comes down to ability, no matter what a player's size. It helps hugely if you're big and strong, but all the more if you can play. A small, slight, skilful player can still have a successful career, but that said, I can't imagine a seventeen- or eighteen-year-old version of myself starting out now. It's difficult to make that comparison because the club game isn't the same breeding ground for a young 10. Sure, in a professional provincial set-up he will be working with a senior, more established 10, but the coach has to give the younger player game time as well.

Could a young Ronan O'Gara still make it in the game today? Without a shadow of a doubt, although he wouldn't be drinking twice a weekend! But that was accepted then. For young players coming into the sport now it's different. Aside from having to look after their bodies, the advent of social media has completely changed the profile of Irish rugby players. In my time, even though I was Ireland's number 10, the public and the media weren't as interested in players as they are now. Indeed, they've more interest in me now than when I was playing, which is very odd!

I would love to have been exposed to weightlifting earlier in my physical development, and been a bigger player. I broke my arse in the gym but I was a slow gainer, and I found it difficult to keep the weight on. I could eat crap and put on another three or four kilos but that was no good. Essentially, I was very fit in terms of endurance but I had very limited fast-twitch fibres. We each have our own genetic make-up. I'd never win a sprint or any one-off fitness test, but if I had to do it ten times, I'd come into my own from rep six or seven and beyond.

The bulk of the Wales and Lions teams which Warren Gatland favoured are big men. It's not just the obvious ones, like Dan Lydiate or Jamie Roberts, who are now both at Racing; Jonathan Davies and even the smallest of them, Leigh Halfpenny, are in very good shape. They seem to place huge emphasis on leg power and leg speed too, all of which shows that Warren knows how to build a good team around him. He knows rugby inside out, yet not only has he employed good assistant coaches, he's taken on the best strength and conditioning coaches as well.

This is a very competitive area in its own right, and identifying the right person or people is critical. I've worked with some superb ones over the years who've had a huge role in my career. I've really trusted them and developed a relationship with them as people, not just as trainers. As a coach, it's an area I need to become even more knowledgeable about, especially the link between S and C and diet and nutrition. If a player trains two hours a day, as Bryce Cavanagh says, what he does with the other twenty-two defines him as a rugby player every bit as much. That ties in with Deccie's bigger vision, what he calls 'balancing the four legs of the stool'. There's only so much physical training you can do and there's only so much tactical work you can do. If you can get the preparation and motivation right from the top man down, you're going to create a squad of thirty or so players thinking along exactly the same lines. Warren has achieved this, because you don't win three Grand Slams without it. At any rate, it's bloody hard to achieve without it. Whenever Wales are in contention they seem to have an uncanny knack of winning the Slam or the Six Nations title.

Like everyone else of my vintage, my own diet was un-recognizable in latter years compared to when I started. I used to be very particular about my diet but since hitting thirty I've chilled out. I realized that taking three protein shakes a day and eating tuna and pasta and green beans or asparagus doesn't make you a better rugby player. It helps to get your body in better shape, but I honestly don't understand how three cups of coffee could be detrimental to me as a rugby player.

We had the best of advice from every quarter, although I wouldn't have been as consistent as others in sticking to the diet. I found solace in the realization that my body fat scores were always average. They weren't superb or anything but they weren't noticeably affected by my diet.

I am a big fan of anything in moderation, although I did effectively cut out alcohol completely bar four or five 'charges' a year. I had to do that for the head. Rugby is highly stressful when it means so much to you and you play for your local team.

No matter what players say, we all care what the public thinks of us.

Today, rugby is big business. A professional squad has a medical team, physios, masseurs/masseuses and rehab specialists, and in addition to the head coach there is a forwards coach, defence coach, kicking coach, scrum coach – the list goes on. Every part of the game has to be accountable now. The media will attack an area where they feel there's a deficiency and ask why more isn't being done to fix it. Hence the temptation in any management team is to cover all bases.

On the other hand, the tighter a squad is the better, and as this is hard to achieve with a group of fifty-plus people, the smaller a management team, the more effective it is likely to be.

I think there is an awful lot of box-ticking in all of this – everyone getting their fifteen minutes of coaching here and there. But I just don't see how essential some of it is. Against that, some specialist coaches would like to have more input, and would use that additional time profitably.

The perception would be that the game has changed on the pitch, but ironically, for all the changes off the pitch and the increased number of coaches with each team, the game itself is essentially not that different. For example, I challenge anyone to watch Munster against Toulouse in 2000 and say that the game has evolved dramatically in the last thirteen years. If I was four weeks into a career as a coach, I would replay that video over and over. The variety of skills involved in the try I finished off from Dominic Crotty's beautiful pass inside out of the tackle were a joy to watch; that try was started in our own 22 and featured seven offloads. In some international games involving

Ireland there wouldn't be seven offloads in the entire match!

Watching that try again a few weeks ago reminded me that it is very, very difficult to build any defensive alignment when the ball is played out of the tackle like that. It is the type of offloading rugby more normally associated with the French. There are ways of counteracting it, but that is essentially rugby at its best.

The biggest improvement with regard to skills I have witnessed is in place-kicking. Goal-kickers achieve a much higher ratio compared with when I started. I have thought about this a lot. I was talented and I was good as a young lad but I improved progressively. If you do the work, with the right technique you get results. Still, the value of a reliable goal-kicker remains as pronounced as ever. This has been proved consistently over the years and it is as pertinent today as it's ever been: if a team is to win a trophy, it needs a reliable kicker.

The game also revolves around the breakdown more than ever, but this area has become increasingly complex as the rules around it keep changing. You just have to go with the times. In the Super 15, they selectively pick which breakdowns to contest, whereas in the Rabo Pro12 and the European Cup, teams smash into virtually every single breakdown.

Players have become so much more adept with their tackle and poaching technique, which scarcely existed ten years ago. For a while, groundhog sevens – which Neil Back took to a new level – became too influential and as a result defences became too dominant. The IRB addressed this effectively by introducing the law whereby the tackler has to release the tackled player before contesting for the ball. Undoubtedly too many games hinge on the referee's interpretation, particularly at the breakdown, of whether or not a player is on his feet and supporting his own body weight. Players are able to do the splits now and keep on their feet. This issue will probably prompt the next IRB law change – namely, a player won't be allowed to poach at forty-five degrees. Your legs will have to be no more than a metre apart, which wouldn't be a bad idea.

Rugby is not an easy game to police, for the IRB or referees, and it amazes me how much players need to improve their knowledge of the rule book. When a team receives a kick-off, for example, and the ball rolls towards the end-goal line, if a player allows it to stop before touching it and putting his foot over the line, the next play is a 22-metre restart for his team; whereas if he places his foot over the line and gathers the ball while it is still moving, his team has a scrum on halfway. Yet within top-level squads there is a surprising amount of uncertainty about this law.

Similarly, although players are more aware of the law preventing them kicking out on the full if they've brought the ball back inside their 22, it's amazing how this can still be forgotten in the heat of the moment – witness Stephen Jones in the Wales–Ireland endgame in 2009 and James O'Connor in the second Lions Test in 2013.

One of the side effects of this law change has been to make the number 9 the new 10. Scrum-halves do so much more of the defensive kicking because there's often little point in passing to a 10 inside the 22, as their one option is to kick long. With the quality of kickers at 9 now you can have a hang time of three and a half seconds for a box-kick of twenty-five metres, which in turn makes it more contestable on the halfway line. That would be our approach in Ireland or Munster, whereas Wales prefer to kick it as long as possible and then set their defensive line further up the pitch. They are effective with that tactic because their whole team buys into it.

In tandem with this, another beneficial law change has been the 'use it or lose it rule' at rucks as well as mauls. Teams in possession with the lead used to be able to run down the clock and it was destroying endgames. I know this may sound rich coming from a Munsterman bearing in mind how we patented this in the 2008 Heineken Cup final in the Millennium Stadium. However, it wasn't much fun being on the receiving end. Wales did it to us in Croke Park, and it is so frustrating.

Restarts have become crucial in recent years also, both receipt and kick-off. Previously the emphasis had been on scrum and line-out for primary set-piece possession, but nowadays the improved quality of restarts has made them a more contestable source of possession.

If a team scores, say, two tries and four penalties, the opposition then have six plays from the exact same spot on the halfway line. In high-scoring games, there could be ten or more restarts. Whether a team wants to win the ball back from a restart or make the opposition resume from deep inside their own half, the out-half has had to add this to his kicking repertoire. Leinster have made it into a very potent weapon in recent years, with reverse restarts to the right for Shaggy or right to left for Nacewa, which more often than not Johnny executed perfectly.

The importance of restarts was hammered home to us by the All Blacks on the three-Test tour to New Zealand in 2012. This was a huge learning curve for us, and particularly for Johnny, because compared with Dan Carter's restarts, ours were nowhere near good enough. Whereas our kick-offs gave them the ball, Carter invariably found Kieran Reid with his. An effective or ineffective restart is the difference between receiving the ball forty yards from the opposition line and attacking on the front foot, and being on the back foot defending straight from the kick-off.

I really enjoyed the challenge of improving my restarts because it was made easier by rugby's increased use of quality soccer pitches. On decent surfaces there are so many more possibilities. I used to have lengthy discussions about this with Ireland's forwards coach Gert Smal, who was familiar with the high veldt, where the Bulls play, and where you can place a restart five metres in from the touchline with a four-second hang time. That is simply not possible in Ireland. On the rare enough occasions when conditions are absolutely perfect you might get three seconds at best.

There is also more variety to the kicking games of both 9s and 10s with the advent of cross-kicks to counter defences which push up hard and leave space out wide. Johnny came up with a big play with the dinked cross-kick to George North from turnover ball inside the Lions 22 in the third Test against the Australians when it was a one-score game. That showed the value of having a good 10 with the vision, the skills set and the balls occasionally to go against the expected or percentage play.

If a play like that doesn't work a coach shouldn't criticize his 10. To do so betrays a weakness in that coach. You have to trust your players. At the elite level, coaches are dealing with elite players. If, say, Johnny's play in that third Test hadn't come off and Warren was unhappy about it, but Johnny tells him 'I saw a bit of space there and went for it', then I don't think the coach can have an argument. He can have a look at it to see if the out-half's skills set or his decision-making let him down, or he was a small bit unlucky with a bounce. But a coach has to trust his players. That's what separates instinctive players from robots.

This begs the question: are modern-day players given their heads as much now as used to be the case, or have they become over-coached and robotic? This question fascinates me because I think that an increasingly high proportion of players want to be told what to do in virtually every circumstance, and use that as a safety net; whereas the better players review their perform-ances and their team's training and deduce how they themselves can make a difference. Many prefer to be spoon-fed, to be given the game plan or the battle plan during the week. Yet there will come a day when it hasn't worked again and they'll eventually have to say to themselves, 'If I really want this team to succeed, I've got to drive this team, not the coaches.' One of the reasons for Munster's consistency over the years, undoubtedly, was the degree to which the players were interested in the game plan.

It was murder for myself in the early stage of my career because you're agreeing with the game plan during the week only to come up with general calls on match day. But you realize it's not fair to do that to the other players around you. There are some calls that are very applicable generally and easy to use, but if you have a game plan you trust in it, and within those game plans there have to be multiple options. There cannot be only a one-option play in certain areas of the pitch, which is happening at times. Teams are doing 8–12, kick, no matter what, off left-hand-side scrums, i.e. the 8 picks and either passes to the 12 or takes it up himself. But if the 8 sees that the 12 is bitten into, and that the opposition 12 hits in and protects the inside, then it's a better option for the 8 to hit the 10 and use the blindside winger as a trailer. But sometimes an 8 just trucks it up without even looking. Having the options and using them may seem complicated, but it's not if you've a good 8. It's all about being made aware by a good coach what man the 8 is trying to attract, and what his keys are for holding the ball and driving into contact, or for passing, because others just pass for the sake of passing. There are over a hundred decisions in a game, but essentially all that is involved in that decision is 'Do I hold it or do I pass it?' It's not that complicated. The 8 has been breaking off the back of the scrum for thirty years; it's just that passing to the 12 is a new addition, and that's not the hardest thing to think up.

Direction is crucial – you have a certain way of playing the game – but you also have to use your instincts. If you are to play as a team you decide early in the week how you want to operate within a broad framework, and within that framework there are certain 'power plays' you might like to try. But what surpasses everything is how you react to the opposition defence. That's what separates the great from the good – the ability to think on their feet.

When I started my international career, one criticism of Warren Gatland was that he didn't have a specialist defensive coach, but it was an easy stick to beat him with. A defensive system has become an integral part of a team's make-up. Players nowadays receive such an earful from their defensive coach that they have become more conscious of their responsibilities in that respect. Having said that, I think defensive rugby has always been strong. Defences appear more sophisticated because for years there were no systems. Obviously the more structured, organized and cohesive a defence is, the harder it is to break down, but while I think it's comparatively easy to coach a good defence, how players implement one is another matter.

That is what has set Brian O'Driscoll apart from everyone else for the last ten years. His ability to come up with the right decision at the right time can make any defensive system look good. It's only the one time in ten, when he might make the wrong decision, that you see the amount of space and opportunity which he covers. The flip side of that is nine times out of ten he's stopping the opposition. In this regard, he is the best I've seen, without a shadow of doubt.

The 'hindmost foot' offside line rule is not applied as strictly as it could be. The only way a team will be caught is if there is one 'outlier'. If one player shoots ahead it's easier for the referee to adjudge it offside, but a disciplined team will never be caught if they keep their line. Teams are taught all week about keeping their line. If they do, even if they start from half a yard or even a yard offside they'll generally get away with it.

The scrum reset is killing the game, but here the IRB have to tread carefully. They cannot afford to dilute the scrum to such an extent that we take the route of rugby league and have flankers as props. The biggest challenge facing the IRB and referees is to make the scrum a proper contest and ref it correctly.

Glen Jackson, like Alain Rolland and John Lacey, is a former player, and the advent of retired players becoming referees is a positive development for the game. However, like all former backs, if I tried refereeing I wouldn't have a clue what's going on in the front row. I'd be guessing if it went down, and I think we all have to be more honest in saying that. Barring a few ex-props turning to refereeing, referees need better education from retired props – although one of the problems with props is that they never, ever, blame themselves; it's always an issue with something, or someone, else. 'He got the better of me.' How many times have any of us heard a prop say that?

Maybe a suggestion worth exploring would be to have an ex-prop sitting next to the TMO, and linked up to the ref. He could then clarify, for example, whether a tight-head is boring in on the opposition loose-head, whether one of the props is the guiltier party in bringing down a scrum, or which prop is legitimately on top.

I don't think I've ever seen the five-metre rule at scrum time enforced, and it has made little difference save for giving the 10 more time and space to kick. Even then I sometimes think the ease with which the 10 finds space in the corners can be interpreted as terrible play by the defending winger. A significant part of my new coaching role will be spending time with the back three to work out if they can visualize what the opposition 10 will do four or five seconds before he even receives the ball, as Girvan Dempsey always seemed able to do. There were so many times when I found space with ease in behind the opposition winger that I'd think, 'Is this fella watching the same game I'm playing in?' However, when the French were tuned in, they were lethal to kick against because their back three played in a pendulum and all knew exactly what was happening. Nowadays, though, it seems that if you're off by a fraction of a second, you get nailed. All you need as a kicker is five metres to make ground. The French were also the most devastating counter-attackers, although there's less counter-attacking in the game generally these days.

I had the honour in my third Lions Tour in 2009 of captaining the team against the Emerging Springboks (**above**), after scoring a try in the opening match against the Royal XV (**left**), but defeat in the Second Test in Pretoria (**bottom**) would prove a crushing disappointment. I felt we had to go for a win to maintain our chances of winning the series, but it wasn't to be, and it hurt like hell.

Above: On the bench with Strings, against South Africa on 6 November 2010. I eventually came on to win my 100th cap, but it should have been a different occasion for me.

Left: The Heineken Cup is obviously close to my heart, and being named the most influential player in the first fifteen years of the tournament by the ERC was a great recognition.

Below: Losing Paul Darbyshire shortly after we beat Leinster in the 2011 Magners League Grand Final put rugby firmly in its place.

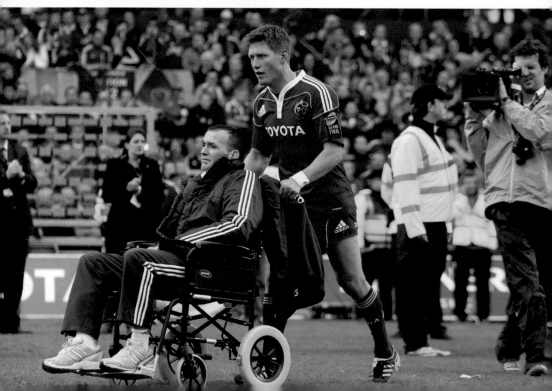

Left: It took this last-minute drop goal to get us out of jail in Rome in the 2011 Six Nations.

Below: I was back as a starter at Murrayfield and evaded Chris Paterson to score this try, but there's no question we'd let standards slip after the Grand Slam.

Above and right: Beating England is always good though, and I had enough time off the bench to get to grips with Chris Ashton.

Our preparations for the 2011 World Cup were spot on, thanks to the IRFU, Deccie and the team operations manager Ger Carmody, and starting off for a week in Queenstown was a masterstroke. There was good craic amongst the players – there always is with Donncha (**top**) – and Kearns and I even enjoyed the obligatory press conference (**above**). On top of that, there were loads of activities to make it a happy camp. How we were allowed on these go-karts (**right**) I'll never know, but I'm showing Tommy Bowe a good turn of speed.

Right: By the time we got to Auckland, we were fired up, and I came on to kick a couple of high-pressure penalties to give us a massive victory over Australia.

Below and bottom: I was more than satisfied to be picked against Italy, and a big win against them gave us the favourable quarter-final draw against Wales. We got the boot in Wellington though – we were just not at our best on the night – and I couldn't help thinking about what might have been.

Above: 12 November 2011, Thomond Park. My favourite drop goal, after 41 phases against Northampton, defined what we, and the Heineken Cup, were all about.

Right and below: Kicking one of my six penalties (after two unforgiveable early misses) and then celebrating with Dougie Howlett after we shocked Harlequins on their own turf in the 2013 quarter-final – another great victory for Munster Rugby.

Above: We came up short against Clermont in the semi-final, where even Nathan Hines had some complimentary words to say to me. That was quality and decent of him.

Left: Paulie knew that I had probably come to the end of the road.

Left and above: Saying my goodbyes at the Stade de la Mosson, first with Rua, and then saluting the fans. Words cannot describe them.

Above: Receiving an honorary doctorate from UCC in September 2012 was a great family celebration.

Left: My 128th and final cap, for fifteen minutes as a substitute against Scotland on 24 February 2013. Drico and I have certainly shared it all.

Below: So Paris with Johnny Sexton and the rest of the Racing Metro boys it now is. Becoming a coach is the start of a new chapter.

One good feature of the third Lions Test: it underlined that the scrum is alive and well. The scrum is still the best place to attack from, especially 'Amber D' scrums, which are scrums from outside your own 22 to the halfway line. Then the defending team have to play a back three, or if they don't then you boot it in behind them for easy yardage.

The law keeping the back rows bound at scrums has been really beneficial, although here again it's rarely penalized unless glaringly obvious. But I suppose if the referee were to apply all the rules he'd be blowing his whistle fifty times a match.

I wouldn't envy a referee. His job is wickedly tough. Over the years, Nigel Owens has been one of the best I've encountered. I've been cranky with him in recent games but over the course of our careers I've found him a very decent person and very easy to get along with.

Alan Lewis and Alain Rolland were probably the best two Irish referees, but because they were Irish they didn't referee many games I was involved in. Now a new breed of referee is coming through in Ireland with John Lacey and Eddie Hogan-O'Connell, fellas I played with.

I've experienced our buddy at Thomond Park, Romain Poite, quite a lot in recent times, but actually I think he's OK. The players weren't able to engage with him much but I think he's a good referee. He's quick to whistle and lay down the law, and he has presence. He also has the same rules for everyone; he doesn't change them for an O'Driscoll or an O'Connell. If you're wrong, you're wrong.

I liked to engage verbally with referees and I suppose I went through every possible experience with them in initially talking too much and then not talking enough. It's about trying to find the balance. For sure Dylan Hartley crossed the line when he was sent off in the English Premiership final at Twickenham for using foul and abusive language at Wayne Barnes and missed the Lions tour through suspension. Yet as a professional sports-person I could completely understand where Hartley was coming from. I've had this argument with plenty of people. Yes, it was disgraceful and of course you can't do it, but I'm telling you, when the red mist hits you in a game it's very easy for someone sitting on his sofa with a cup of tea or perched on a high stool with a pint to air his opinion about it, but very few have been in that highly pressurized, high-intensity environment.

I have had to apologize to referees after games, most recently with Nigel Owens when he called Paulie's pass forward in the endgame against Clermont. The result means so much to you crazy things come into your head. But that's part of what makes sport interesting.

I never had any strong opinions on Wayne Barnes one way or the other, but he does seem to be attracting more controversy lately. Paddy O'Brien was a referee who you could have a chat with, and he had a sense of humour, which is important.

In the last few years rugby has gone in so many directions, and there have been so many law changes. With some being applied differently depending on whether you're in the southern or northern hemisphere, it's very hard to keep track of what's new and what isn't. Referees are only human as well and have their own career ambitions, so the degree to which a coach can influence or build a good relationship with a referee has become more important than ever.

The same is true of captains and referees. Even though I didn't mind him personally, the prospect of Poite being in charge of a game I was playing in might have me more on edge than most other referees. You knew you were going to be in for a long day because he and Paulie clashed, and that always makes it difficult.

The single most important factor in being a good referee – and it's hard for them, and they'll contest it until the day they die – is that they have to make sure it's not about them. Some clearly want it to be about themselves. It doesn't help that they seem to enjoy a higher profile than ever before.

The addition of, and use of, a TMO has been a brilliant development for the game. It has added intrigue and increased the entertainment value for the public, and while it hasn't been foolproof, it has ensured more decisions are made correctly. Extending the role of the TMO, as in rugby league, so that a referee can ask them to rewind for foul play, obstruction or a forward pass in the build-up to a try, would be a good move, but here rugby union needs to be careful again. There's no need to over-sanitize the game; there has to be some leeway for a little clip or shoulder or block off the ball. What made some players really good was their ability to cheat and torment the opposition. The game needs characters, like Quinny, although I fear we're losing them. Players are coming into the game as athletes, not as players who learned a few tricks of the trade in the AIL.

The game also needs tries, and therefore doesn't require block lines to be penalized too severely, particularly if players run good dummy lines and check before contact. In rugby league, if there's any contact the try is ruled out. However, to be effective in your block line you have to check an opposing defender. There could be a danger of blurring the distinction between obstruction and running an effective decoy line.

When Johnny Sexton hit Alex Cuthbert for his try in the Lions' first Test in Australia, for example, Chris Pollock asked the TMO, Vinny Munro, to review the move and check if there was blocking in the build-up when Brian ran a dummy line which checked James O'Connor. Rugby can never favour the defending team and disallow a try like that one. It has to be a try every time.

CHAPTER 11

The Home Team

In the last two years particularly I've noticed a huge difference in my body's reaction to playing matches. I never slept well after games, and the advent of more night matches – involving a return from playing abroad with Munster on the same night – meant it could be all hours of the morning by the time I got home. Even after a home game I'd drive back from Thomond Park or Musgrave Park, be home by one a.m., generally watch the game again and be up until four. I followed this routine even more in latter years because I realized that they were my best hours for concentrating and the game was fresher in my mind.

But with the arrival of kids, I liked Sundays to be family days, so after a Saturday night match I didn't want to use up a chunk of time watching a rugby video. Not that I'd have had much choice, as even if I got to bed at four I usually had one of the kids jumping on me by 7.30.

I was always wrecked on Sundays, and I'd be sore after a game, but Monday was when I really suffered. The younger players would be preparing to train without a care, as I used to, but now my knees or ankles would be sore, the rest of my body as stiff as a board.

In my last playing year I had severe pain in my gluteus muscles. It was very sore the day after a match and wasn't much better the following day either. I can't stress enough the benefit of deep-tissue massage for three hours a week. It did wonders for me, and I attribute so much of my longevity to physical therapists Ger Hartmann, Willie Bennett, Alan Kelly, Paddy Quinlan and, primarily, Dave Revins. Dave worked his arse off on my arse; he allotted an hour and a half per patient, an hour of which was normally set aside for actual treatment, with a half-hour gap between appointments, be they other players or private clients. I'd say an hour and twenty-five minutes was the shortest time I ever spent with him.

In 2007, he became the massage therapist with the Ireland squad, as well as the Munster's. An ability to work hard no matter the discipline is a rare trait. Youghal-born and from Glanmire, he's pure Cork and is a great lad, but gets an absolute hammering from all the lads. Donncha and Tomas have tormented him over the years. Dave is great craic, always in good form. He doesn't drink so he'd be full of energy every morning, every day – he's very appreciative of being both the Munster and the Ireland 'rub man', and carries himself very well. He's very humble, although for a masseur he's a great man for the opportunist photo or manoeuvring his way into the view of a Sky Sports camera. The boys, of course, spotted this pretty quickly and gave him an awful roasting.

Now that he's doing Ireland as well as Munster, the boys who aren't playing with Ireland just tear into him – 'Drico' this and

'Drico' that. I say to him, 'Dave, I remember when I was top of your queue, now it's Johnny.' I might ask, 'What's Johnny like before a match? What does Johnny need done?' It's a tough job doing both, but I've never heard a complaint, never got the quick lick you get from some masseurs. Dave has, essentially, been looking after my body since 2007.

Luckily I've had very few injuries, even of the soft-tissue kind. I suffered a bit of a freak hamstring injury against Racing Metro last season at the Stade de France, which can happen more easily on a waterlogged pitch. Sometimes you can sustain a nasty tweak, as Johnny did in the 2013 Six Nations game against England at the Aviva. You have to accept them. There are fewer of them nowadays, but there's obviously a weakness in the body too when something like that happens. A gluey pitch can't be the sole cause.

Soft-tissue injuries can be stress-related. As Rob Penney says, the body will go where the mind tells it. I agree. The first to go isn't the body, it's the mind.

Adrenalin is a wonderful thing, and there's a comfort to it, but it was also why I always struggled to sleep after games. My mind would be racing. Tony McGahan was very keen on 100 per cent effort at every training session, but I never agreed. I always liked to tip away at 80 per cent and then have to reach the final push for game day. Make a difference – I enjoyed that. To maintain 100 per cent all the time is too intense. Where does the step up come from? Where does your raised performance come from? And when would you have a proper night's sleep?

I went through periods of being very strict with my diet, and periods of being loose enough, before settling on keeping 'everything in moderation', and as I said, I barely touched alcohol in the last six years of my career (apart from those essential nights out). With the kids' wake-up call you've no choice anyway, but after a Saturday session, with my metabolism, not only would I struggle on the Sunday but on the Monday as well. I'd just get through training. So I came to the conclusion that if I skipped a Saturday night out, Sunday would be a good eating day and I was ready to improve on Monday. If you're doing speed and reactions on a Monday morning you need to feel sharp.

Rua and Molly were born on 11 October 2008. JJ came into the world on 30 June 2010 and Zac on 22 July 2012. They changed my life, not just by waking me up early on the mornings after games. They were the best thing that ever happened to me, and I don't say that lightly.

I remember arguing with Ken O'Connell once, saying the Heineken Cup was the be-all and end-all. He said, 'Rog, just fucking stop, will ye? When you have a kid, right, it changes your life.' It's one of those things you only appreciate when you go through it. Jonathan Wisniewski, the other 10 here in Racing, told me recently he has a completely different outlook on rugby already after becoming a father – and at the time his baby boy was only a few weeks old. If you're lucky enough to become a father it has a huge impact on you. It comes back to perspective. I think it can make you more focused too, because you're not spending all day every day thinking about rugby. A really enjoyable home life allows you to get stuck into rugby and appreciate what you're doing.

Becoming a little older also provides you with another source of motivation: to a degree, you begin playing for your kids as well.

I don't believe you take the game any less seriously for having a young family. I don't believe in any of that. It didn't affect my work. I suppose one of the benefits about going out with Jess for so long before we married was that she understood what was involved, that I took it very seriously. When the kids came along, the biggest difference was in the quality and the amount of sleep, and the amount of coffee I drank. That was my way of dealing with reduced sleep. When in Irish camp in Carton House there was a routine, and you lived like a king. It was a surreal world compared with home life and a family, although Jess was always the primary carer and especially on nights before games. That will have to change now, but I'm a hands-on dad anyway. I like getting stuck in. I've been extremely selfish my whole career. You want to pass on good things to your children, be a good parent, and that invariably involves doing things which aren't the easiest. You have to get up when it doesn't suit you to get up, but I don't mind that stuff.

Rugby has been a dominant feature of my life, and my dad has been my mentor. He understands the technical and the mental side of the game, but the role of my mum, Joan, has been underplayed. She showed her love, patience and tolerance in not saying anything through all the hassle, rumours and media coverage which came my way during and after the 2007 World Cup, but most of all through the loving home she created. You can't put a value on that.

My upbringing, with private tennis lessons and so on, wasn't the norm. Every single thing my mum could possibly have done, she did. But the most important thing – and I see it with Jess – is the love they give their children. There's a special bond between a mother and her children. It's different from fathers', although I look forward to working on my bond more in the years ahead.

I hope I haven't neglected my mum. I talked more with my dad because of his expertise and my faith in him. As important, though, has been the love my mum has given me and my three brothers. People think that because you're writing a book you're obliged to say these things, but this genuinely is the case.

I see loads of Jess's parents, Dom and Judy Daly. Dom is a big auctioneer around Cork city and Jess is close to both of them. I always enjoy heading up to Judy's for the Sunday dinner, be it roast chicken or roast lamb with mint jelly. It's incredible. I miss those roast potatoes. She has some technique. I don't know how she does it, but you can't beat experience. The mint jelly is made fresh from the garden. But she'll be here in Paris plenty of times too, so I hope she finds some way of recreating it.

Because I've been with Jess for so long, Judy has been like another mother to me. The most pleasing thing is that my mum never had a daughter, and herself and Jess are close too. It's lovely that they have their own relationship without me.

As is commonplace throughout rugby, as players we can become quite insular and think we're more important than we actually are, so the information which is relayed back to the parents is usually from the other half of the relationship. Jess has made me cop on about this. Sometimes, when I'm shattered at the end of the day and my dad rings but I'm too tired to answer, after a few rings Jess would say, 'Would you like Rua to do that to you?'

Argument over, there and then.

I'm not sure I'd want to see Rua, JJ or Zac picking up where I left off, given that standards and the level of competition are rising all the time, along with the stresses involved in the modern game. They would have additional pressures with the O'Gara name, and people can be nasty too. I've seen that already with my brothers. I've had very little interaction with Colin, Fergal and Morgan because of the increased demands of the game and my desire to succeed. For ten months or so of every year for the last sixteen years I've had to go into match mode, and I wouldn't be good company. I'd openly admit that. After a game, all the more so if it's a big occasion, there's usually a post-match meal. It's very hard to fit in family members.

Some will say there's always a solution, but I've only had two or three weeks' holiday abroad at most before resuming light training and then official pre-season. It has been hard to arrange any quality time with my family. That's another trade-off. But would I swap it? No, I wouldn't, to be honest, because I had limited time to play rugby. Sixteen years might seem like a long time, but you need to be doing everything possible to maximize your performance. The minute you take your eye off the ball someone will take your place.

Some sons of former players have cut it at professional level. TJ Anderson, Willie's boy, has played at Ulster and Connacht, while the most high-profile is probably Luke Fitzgerald, Des's son. One of Lukey's best virtues is his mental strength. It's a very impressive trait to have, and I think he's needed it because he's had plenty of adversity. Luke was a Lion in 2009, and I'm sure, like myself and many others, he'd have expected to be a Lion in 2013. That's the way fellas who've been there think about it.

The importance of balancing sport with education was instilled into Luke, as it was in me by my parents. For this and many other reasons, one of the proudest days of my life wasn't on the rugby pitch: 5 September 2012 was the day I received an honorary doctorate in UCC, one of five sportspeople honoured by the college for their contributions to various sports. I was alongside Kilkenny hurling manager Brian Cody, footballer Denis Irwin, horse trainer Aidan O'Brien and the dual ladies footballer and camogie player Mary O'Connor. The awards were in celebration of a hundred years of sport at UCC, which made it all the more prestigious, not to mention the company I was in that day. There's only ever going to be one Aidan O'Brien, one Brian Cody, one Denis Irwin and one Mary O'Connor.

The whole occasion got to everybody. Mícheál Ó Muircheartaigh was the MC, and when he speaks with that iconic voice of his, he makes it emotional. Brian Cody spoke beautifully, and Aidan O'Brien admitted the occasion was just too much for him. It was one of those ceremonies you'll never forget. Denis Irwin spoke brilliantly, and it was class being in such company. When I was a young fella, to think I'd be part of such a ceremony – beyond a dream.

I did do a Masters degree, though at the time I didn't value it. But this honorary doctorate was special. It was an almost overpoweringly humbling occasion, and it's something you especially appreciate when you have finished playing. The careers of John Hayes, Quinny, Donncha, Wally, Axel and others were every bit as long, and I received that award because of the good days we'd had together. Team sport is different: it felt like I was receiving the award on their behalf as well.

It was a beautiful day, the sun shone brightly, and it was just lovely to be part of it. Each of the five recipients wore suits with red-and-white robes and black hats. Along with the official dignitaries, each of us was allowed to invite twenty guests for the ceremony. I invited my family, my brothers and all of Jess's family, and Michael O'Flynn, because of his contribution, and Joan O'Flynn, as well as my friends from school: Paul O'Mahoney, John Powell, Conor Howell, Eoin Walsh and Aidan Fitzgerald. I have stayed very tight with them, and they've been important in my life because they're not directly involved in rugby. It's vital to have friends outside the circle who are able to give you a different perspective on things, and that's what they do. True friends are great friends. I also invited team-mates Rob Penney and Noel Murphy, and Donal Lenihan spoke about me.

It was nice to see my dad dust down his old gown as a former Professor of Microbiology in UCC and one of the university's alumni, given how much store my parents placed on education. At the time you think they're stupid and you're different – I'll be the one that will break this tradition. But – and there's a recurring theme here – it's hard to beat experience. They're telling you things for a reason, because they think it's right, not to try and make their relationship with you difficult, which as a young lad is how you see it. So I'm prepared for Rua and the rest of them not to listen to me or agree with me. It's happening already.

I had my speech prepared for weeks, and the same people helped me again: Michael O'Flynn and my dad. Another benefit of a rugby career is that virtually all players learn to speak in front of an audience, whereas others can become intimidated by it. We have to speak in front of our peers regularly, or sometimes make presentations, or speak to an invited audience after matches, and it's a great skill to develop. Indeed, when you think about the positive effects of being in a dressing-room of forty players, and the number of things that are discussed, this can only enhance your mental health. Exercise is wonderful too for making us feel good about ourselves, mentally as well as physically.

In fact words can scarcely describe how much better you feel after exercise. We should all exercise, but not enough people do. If you've been drinking late into the night, the next day you have little interest in doing anything. If you do two nights in a row, you're depressed for three days. Exercise is crucial for a person's well-being; when you also become very tight with a group, as was the case for me with Munster and Ireland, anything and everything can be aired and spoken about. Even if you've a lump on your balls, something like that will be discussed and everyone'll make the player have it checked. That's the nature of a dressing-room, whereas I would imagine it's more difficult in an office, where there might be more embarrassment, and maybe less trust also.

Exercise and camaraderie are also proven antidotes to loneliness, anxiety, depression and other emotional issues. Obviously exercise has to be done alone at times, but there is always an option of playing five-a-side, or tag in summer months, hurling, football, tennis, golf (with others) – whatever you fancy. I think the key is to do *something*. You'll just feel better.

I've sometimes wondered if I could have played an individual sport, and I've toyed with the idea of having a crack on the senior tour in golf when I'm fifty. I think I have a good head for golf. I wouldn't have learned enough of the skills at a young age, when it's easier to learn, and hence my golf game wouldn't be good enough. But I love matchplay golf, because it's not only you against the course, like normal golf, it's you against your opponent. Then again, I'd probably be disqualified because you're not allowed to talk when a fella is hitting a shot! This is a big part of 'rugby' golf. If you were allowed to play golf with commentary I think I'd excel!

Maybe I had the best balance in terms of personality, in the sense that an out-half and goal-kicker has to master an individualistic aspect of a team sport. This is what young out-halves and goal-kickers coming into the game have to do: they have to compartmentalize their game and, as crazy as it may sound, separate the kicking from the rest of the game. Effectively, you have to excel in two areas now. A young lad who is a very good kicker but a dud as a player is not going to be picked. I think it's really crucial to have the ability – and I've been in this position many times – to come back into it after bad moments in a game and finish strongly. Some out-halves may have had a bad first kick, or a bad period at the start of a match, and then they'll have a bad day. I nearly enjoyed missing the first kick at times because I'd convince myself 'I'm going to get the next'.

I needed plenty of help along the way, though. My dad and Michael O'Flynn were the two constants, and there were so many coaches and team-mates too. But even individual sports-people are leaning more on those around them. When Novak Djokovic or Andy Murray wins a major, the first people they thank – and it's clearly genuine – is their 'team', be it their loved ones, their coaches, their physio, their agent, whoever. And most of that 'team' works full-time with the tennis player.

The benefits are enormous when a player has a team with him for a long time which is pulling together. If you're on your own you've no one to bounce things off. A player's personal team plays a key role. There are plenty of 'yes men' out there, and I've seen that with a lot of rugby players. They get told what they want to hear and have their backs slapped but essentially these advisers damage the individual by doing this. It takes a strong person to tell a player the truth. I certainly benefited from my dad and Michael sometimes seeing it completely differently and then having the conviction to tell me.

I realize I'm not the easiest person at times to be told stuff and that comes from being a strong personality and having so many caps, but I need to learn every day. I want to learn every day. I need to be challenged every day, and no matter how many senior players are in a squad they need to be motivated. They need to be challenged and they need to learn every day too.

I'd like my kids to be happy, and as I've said, I think exercise and sport contribute to a balanced lifestyle. That's exactly what my parents gave me. I was mad into rugby, and of course I wanted to play for Ireland, but I didn't expect it to work out the way it did. Rugby at that stage was Tuesday and Thursday nights in Con, and then it took off and you go with it. So I'll give them every opportunity to do what they want, and if I've learned one thing it is that they need guidance, not firm direction.

I managed to complete a degree and a Masters, but the demands of the game from an early age are such now that it's tougher for kids to achieve that same balance between education and sport. This is another trade-off. I've noticed this especially in the last two years. Whereas 80 per cent of my career was training for an hour in the morning, then home to chill out and have lunch before going training again, in the last couple of years my working rugby day has been 8.30 a.m. to four p.m. minimum every day. You'd have to question – and I did question it too – what are we doing? If those are the demands, when do you fit in education? That's why I admire Jamie Roberts for completing his degree in medicine. I think this achievement will only become appreciated with time. I admire Felipe Contepomi for doing it as well, but Felipe is from the same era as me. I'd say he had a lot of the groundwork done by the time he turned professional. Jamie Roberts is twenty-six. It took him eight years. Times have changed. Nowadays it's so bloody hard to get a job in Ireland, and players realize that the rugby name isn't going to have the same influence as used to be the case. The name can be helpful, of course, but they need qualifications as well. There are groups in the provincial squads taking evening courses, and for more reasons than keeping the brain ticking over and ensuring the kind of balance Deccie always encouraged.

I'm not best placed to comment, because I'm still in a rugby bubble, but I believe playing professionally for a province and for your country is an achievement. Thousands of young kids are trying to do the same. Former players would bring an awful lot to an organization or a business, or whatever they choose. So they shouldn't be too hard on themselves and think they need to start from scratch. They do have an advantage. However, some additional education, no matter how small, demonstrates to a potential employer that they're prepared to do extra graft and are willing to challenge themselves outside the comfort zone.

I'm obliged to further my education in rugby now, and to be honest, I don't know how I'll go about it. I'd like to do it in Ireland but I'd also like to do it in France, so I have to find out what's the best route. I've enquired in France because I'm here, but my French isn't good enough as you have to be fluent. This is a decision I have to make at the end of this 2013/14 season, and I have yet to talk to Stephen Aboud, the IRFU's technical director, to see what my possibilities are at home. Either way, I'm intent on acquiring my coaching badges. You have to do things by the book, no matter who you are.

If the coaching doesn't work out for whatever reason I'm very interested in business and in trying to drive something I believe in, but at this point in my life rugby remains dominant. I think I know plenty about the game and I'd like to give something back, so I want to explore this.

But who's to say that in two years' time I'll still be in rugby? That's a realistic question, and I've no problem with that. The most important thing is my family. If my family don't like it in France it will narrow my options and make things extremely difficult. But one thing's for sure: I'm not going to put rugby before them.

CHAPTER 12

The Final Curtain

Saturday, 27 April 2013: Stade de la Mosson, Montpellier

I had roomed on my own and I didn't like it. It was so boring. No one to talk to. Time went very slowly. But as usual ahead of match days I received an email from my dad, with a few check points about what he thinks is important. It's very valuable to me, and it brightened my mood. Here's what he wrote that week:

Munster v Clermont. Sat 27th April
This ERC Semifinal is a Scenario where you really thrive;- French soil; Total underdogs; Cocky and disrespectful opposition;
So from the off make your mark.

(1) Play your own game.
(2) Play as ROG at 10 – no other position (others play their own positions).
(3) Do not get distracted in the lead-up or during the game.

(4) Nothing else matters; Be in 'match mode and in the Zone' when you get on plane on Friday.

(5) Must do your homework and visualize how you will play this game taking every eventuality into consideration. Then be fully confident and believe you will perform to your ROG standards and level.

(6) Stay cool and calculating.

(7) Take every score you possibly can.

(8) You will be targeted so make sure your back row/centres do their job.

(9) Defensively – just low tackling when it's your own man.

(10) Use your rugby brain; don't get frustrated/distracted or lose the cool; stay focused and total concentration.

Come off the pitch at end having given 100% and no 'ifs', 'buts' or regrets.

Go for it and Good luck. No better Man.

My dad has always been very helpful to me on the mental side of things. When I was at school he encouraged me to have my homework done early in the week so that thereafter it wouldn't clutter my mind. 'Just go on autopilot,' he would say to me before a game. 'You've always trusted your instincts and that's when you play your best.' I'd also receive a text from Michael O'Flynn twenty-four hours before a game which would be very specific, whereas my dad's would be broader and come earlier in the week. Then, the bigger the game, the more times I would go over it.

I looked at the email again, and then after breakfast, at 11.15, we had a 'move and groove' – a bit of stretching and flexibility. The boys went downtown for coffee but it was pissing with rain so I said, 'Not for me, I'm not going near that.' Instead I went back to the team room. It was myself and Varley again, and we looked at each other. There was nothing to chat about, though he's great company. I was in match mode now. He talked about being on the bench and the difference between being on the bench and starting. I said, 'Jesus, I know all about that.' I hadn't started for Ireland since the World Cup quarter-final defeat to Wales in 2011, winning my last dozen caps since then off the bench. For me it was just a case of 'come on, let's get this on'.

With a six p.m. kick-off, the preparation starts about four hours beforehand. The backs met to check if there was anything to go through, and there was nothing really, except for one thing: given the weather, we discussed doing a few blitz defences off scrums more often than we would normally, with our right winger leading it up on the outside as it's harder to cross-kick on that side. Usually you've everything else covered on the blitz, so it's just man on man. I was promoting that because it would mean I could stay on their 10, Brock James. I wouldn't have to hit Nalaga or Sivivatu or Fofana off a pop! But no dice.

Our pre-match meal was three and a half hours before kick-off. Chicken and pasta. Terrible. Brutal. And the appetite isn't great when you're nervous. But I told myself: 'Enjoy this. This is why you're playing. This is what you do.' I also had to back up my Harlequins performance. People are fickle, and I'd say plenty were saying 'this fella is losing it' and asking, 'Is he over the hill?' I knew from training that I certainly wasn't over the hill. I was itching to play.

Perhaps I was in my own world more than usual. I went back to my room to shower and get ready. In the back of my head I also knew this could be my last game, so I wanted it to be a good feeling just for myself. There had been an item about me on French TV the night before. This was my 110th cap in the Heineken Cup, and I'd scored 1,360 points. No matter who you are, that gives you confidence. Sometimes I'm so hard on myself that I don't see that. Perhaps that's what helped me last so long. I look at the young players in the Irish set-up now, especially those from Leinster, and the confidence they have is incredible. In the last few years I have asked myself, 'Jesus, would I have been a better player if I'd had that starting off?' I wish I'd had it, but then I don't think I would have developed the mental side of my game to the same extent, and I just question how deep the desire is in some players. Even then, once you get to the top the trick is trying to stay there. It's one thing getting there; it's harder to stay there.

I loved travelling to France too – always a cracking atmosphere. Playing for Munster, you're the underdog. Not that I was thinking we were the underdog that day. I was thinking, 'Let's have a go here. Let's go. I can't wait for it. If this is my last game, I'm going to give an account of myself that I'll be happy with and proud of.' Before every game I remind myself that as long as I can look myself in the mirror going to bed that night I don't really care what other people think.

I took the same seat as always on the bus to the ground, two from the back. Paulie is usually one in front of me for Ireland and Brian is behind me. For Munster, Paulie is one ahead too, but today he'd moved down to the back, so I had Billy Holland in front of me. There was no chat anyway. Billy was outside the playing squad today but his attitude was always exemplary.

You're questioning everything really. On the one hand I'm really looking forward to it; on the other hand I'm just hoping that it doesn't go pear-shaped. 'Fuck, do I have to play this?' All kinds of thoughts go through my head. 'I can kick six drop goals here today. We can win on that.' Crazy stuff. But the one I kept repeating was 'this could be a great day'.

There was plenty of red on the way to the ground. We arrived an hour and a quarter before kick-off, in good time, and we each had large travel bags with plenty of space because we were going straight to the airport afterwards. I just took out what I needed for the game and put it down in my slot. We all had our own individual changing seat and I put my bag on the other side of the dressing-room where there was plenty of space. It was wrecking my head that the boys wouldn't move their bags over there too to make us a bit more organized.

Jack Kiely, our bag man, had laid out and prepared the seats, and I had Murray (number 9) and Zeebs (11) either side of me. We each had our own warm-up tops and GPS vests. Some fellas had caffeine tablets, others had shakes. I don't take any of that. I don't need my heart rate going any faster. Adrenalin is enough for me.

Zebo was bopping and dancing, getting into a rhythm. Fucking crazy cool. Conor was nervous. I could see he was up for it, and I think he's turned a corner. I think it was a massive benefit for him being the senior partner in the Irish half-backs for the last two games beside Paddy Jackson. I think that has advanced his game big time. Before then, when I played with him I thought he always felt like he had to run the decision by me because he is a very respectful young fella – not that I'd be looking for anything like that. Since returning from the Six Nations he has been doing things more instinctively, and quicker and better, and I'm sure he's going to come into his own when I'm gone. Touring with the Lions will benefit him hugely too, I think to myself. He's twenty-four now with nineteen caps. I was twenty-four and had fourteen caps when I went with the Lions to Australia in 2001, so I know. I would say that Conor was in the top five most impressive players on the Lions trip in 2013.

The big difference is that back in 2001 Ireland were the poor relation. We're not any more, and that's thanks to many of the current or recently retired internationals. We've brought standards way up. Nowadays, the fellas coming in at Munster expect to win Heineken Cups. Back in 1997 we were trying to keep it under fifty away to Toulouse (and lost 60–19). I'm thinking the Irish lads will experience good standards with the Lions, but it won't be the same quantum leap I was exposed to with Dallaglio, Johnson, Hill, Back, Healy, Dawson and those lads. Incredible players. That was the nucleus of England's World Cup-winning team two years later.

Conor has the talent. What may be of benefit to him and a lot of the other young players is finding a mentor who gives them accurate feedback after every game. It's so crucial, and can really advance their progress. It takes an O'Driscoll or a Horgan or a Hickie to sit down with these fellas, or a Paulie, Quinny or Wally – someone they'd respect.

Conor's a good lad and a hard-working lad. I said to him in the warm-up, 'This is a great opportunity now, against Parra and James, this is where we're going to get an advantage. You fucking destroyed Parra in the Aviva,' I reminded him. 'More of the same now today. He doesn't like playing against you.'

I could see him literally growing in front of me. He kind of thought about it and said, 'I fucking manhandled him.'

'Do it again now, today.'

I think Morgan Parra does have a small bit of a doubt playing against Conor. Parra was good that day, but by his standards he was quiet enough, while Conor worked unbelievably hard and had a big game.

I went through my kicking, and I was relaxed and going well. The Munster fans were all to one side of me and shouting 'Come on, Rog!' and so on. You can feed off that.

Suddenly the French crowd were going mental. Booing echoed around the ground, and I see the big red monster, Paulie, running across the pitch. The twice-weekly *Midi Olimpique* rugby paper had demonized him all week, using still photographs from television pictures of him kicking Dave Kearney during the Leinster game a couple of weeks before. Then Paulie copped that it was directed at him. I could see him talking to himself: 'Come on, ye *****, come on, ye *****.' I put out my hand, and as he ran by he slapped it and shouted, 'Let's fucking kill these *****, Rog!' It was fucking special. He nearly knocked my fucking shoulder out of its socket with the force of his high five. I'd say he hadn't expected it at all and yet his initial reaction was 'Bring it on! We're going to fucking do it today!' I loved it. He was fit to play all right. He was ready to go there and then, and there was still half an hour to kick-off!

Paulie had told the senior players the night before that he was doing a fitness test at 9.30 a.m. It had been in my head all night, and when I came down to breakfast I asked Bryce Cavanagh. 'What's the story with Paulie?'

And he went: 'All good.'

'How did the tests go?'

'No, he didn't need to do them.'

I thought, 'what the hell is he playing at so?' I hadn't thought about it since, and then Paulie's reaction to the booing gave me confidence.

Back in the dressing-room there was a good buzz, with a nice focus. Before the majority of games much of what's said is noise, and sometimes fellas say things as much for themselves as for everyone else. This must have been one of those times, because I only remember saying something like 'Lads, we'll be on the ropes, but don't break. Don't fucking break. Just hang in there. I'm telling you they'll have fucking purple patches, but do not break. Just let them be the first fuckers to break. You might think we are being steamrollered at times, but just don't break.'

We made a good start. The first scrum was good. Penalty to us. It was a bit of a nothing kick but I just pushed the ball about thirty yards up the line, so the line-out was in their half. A good take; a good maul. Nigel Owens penalized them for bringing it down and I nailed the kick. I picked out my target and nailed it. I had started slowly against Harlequins but I was conscious that I couldn't afford to miss opportunities this time. 'Get your shit together.' Against this lot, we had to take everything going.

Straight from their restart, they came at us in waves, King and Fofana offloading for fun, and within three minutes Nalaga straightened through under the posts: 7–3 to them. The ease with which they scored had me thinking these boys could score at any attack. They hadn't seemed to do anything much. 'Where are our numbers?' I was wondering.

Word came on that we were committing too many to rucks, to dead rucks. But we still couldn't do anything for twenty minutes. Nalaga and Sivivatu had some work rate off the rucks because they obviously identified catch-and-drive line-outs as their best tactic and then got their wingers running inside. I missed Fofana too. Just got burned by him. I thought I had him and then he was gone. We talked about him in the dressing-room afterwards. It was a bad miss, but he's a serious player. Regan King had a great step on me in the second half too, when Paulie was inside to my left. Thank God we scrambled back and nothing came of that.

We were hanging on for long stretches but it felt like the more we could hang in there, we'd be all right. Parra tapped over a couple of penalties, one of which was very hard on Peter O'Mahony. But Nigel Owens is human too and I'd say the fall-out from the Munster–Leinster game, which he'd also refereed, meant that subconsciously he had an issue with Paulie. Whenever Paulie and he spoke as captain and referee, the din from twenty-five thousand Clermont supporters was deafening. Nigel couldn't have not heard it. It had to get into his head. Nothing surer.

When Nigel came in before the game, Paulie had been good with him. He was professional. They even had a bit of a joke. Paulie is a huge presence, but Nigel has a bit of a presence too. You'd be thinking after that 'hopefully the slate is clean and let's get on with it', but I don't think Nigel reffed it like that. That was my gut feeling.

Coming up to half-time, I moved the ball wide to Felix Jones, Earlsy chipped and chased up the line, and they had a chance to clear the ball but made a mess of it. I thought the decision then not to give us a penalty was crucial. We were under their posts and Julien Bonnaire came in from the side to kill the ball, and

13–6 at half-time instead of 13–3 is a big difference. I'm maybe being a small bit critical, but that's where Conor needs to get the ball and whip it, or else let the forwards do it, or manipulate the ref. Eoin Reddan is very good at influencing refs.

At half-time, Earlsy was struggling with his shoulder. Mannix told me, and I said, 'Leave him on as long as you can. He'll be grand.'

Axel gave us a bollocking. 'You're talking about taking the game to these guys. I don't fucking see it. You're full of shit! Where's the physicality you're talking about?' He told the forwards to start getting into them, as opposed to feeling sorry for themselves for being run around the pitch. It was fucking class. I liked it anyway.

We botched another opportunity in the green zone at the start of the second half, and Parra made it 16–3, but gradually we got our game going. Part of the game plan was for me to put the ball in behind them because their two wingers can't kick and their full-back, Lee Byrne, is very one-sided, but we had no ball in the first half. I began doing that probably a bit further up the pitch than you'd like. You'd like to be doing that from your own ten-yard line, but that's where we were, and they're big men, so it made sense to make them turn and go back. I had one extraordinary bounce that virtually backspinned into touch, then the one I nailed went out by a metre on the full. But we needed to stay down there, and then put pressure on them.

We identified a few moves, like getting Zebo outside their 13, but we were a little bit hesitant in our execution and I don't think Zeebs was going hard enough to beat them on the outside.

Felix was good all day. That game may have been a turning point for him. He's a great fella. Great attitude. Really wants it. For a fella who was going to the 2011 World Cup until he got injured he hadn't hit anywhere near that form since, but I thought this was a big, big step up by him from the Harlequins game.

From a phase play I saw there was a fair bit of width, and they were struggling to fill, so Felix just came hard off his right foot and got us over the gain line. A couple of rucks later they were stretched. I could just see Lee Byrne closing, and I put through a grubber for Denis Hurley, now on for Earlsy. I didn't expect it to land in Denis's lap but it gave us a big lift. That made it an eight-point game, so the conversion was crucial, and I hit it really well.

Six points behind. Game on.

If there's one decision I could take back it would be the play we went for from the next kick-off. We caught the restart really well but Conor boxed it and we should have gone left. If there was more vision or communication outside me we would have got to forty yards from our line and we could have kicked on our terms. However, the box-kick gave it back to them, they re-cycled it, King stepped me, and they were on the attack again. If we'd run at them God knows what would have happened. Instead they counteracted by having the ball for two or three minutes and we lost the momentum. I didn't express myself at the time but watching it again confirmed what I was thinking. We had eight of our fellas outside me, and three on one out wide, because they had five players back.

We still had chances. I hit Casey on a miss pass and he put through a great grubber. He'd been practising them too, but the ball just eluded him and Felix over their line. That was a snapshot of our season. With a small bit more organization or belief I think you score them.

I still definitely thought we were going to do it, that I'd have a conversion to win it. Jess said afterwards, 'It would have been awful if you'd missed it.' But I was thinking 'just give me the opportunity'.

We managed the game really well and then we had a penalty with three and a half minutes left. I said to Paulie, 'Let's kick this and then we've two and a half minutes for a drop goal,' which would have brought us level and forced extra time.

He goes, 'We're six points down, kid.'

I said, 'Yeah, I know, kick this and then—'

'No, no, we go to the corner.'

I still think it was good that we discussed it, but on the day, if we'd got them into extra time it would have been interesting.

We had a couple of mauls, but we had an overthrow. We'd a peel organized and it was going to be a 'gooseball' to Zeebs in behind one of the forwards. It was an all-or-nothing play if we got it. But we had a few opportunities and then, with the last play of the game, Nigel called Paulie for a forward pass that was never forward.

I'm not saying we would have scored, but it would have been interesting. I lost the plot with Nigel there and then. 'You're fucking joking me. You're fucking robbing us all day' – or something like that.

Paulie said, 'Shut the fuck up, will you.'

Tommy said he was going to try and do something off their final scrum, but what can you do? Game over.

Nathan Hines was the first Clermont player I shook hands with. He was very complimentary. There's a bit of history there in terms of Scotland and Leinster games, and he gave me an awful stamp a few years ago behind my knee, a nasty one. But by all accounts he's a good fella.

I said, 'Well done. Thanks. I think that's me done now.'

And he said, 'Well, for what it's worth, you're the best I've come up against,' or words to that effect. Right there and then. It was quality. It was decent of him. I wouldn't be getting that from a fella like him too often. It's bred into him to hate me because he's been in Leinster, and I know what they think of me! And that's what makes him successful.

That sparked a few tears. But it also wrecked my head. The younger fellas don't understand that you don't just get back to the semi-final next year. When you have momentum in sport it's so easy to keep it going, whereas it's so difficult to regenerate from the start. And it hit me. I realized, 'That's fucking it now.' It had all been so good – the atmosphere, the fans' jumping in the stadium. It was a great game to be a part of. Not the losing, but I could see all the good of it. This was why I got into this great game from day one. That's exactly why you play. There's such a buzz and a challenge with your friends, and the feeling before the game makes you sick. 'Am I fucking good enough for this any more? What shit is going to be written about me? What are people thinking?' Everything goes through your head, and then you play like that in a game like that. There's no better feeling than hitting your peak performance on the biggest stage.

I thought of Deccie too. I wished he'd backed me, and thought for a moment, 'You could have done with that in the Six Nations.' I said that once or twice in my own head, but then again, having a point to prove was another motivation. That's the fuel that makes me tick.

I knew it was all over, but time is a healer, and as the minutes passed I became kind of content, thinking, 'I'll go to bed tonight happy. That's me done. I'll sign out. There's my record. Thanks, good luck.' I have given everything to this game. Being the kicker, the chief decision-maker, I've put my whole life into it, but I've got such reward out of it that I absolutely loved it. Now when I thought 'that's it, that's the end', it actually felt very natural.

My 110th game in the Heineken Cup. My tenth semi-final. It obviously wasn't the perfect ending, but I would have preferred to have lost in that game than the final. It's easier to accept.

Donnacha Ryan gave me a big hug. I was a bit hazy at that stage and was getting myself together. He's a decent lad, and I'd told him I was finishing. I shook hands with and hugged the rest of my team-mates and joined Paulie at the end of the corridor we had formed for Clermont. They were still on the far corner of the pitch, just starting their lap of honour. Paulie told us to wait, and I thought that was class. Bonnaire saw this and cut their lap short, motioning his players to come over to us. It was a class occasion in every sense, but it's a class competition. There's respect there. I don't know if you get that in soccer. Them boys would have been milking it if it was a soccer team, but they did stop. They came over and he hurried them up, and it was important for us, as losers, to be there first. To lose gracefully. It's hard. You're hurt. You're angry. But it has to be done.

Rua just landed into my arms. Jess had made her way down towards the sidelines. Dave Revins had Rua in his arms and passed him on to me. That was nice. That's what life is all about. I didn't see it before having kids, but now I see that's what it's all about.

'Did you enjoy it?' I asked Rua.

'Daddy, it was too loud.'

I said, 'Are you OK?'

And he goes, 'Yeah, but too loud. And you didn't win the match.'

'I know, I know, I know.'

I tried to explain to him that you can't always win, but I was thrilled he was there. I didn't expect him to be on the pitch. That probably suggested to people that this fella knew in his own mind he was finished, but carrying my child doesn't make it any more final for me. That's the way it happened. Sometimes I've thought scenes like these are PR stunts, but that wasn't pre-planned. I'd had it in my head to thank the Munster fans on either side of the pitch anyway. They'd been bloody good, and I'd spotted Jess five or six rows back from the front behind Dougie. When the final whistle went it would have been nice to give her a kiss, but I couldn't get near her. I could see she looked a little sad, or upset. I tried to make her smile. Mick O'Driscoll and a few fellas from Pres and Christians were there too, guys I recognized and all good lads, and a few of them were crying. I found that a little strange.

In the dressing-room, Axel spoke well again. 'Don't presume we'll get into the semi-final next year,' he told the players. 'We won't have any more right to get there again. We've got to work hard. Do everything right.' It was good because he's pure Munster.

There was a nice big bath in the changing-room and Paulie had talked the day before the game about how we were all going to be in there celebrating and having the craic, and to picture it. I went in and, of course, after the loss there wasn't a bead of water in it. We filled it up anyway. It was a nice hot bath and a few of us got into it and started chatting there – Felix, Donnacha and others. We relived the match. Everyone always comes at it from a different angle, and so you try to think about it from their perspective. Rugby is crazy. It's all so different yet it's all so close, almost like fifteen mini-matches going on simultaneously.

I had some really decent text messages and emails, including one from Humphs: 'Rog, bad luck today. Thought you were going to write another chapter on the O'Gara story with a last-kick conversion to seal another dramatic Munster win. Watching your reaction after the game suggested it might be your last ERC match, and I just wanted to say it will never be the same watching Munster in Europe without you at 10. As someone who has cursed you, cheered for you, but generally come off second best in head-to-head battles, your record for Munster and Ireland is incredible and I don't think the Heineken Cup will ever again have a decade of competition influenced so much by one person. I still stand by what I said to you a few weeks ago about retirement but you know what's right better than anyone else. Have a good night and I'm sure our paths will cross again over the next few months. Regards to Jess and your mum and dad. Congrats again.'

I thought in my own head I had played well, but some people who are good judges were complimentary. It was crucial, it was affirmation.

When I emerged from the dressing-room, Pat Geraghty, our press officer, whisked me around to the tent where the reception was being held. On the way I met a neighbour from across the road in Cork I hadn't seen in a decade and a half, Cathal Daly. He's a publican in Barcelona now but he hasn't changed a day. A right funny little fella. I was calling him Niall Horan from the group One Direction because he's the head off him, and he was loving it.

Pat said, 'Rog, you've got to move. You've got to go.'

There were a few French people looking for autographs and photos en route to the reception, where virtually the first person I met was the Stade Français president, Thomas Savare. I had no idea why he was there. It was just so bizarre, with everything that was happening in the background. I'd had the full interview with Stade but I had become aware by email that something had happened in the club and Diego Dominguez said he would explain when he saw me. Right then and there the president of the club explained that while he'd love me to come to Paris, the senior team had only three coaches, those positions had been filled and they were not going to put me into their academy. I told him I appreciated the explanation.

I bumped into Mehrts, who'd just had five years in French club rugby with Toulon, Racing Metro and Beziers. We've had a few good nights together, usually revolving around 'the red zone'. This is a game involving bottles of Steinlager. They have a red label about the size of your baby finger. It's three quarters of the way down the bottle and the beer level after your first gulp has to land perfectly on that red zone or you go again. I chatted to him for a while, then from there it was straight to the airport. I like quick getaways.

We flew to Cork via Shannon. The same four of us who started out from Cork three days before – myself, Casey, Dougie and Peter – stopped off in McCurtain's Street in Cork to buy a 'hillbillies', which is curried chips and a breast of chicken in a bun, and a bottle of Coke, at about 2.30 a.m. The number of drunken people around the place was an incredible sight. Fellas that could talk were very complimentary but others were just sprawled out on tables, wrecked.

I got home at about three and slept from about four until six. Wired. Too much going on in the head. It was an opportunity lost, and it could have been the greatest one. I took comfort from having given it a good shot. If you're completely outplayed or outfought then you're demoralized, thinking this game isn't for you.

That briefly made me reconsider. 'Am I making the right decision? Should I play on?' But then I thought, no, that wasn't a bad way to leave.

CHAPTER 13

Moving On

Saturday, 18 May

Yesterday was an eventful day. It began with a 7.15 a.m. flight from Cork to Heathrow. Having been a pampered professional sportsman for so long, I hadn't experienced travelling on my own for a very long time. A fourteen-year-old boy would have made a better effort. I managed the Heathrow Express into Paddington all by myself. Then I bought a Tube ticket because I had to find my way to Berry Brothers and Rudd, a posh wine cellar, and one of the top restaurants in London. Monsieur Jacky Lorenzetti, the Racing Metro president, was hosting a private lunch there.

I was pathetic. I was disappointed with myself. Rugby has taken me all over the world yet I had no idea how to negotiate the Tube. I suppose it's the same as anything: the first or second time is awkward, then it becomes progressively easier. At one point I was actually laughing at myself. 'Jesus, you'd want to have a good look at yourself now. Thirty-six years of age and you can't get on the Underground and follow the Tube lines and the coloured codes.' Everyone moves at a fierce pace and you can be virtually swallowed up unless you know what you're doing. I was the most indecisive person in the train station, and I'd always thought decision-making came naturally to me.

The lunch had been in the pipeline for three weeks, ever since my meeting with Thomas Savare after the Clermont semi-final. He was with Laurent Lafitte, an agent with the global management group Essentially whom I've known for a few years. He told me Clermont would be interested in signing me on a four-month contract. I told him I wasn't interested in playing but I wouldn't mind trying to get into an academy in France. 'What are the chances of a coaching job in France?'

He said, 'Oh, why didn't you say that? Clermont only made an appointment two weeks ago. You would have been perfect for that.'

'Yeah, but sure I wasn't thinking about that two weeks ago.'

'Leave it with me,' he said, and then he came back with this. The contract arrived on Tuesday along with notification to attend the lunch in London. Racing had to get clearance from Castres to speak to their incoming coaches, Laurent Labit and Laurent Travers. To their credit, they were open-minded as opposed to seeing me as a threat. I told Racing that the salary wasn't as important as bringing my family to France, and that I'd need a house in Paris.

I think it will be easier for me than for Johnny Sexton. I'll have my wife and four kids, and I'm finished playing. There are no issues between us now. Myself and Johnny have come full circle; he invited me to his wedding and you don't do that unless you are friends. Out of courtesy, he was one of the first people I rang.

'I'm not messing, Johnny.'

I'd say I've been dominant enough in his head over the years, and he goes, 'Ah Jesus, I don't believe it. So when I go playing for Ireland you're going to be playing for Racing. Is that what you're telling me?'

I told him, 'I'm finished playing, Johnny, will you relax for God's sake!'

His immediate reaction was that I would be playing and still be a rival! It was funny. It should actually be good for both of us and for Irish rugby, while Irish supporters will be interested in Racing now.

Monsieur Lorenzetti, who has bought a few castles and estates in his time, was hosting the wine-tasting lunch for Danish wine importers. It was pretty impressive, a different world from the one I inhabit. When I walked through the door everyone was upstairs and I first spoke to Juan Hernandez and Maxime Machenaud, both of whom play for Racing. I was handed an unbelievably nice glass of the finest champagne at 11.45 in the morning! Machenaud was travelling to New Zealand with the French squad and Hernandez was heading off to the Rugby Championship with Argentina and wouldn't be back in Paris until October. There was no mention of me joining Racing because they had been told I was there as a guest. Lorenzetti, however, revealed this in his welcoming speech, so the cat was out of the bag. There were a few claps from those in attendance, which included a few English businessmen.

Two new Racing signings, the Northampton props Soane Tonga'uiha and Brian Mujati, were also there. Jesus, Tonga'uiha is a big man. We only chatted for a short while as the players were there to mingle with the other guests.

Before lunch, four of us went into what seemed to me a very prestigious smaller room. Laurent Lafitte sat next to me, with Jacky and Georges-Henry Bediou, his director of communications, on the opposite side of the table. There were three contracts, duplicated in English as well as French, so there was a fair bit of shuffling of paperwork. We spoke slowly in French and went through the contracts. I'm not in the elite playing bracket any more, that's for sure, but the deal included a car and a house, and at least we were moving to Paris. It's not as if I was moving to Limerick! Monsieur Lorenzetti was most helpful and very keen in making sure Jessica and the kids would be happy to move to France.

I signed the contract there and then.

I am not moving for financial reasons but to give my coaching career the best possible start. I think it's the perfect club. Racing Metro have ambition. They've proper players and we should do something there in the next twenty-four to thirty-six months. I know Johnny's mindset too. He's not going there to pick up cash, even if he is getting shedloads of it! He's a good operator, and if he's driving it, things will happen.

The need for a house was paramount, though, because if Jess and the kids aren't happy it's not going to work. As I was due on Sky Sports and I'm not good at telling porkies I wanted to conclude everything and so be able to come clean. It had been in my head since the Clermont game. You have to retire for a decent reason, and with a future direction, as opposed to just finishing. Other opportunities might have materialized if I'd announced my retirement first, but in this financial environment they might not have. I wanted to give the coaching a go anyway, so let's see.

I saw in my contract that training 'commence le premier juillet'. My first reaction was: 'And when are the Lions back?' Oh well, I was once one of the big shots myself, coming back late after summer tours. I thought I'd go over on my own for the first few weeks. No point in bringing Jess and the kids until it's really necessary.

I told them I planned to do a mini coaching blitz in rugby league – watch Tony Smith, a renowned Australian coach with Warrington, and take in Wigan and St Helens. I'd miss the main strategy meetings at Racing on 6 and 7 June because our holiday in the British Virgin Islands was booked for the first two weeks of that month. They understood.

I then asked Lorenzetti what he expected from me.

He said, 'I spend a lot of money, and we have a good base. Berbizier was happy with us, and created a base, but I need success. I look to you for success. You bring a strong mind!'

I said, 'Yeah, well, I hope so.'

My role, he continued, would be to oversee all the kicking strategy, working under the two head coaches: Travers, who is the head coach and will direct operations, and Labit, who works with the backs.

I asked him how many players were at Racing, expecting him to say thirty or so; he said there were forty-two players plus the two coaches and myself, so I'm going to have my hands full. Travers also does defence as well as the forwards, and I'll work alongside Labit and the backs. I'll also be involved in the game plans and tactical approach of the Under-17, 19, 21 and Academy teams, and I'll be liaising with the head of the youth system. All good, even if it seems like a lot of work. As part of my remit I will of course be working with the kickers, but it will be good to have a taste of something else. I will never go down the line of becoming a specialist kicking coach. It wouldn't be enough to stimulate me. I don't have any coaching experience and I'm not fluent in the language, and in coaching, how you deliver your message is almost as important as what you actually say.

My French is rustier than I thought. I'm fine talking to a fella in French if he's speaking slowly to me, but in that meeting, when the agent, the director of communications or Jackie Lorenzetti was in full flow, I was lost. So it will be a big, big challenge, but it should help, from my point of view, that Johnny will be there, and I can build an even better relationship with him.

Last night I texted him before the Leinster–Stade Français Amlin Challenge Cup final in the RDS, prior to my news breaking, and sent him a picture of me shaking hands with Lorenzetti. I expected him to receive it after the game when he turned on his phone, but he responded immediately. He was at ease with our new working relationship.

As a professional rugby player I've been spoiled over the years, especially with so many Italian and French post-match dinners in beautiful settings. This was in a cellar underground that is apparently connected to Buckingham Palace via a tunnel. There were seven big wine glasses in front of each of us to taste seven fine red wines, with coloured stickers to signify which one was which. We sampled three or four fingers' full of each one. I'm no connoisseur, but I've obviously been drinking cheap wine for the last few years: even on an empty stomach, these were delicious. You get what you pay for, as the man says.

The starter was a delicious beef carpaccio with little rib cubes, which I'd never seen before, followed by a beautiful breast of duck with a few greens and, of course, some cheese and wine and crackers, and two glasses of port to finish it off. The seven glasses weren't taken away, so it would have been some session if you were up for it, and an enjoyable one! If I was only with players we'd have hoovered everything, but the other players had to go, so I included myself in that group, and left at around 3.30.

I had learned from my underground escapade in the morning and took a taxi to Paddington for the Heathrow Express. As soon as I walked on it I met Stephen Ferris and 'GG', the Ulster physio. Fez was having more assessments on his ankle, which will need another operation, sidelining him for another six months, and it was wrecking his head. Otherwise, though, he was in good shape – his arms as massive as ever.

'What about ye? Ah right, oh you're fucking on an earner,' he said to me immediately.

'Yeah,' I said. 'I'm on a full-time earner.'

There was no point in hiding it. Fez is a good fella, great company. Completely black and white. I thought I was bad, but he is on a different level altogether. It was enjoyable chatting away with him but my phone was hopping because the story was out. I tried to ignore it.

I reflected on the day's events on the flight home. Being with the French in London brought home to me how different it would be. I've played with friends all my career, people I've really cared about, but now I'm going to a place where, essentially, they won't care about me at all. That's the reality of it, so it will be tough, and as is the case going into any new job, I'll have to build trusting relationships.

Until now, I've taken that as a given. I've had huge rewards from treating team-mates like brothers as opposed to team-mates. Sitting there, the thought came into my head that it would actually be different if Johnny wasn't there – as bizarre as that might sound to others. I was thinking, 'This could be great. People will have an interest in him because he's the Irish out-half and they'll have an interest in me now as well.' It will, hopefully, be good for Racing too.

The reaction over the ensuing twenty-four hours was over-whelmingly supportive. I could easily have moved to play somewhere else but I didn't. There are always one or two lunatics in every walk of life who find some fault in what you do, but everyone appeared to approve of this decision. They saw the bigger picture: Rog is doing this to better himself and per-haps become Munster coach one day.

I rang Garrett Fitzgerald, out of courtesy, when I arrived off the Heathrow Express. I told him I'd be joining Racing. We've always had a good relationship, even through the negotiations this year, when I was dropping from a national to a provincial contract, all of which I totally accepted. He said he appreciated the phone call, and thanked me. He rang me back later to say that because the story was out 'we need to make a comment on it'.

I said, 'No, you can't make a comment until tomorrow. Please, I've a deal here and I need to break this myself in the morning.'

He said OK, and then Pat Geraghty contacted me, of course, wondering what he could say when he started fielding calls. 'Pat, you can't say anything,' I repeated, and Pat, in fairness, was fine with that. Munster would release something at nine in the morning. He also told me the *Examiner* would have my retirement on Twitter that night, which they did, but it was important that I didn't comment until my first column in the *Examiner* confirmed it in the morning.

I only texted Rob Penney that night when I got home because I was absolutely shattered. 'Hi, Rob, just a quick text to confirm my retirement. Thank you for all your time and input on all fronts.' But I'd been in contact with him over the previous weeks and had forewarned him: 'Rob, it's not looking like I'll be playing on.'

He texted back: 'Sad for us, mate. I hope your future is as prosperous as your past. I'd love to have had an opportunity to work with you. Coffee when you are free?'

And I said: 'Yes, we'll text on Monday to arrange.' That was it really.

I also sent a group text to the players. 'Lads, officially retired. Joining Racing Metro as a coach. Thanks.'

Since the Clermont game there had been three piss-ups so it wasn't as if I was throwing dummies to any of them. I'd had a chat with virtually all of them on their own. I talked to Paulie twice, and although I didn't have anything definitely lined up then I'd told him 'playing-wise I'm done' on the Tuesday night after the Clermont game. Then last Monday, late at night, I rang him from my couch to confirm it. I told him I wanted to coach but that I hadn't anything sorted out, so until then I would not be saying anything publicly.

He was calm. He was fine. He didn't say 'Jesus, play on' or anything. He said, 'Yah, I can see where you're coming from, I can see where you're coming from.'

I said: 'It's tough. It's kind of hard to know and hard to call; just mentally I feel like I'm kind of empty. I just feel like I've given everything now. I think there's not much more to give.'

And he was saying, 'Yah, I can see where you're coming from. Yah. Yah.'

I said: 'I'm kind of happy with the way things finished up.'

'Yah, yah,' he repeated. 'I think that sounds good.'

I had initially texted him to say 'sorry to hear about your buddy', referring to Donal Walsh, who had passed away from cancer at the age of sixteen the day before. And from the text he sent back he was clearly rattled about it, so we got talking. I offered to represent him at the funeral because I knew he was in London on Lions duty.

The funeral was horrific. Just terrible. I'd met Donal two or three times and when I went up to console the family his mother reminded me that I'd met him at a Westlife gig long before he was sick. Another time, I borrowed his sleeping bag in Tralee when we were camping in the pissing rain.

Earlier that month, on Wednesday 8 May, something had come over me. We were following each other on Twitter so I direct-mailed him, at 10.30 p.m. 'Can I just compliment you on what you are, a beautiful inspiring boy,' I wrote. 'What extraordinary, wonderful qualities you have.'

He got back: 'Thank you so much. You've no idea what this means to me, coming from someone like you. I honestly appreciate this from the bottom of my heart and wish you and your family nothing but the best for the next few months and years.'

'Thank you so much,' I wrote back. 'How are you feeling?'

'I'm doing OK thankfully. The pain is manageable. But I still feel it catching up on me these days.'

'Can you remember your sleeping bag in Tralee last summer?' he added in another text the next day.

I said: 'I sure can. Slept like a baby in the pissing rain. Thanks for looking after me. I owe you one. Is Paul calling down to you soon?'

And he said: 'Ah ha, anytime, I'm not sure. He was on about it all right but I don't know if he'll get the time? Actually he texted me there. I must get back on to him.'

That was at 4.37 p.m. on 9 May, the day before the Munster annual awards lunch in the Maryborough House Hotel. He died on the Sunday. We'd had a big session on the Friday night, recovered all day Saturday, and on Sunday I saw on Twitter 'RIP Donal Walsh'. I thought 'no way' because he'd said 'I'm doing OK, the pain is manageable'.

It was shocking, more so I think because I was a father. You have different feelings about everything. At his funeral I felt I was representing Paul and Munster. A huge number of people wanted to attend, so a bus to Tralee was organized. We all met up, and everyone was on time. Everyone was in the right suit. Everyone was in the right tie. Everyone looked well. We went to his home and then to the church – St John's Church in Tralee. Hundreds and hundreds of people. Too many for the church to accommodate. The mass started at twelve and it was one of those emotionally draining days. Donal was such an intelligent, bright and motivated young fella. His campaign to prevent young people from committing suicide and the way he spoke about it was truly inspiring.

Donal's father and his brothers carried the coffin to the end of the church. Six Munster players were chosen as pallbearers, so myself, Felix, Donncha O'Callaghan, Tommy, Zebo and

Varley then carried the coffin from the door of the church to the hearse. All his schoolmates from CBS the Green, Tralee, lined the road, with others filling the banks on either side. The Munster boys walked alongside us. It was particularly sad, and after we'd placed him in the hearse, lads from the Tralee Rugby Club formed a guard of honour. A sixteen-year-old Kiwi, Dan Cournan, whom Donal had coached, presented the medals which the team had won, and then performed a really strong haka. I've seen a few hakas in my life, but this was different, performed by one person in that setting. It was very powerful, yet almost peaceful too. It was a pity Dougie's arm was in a sling because I'm sure otherwise he'd have joined in.

I'm glad I texted Donal the preceding Wednesday. I don't know what came over me; maybe it was fate. I'm a believer in the man above shaping everything you do, and this was another example of it. There are days when you wonder is there anyone up there at all, but I thank God for what he's given me. I don't really ask for any more, but early in my career I'd ask him 'please God, make this kick go over', which is crazy stuff, but that's what young fellas do. After a while I think you become appreciative and all you ask is for your family to be healthy. In that regard I would be a massive believer.

By the time I arrived home from my London trip, the kids were asleep. I went in to check on them and give them a kiss but Jess said to leave them alone and not wake them.

I have my own little black chair in the corner of the TV room and I can go into a world of my own in there. I quickly put on the Leinster–Stade game. I told Jess that I'd signed with Racing and that we were going. She was up for it but said 'we need to have a family meeting', which sounded very serious.

'About what?'

'To tell the kids.'

'They'll be grand.'

'You're hoping they'll be grand, but it's still a big move for them.'

I love watching rugby matches. Most players say they don't, but I think they're lying. It's our sport! I can maybe believe Jamie Heaslip. That's him. You don't have to watch hours and hours of it, but if there's a game on television it's like putting homework into the subconscious.

This time I was watching a game with my coaching hat on for the first time. I was checking to see if Johnny was spiralling the ball. That was bugging me. He's well able to spiral, so he should keep spiralling. It's such a good skill to have. When you nail that kick, it brings such value to a team. Johnny is fluent off both feet in spiralling so I just don't understand why he doesn't use this more. I can understand other fellas not doing it because their technique breaks down, but not Johnny. The end-over-end is comparatively low-risk, and easier, but once you become more comfortable with the spiral it actually, in my opinion, is a far more accurate kick.

Johnny wasn't spiralling it off penalties, but Leinster took their chances really well. The first try was a lovely score, Andrew Conway did really well for the second, and Nacewa's try was all in the kick by Johnny. Nacewa didn't have to change his line of running or stop. Watch it from the reverse angle and it was all in the kick. The kick had to be exactly where Johnny put it, because the Stade winger had covered virtually 90 per cent of the space; the one area he couldn't cover was where he thought

Johnny couldn't put it, yet he put it there beautifully. It was out-side the five-metre line, exactly where it should be – a belting kick from right to left. Game over. Stade huffed and puffed but they didn't make any progress.

I also wrote my first column for the *Examiner*, confirming my retirement and my move to Racing, and I did actually write it myself. It took me four attempts, and it was corrected and edited a bit – they asked me to flesh some things out, or add something here and there. But that's the only way I'll do it. That gives me more satisfaction, and it will be good to learn another skill. It is more work, and as a former player you can take shortcuts, but if you do it yourself, you're going to take pride in it and you'll want to put your name to it legitimately.

Today I'm making my debut as a pundit on Sky, for the Heineken Cup final – Clermont against Toulon. It's going to be sickening walking in there. Driving through Dublin I could feel myself getting angry watching the Clermont fans, thinking 'this could be Munster'. Ours is the Red Army, and theirs is the Yellow Army, and they are on a journey like Munster's. The Heineken Cup is very special. This is Jonny Wilkinson's first final. It's the culmination of everything you put into a season. Whoever loses is not going to do much wrong, so there shouldn't be an over-reaction, but that is inevitably the case. I am looking forward to it. I'm going to put myself in the jersey of the two 10s. If Mike Ross was watching, he'd probably see the game as a number 3, whereas I still wouldn't have an idea of what's going on in the front row, unless a fella is being absolutely hammered.

I've been to four Heineken Cup finals, all as a player. They said 'just be yourself'. I won't be waving my arms in the air, and get over-excited, but I'll hopefully speak what comes into my mind and let's see where that takes us.

Pre-match nerves rattled me throughout my career, although I wouldn't be nervous on the pitch, due to the responsibility I felt playing for the team. 'I've got to walk the streets' was my attitude, and in every game I had a direct influence on the scoreboard. Of all the players in any team, the 10 exerts a huge influence in every game, and to have done that for such a long period of time is probably what pleases me the most. A good time to quit is when your stock is high and you're still wanted. It's a nice feeling. Out-half is not a position you can cruise in. You're either on your game or you're gone really, and that's become harder. The fitness is there, but it's tougher when other players are five, ten, even fifteen years younger. It would be different if the whole team was my age. We'd have some craic then. But I don't have Quinny or Hayes or Flannery or Leams or Wally pulling each other off the ground. As good a fellow as, say, Stephen Archer is, it's their time. Let them go. Let them off. I'll wait to see it now. And watching Munster will be fascinating next season. I want their development to be like it was for me. That's all you'd ask, that the young fellas are getting every possible help to show their best.

I'm feeling it: this is a career-defining, even life-defining, couple of days for me. Today is the day it became official. 'Rog has retired'. Today my first column appears in the *Examiner*, it's my first day as a TV pundit, and then I move on to coach in France, having signed the contracts yesterday. A little bizarrely, there's a sense of relief. I feel like I've given it everything, it's over now, and I'm so satisfied with the way it went.

At the same time, I don't know if I have truly accepted it's over. It's probably good that I won't be in Cork. I won't have to read all the local papers or listen to the local radio stations about how Munster are going.

It's comforting that people who are, I think, good judges and whom I respect have said it was a very mature decision. In the *Examiner* I had a little snipe about people saying that he cares more about Munster. Absolute horseshit. It's all about Ireland. I think I could easily get back and be back-up to Johnny if I really, really, really, really wanted to and if an obliging coach was willing to give me that crack, but what's the point? I've had my day with Ireland.

It would have been horrible if it had finished in a damp squib with Munster and people said, 'Jesus, Rog was bad in his last year. He should have gone.' Instead, they can look at the Harlequins game and at the Clermont game and say, 'He produced in all European games.' And that's all you want. It's massive. I can walk away with my head held high. I could have convinced myself I'd had a great career based on figures, and records, and statistics, but the last game was as good as most of them.

I have chatted with recently retired friends and it was all fairly negative for a while in Munster because some of them appeared to be struggling. Now fellas like Anthony Horgan, John O'Neill, Leamy, Flannery, Barry Murphy, Ian Dowling, Frankie Sheahan, Wally and Hayes are all loving it. Leams is the happiest of all. 'It's a great life out there.' This is good to hear. Wally is very busy, and Fla is embracing it. He is as big a personality now as he ever was. He has his pub. He's a mad man on Twitter. He does his TG4 punditry. I think the key is being organized, and that's probably what's going to make it very easy for me: I know what

I'm moving on to next. I know where I'm going. I always wanted to go to France. Let's go. Bring it on. Try and get the kids settled. If they're happy in school, we'll be happy.

I did French in school and one year in university, and when we went to France on summer holidays I always made the effort to speak the language, even slipping away to the boulangerie for the old 'chocolat chaud' and 'pain au chocolat', and the country has always attracted me. Still, on the way to Dublin in the car this morning, Paulie advised me to take French lessons immediately. Typical Paulie. Always one step ahead.

I rang him to tell him the plan: off to Paris for two years and develop as a coach, and see where it takes me. It's like starting all over again for me, although some people haven't a clue. They think the deal in Racing is huge. It's not huge, but it's an opportunity for me to start a coaching career. Donal Walsh's dream was to travel the world and play for Munster, and I thought to myself in the church at his funeral, 'I've been living that dream for sixteen years.' Even if you asked for that as a ten-year-old, you'd hardly believe it. I am very grateful.

CHAPTER 14

A Coach in Paris

I arrived in Charles de Gaulle airport on 30 June, a Sunday, ahead of my first day's work with Racing Metro the next day. The club's finance director Julien Albinet, who has been very helpful in the initial stages of my settling-in period, was waiting for me, along with my car. I was driven to an apartment in Bourg-la-Reine, a suburb to the south-west of Paris.

On my first night in France I wanted to go home to Ireland.

I wasn't used to apartments and it was dark. The electricity wasn't working – or, to be more accurate, the trip switch was off, and I never flicked it (I am hopeless around the house). There was no furniture save for a bed. As it was a Sunday night, all the shops were closed, so I couldn't buy bed sheets and had to use two adidas towels. I woke up, freezing, throughout the night.

I kept thinking: 'Is this what I've signed up to?'

Aside from being the Racing Metro president, Jacky Lorenzetti's company is Foncia, an estate agency, and the club said there was no problem if I wanted to change apartments. In the meantime I bought some supplies and a duvet. Brigid, an employee at the training centre, found other accommodation options and the following Thursday we visited a house where one of the former players, Benjamin Sa, used to live with his family.

You get a vibe from a place, and I immediately thought, 'Yep, this is it.' It has four bedrooms, with bunk beds for the twins, and a nice long garden in a quiet, leafy suburb. This will be 'home' for us.

It helps that I'm familiar with the country. Between family holidays and matches with Munster and Ireland I've lost count of the number of times I've been in France. I'm comfortable here. It's the country I know best outside Ireland. In latter years especially, I didn't play that many Magners/Rabo games in Scotland or Wales, just Six Nations matches there every other year.

I had been over for two meetings in June before I officially started work. Each employee has his or her own car parking berth and I was allotted Bay 28. You are given a badge/security key to access the entrance gate to the training centre. Every morning the sun shone warmly – and got warmer by the minute – from a cloudless sky as I parked my car, and then it's like walking into a hotel. When you go through the revolving glass doors into the main entrance, you're obliged to change your shoes and put on house shoes – be it flip-flops, runners or whatever – and then you swipe yourself in. I go straight upstairs for the old espresso and then to my office.

There are four of us in this room: Simon Raiwalui, Racing's Fijian former player and now team manager; René Bonnefont, who's been a Racing player, captain and president; Paul Martini, the chief bagman; and me. The gym and weights room, and the pitches, are perfect. We've a Racing Metro café on site as well.

The Le Plessis Robinson Training and Learning Centre, to give it its proper name, is 6,000 square metres and has been open since October 2012. In pre-season the whole club moved into the two buildings – one for the professionals and the administrative staff and one for the training centre. There are two rugby pitches, including an artificial one. The centre was built along the lines of Arsenal's training complex, and according to the club's website 'the access to the "sanctuary", the centre and its buildings are equipped to low-energy consumption standards: solar panels on the roof which produce part of the electricity used and triple-glazed windows. There's also an energy recovery system to reduce heating and air-conditioning consumption. The façades are insulated on the outside and covered with particle board. In order to develop links between young players and the elite, the professional squad shares space with youngsters from the training centre who live, study and train on site.'

It's a different world, all right.

Jamie Roberts is working in the gym on his own these days, as he's still recovering from the hamstring injury which limited him to just the last of the Lions' three Tests. He reckons the facilities are the best in Europe. Next to the weights room are the physio and medical rooms; the doctor has his own office. Next comes the changing-room, which has a separate shower room with nine showers, hot and cold baths, and a swimming pool. Then there's another room adjoining the main pitch, purely for changing into the runners or boots required for training – again to the design of the Arsenal module. The white walls are decorated with the following words in Racing's sky blue:

PLAISIR. DISCIPLINE. PASSION. EXIGENCE. HUMILITÉ. COURAGE. GAGNER. PROFESSIONNEL.

The first person I met on my first day was Yann Marques, the club house manager. I came in early. That's the key. That way you don't feel intimidated. You're not met by a big group. People are meeting you as opposed to you meeting them before you become an established figure in the set-up.

The head coaches, Laurent Travers and Laurent Labit – Toto and Lolo – have been hugely accommodating and friendly. They are making a big effort with me, which is very good. I'm here to learn and hopefully give something back, but if I wasn't enjoying it or if I felt the relationships were strained, I'd be gone.

Pre-season is different. I've been coming in at 7.30 a.m. Have a coffee. Have another coffee, and have some skills drills organized if I'm called upon. It's progressing every day. Until the games start there's a greater emphasis on team drills, whereas in the first three weeks we were doing plenty of skills work every day. The forwards and backs were separated twice a day, so I had four sessions each day, which was good. It forced me to hit the ground running. This week, week five, there have been more plays off line-outs and scrums, and I've been more of an observer.

Apart from 1 July, the other big day was the 29th when the Lions and the other internationals who had been on summer tours arrived in camp. It was like a split start, with a new team arriving. We also had the president's address. The club president is a very big figure in French rugby. I suppose it's comparable with Roman Abramovich at Chelsea. A few boys took it in turns to translate Jacky Lorenzetti's words, including my ex-Munster team-mate Julien Brugnaut, who has developed into a monster. He's a loose-head whom Munster tried to play as a tight-head; now he's apparently an animal on the other side of the scrum.

Travers outlined his coaching philosophy. He and Lolo are big into humility and respect, and being united. Everyone is as important as the next fella and should be treated the same, be it either of the coaches, any of the players, Hadj who cleans the dressing-room, or anyone else on the staff. That's the way it should be, but unfortunately that isn't always the way the world works.

This had been the way when they coached Montauban and Castres. They guided Montauban from ProD2 to the Top 14 and qualification for the Heineken Cup, then on 1 June won the Bouclier de Brennus – the winners' shield in the French league – in their third season with Castres, beating Toulon in the final. Montauban were beaten 19–17 on their Heineken Cup debut by Munster at Thomond Park when I landed a 78th-minute penalty. We've discussed it – often. They're still riled about it. Munster would have been a serious scalp and a springboard for the two coaches. Pushing them close in Thomond Park was one thing, beating them another. And the late penalty was a very marginal decision by Wayne Barnes.

I'm beginning to appreciate that Toto and Lolo have serious knowledge. Today we were doing five-man line-outs off-the-cuff and Travers was explaining the role of the back row in the defensive line. This is very good detail for players who are tuned in, but some wouldn't even understand it.

A big difference between club or interprovincial rugby and international rugby is the ability of players to know exactly what they are trying to achieve. At club level some players might not understand why they're doing a certain play. Some think they're doing a play for the sake of doing a play, because it looks good, but you're always trying to create a mismatch or an opportunity.

My responsibility for the goal-kicking game, and the kicking game of all the backs, is only part of my brief. There is a bigger picture. As there are only two other coaches here, and given that there can be up to seven coaches with an international team, my daily and weekly briefs from Toto and Lolo are very extensive. So far they've given me my head and an opportunity to have an input in all aspects. Due to the uncertainty about whether or not I would be playing on, there was general disbelief when it was announced that I was joining Racing Metro – and of course my becoming Johnny Sexton's kicking coach is a great story for the media. I did say that I wasn't going to Paris to be Johnny's kicking coach. Part of my job will involve working with him, but there's a huge amount of other work as well. But you're never going to beat the media, you just have to work with them on something.

I know an awful lot about attacking play and backline play, but nothing about presenting them as a coach. I need to learn. I have to know my place here. Laurent Labit is here to coach the backs so I'm watching him and working out if I am thinking the same things. I'm taking the first small steps to, hopefully, becoming a backs coach and then a full coach, and that's exactly why I'm here. I'm not here to be a kicking coach and switch off, far from it. I have to learn a different culture as well and see how others operate.

The main pitch is still bedding in so we've been travelling from the training centre to a pitch in Versailles each morning, before returning here for lunch and going back out on to the

pitch again for a long session at three p.m. Today, like most days
– although now with the opening friendly away to Toulon
(tomorrow night, 2 August) just hours away – we did weights
and skills in the morning, splitting the forwards and the
backs, and drills in the afternoon.

Hadj, or Hadj Hamida Khelifa to give him his full name, is the
first Tunisian I've ever met. He is the Aki of the operation. He's
responsible for having the gear and the dressing-room cleaned,
and everything around here is spotless. Normally chirpy, he's in
bad form these days as he's doing Ramadan. I never knew what
Ramadan was, but eating or drinking are forbidden during
sunlight.

'C'est vrai, Hadji boy? Pas manger ou boire quand il fait du
soleil?' (Is that right, Hadji boy? No eating or drinking when
there's sun?)

'Oui, c'est vrai, mais c'est bien.' (Yeah, it's true, but that's
fine.)

I've been impressed with the attitude of the players, too.
There's a perception of the French as moody and grumpy, but
they've all been hugely respectful and very friendly, which has
made the transition so much easier. Of course, it will change
as the season progresses, especially when we have bad results
along the way. Each morning, everyone says 'bonjour' and
shakes hands with everyone else, as is the formal way in France.
Munster was so different, with mostly local players and a few
quality imports added every few years. This is a global club that
has attracted some of the best players from around the world.

Here it's a business, and it's going to be interesting to see how
it develops. But I'm glad Toto and Lolo are conscious of the
human side of things – without a close bond you don't win

anything. Players have to be close to each other. The coaches' body language is very good. The players feel they are approachable. They carry themselves very well. They're organized, they know their stuff, they're prepared and they're personable. Travers is 'touchy-feely' in a good way. He nearly massages his players, and perhaps that comes in part from winning the Top 14 last season.

Every day I've kept notes. I've everything written down. Essentially, at the end of my first season here I'll have a note of what has been done each day every week. Pre-season has been a massive learning curve for me. Not only do the two Laurents have forty players, they also have a staff of about twenty. As a player you never appreciate the full scale of a professional organization and that coaches have to manage the staff as well. As a player, it's all about the match. I loved the match. I didn't mind training, in decent weather – though sometimes it felt like there were contact sessions for the sake of them. I didn't mind running either. I had to do my own skills sessions so I enjoyed them because it was my responsibility: I had to research them and I had to do them. I have drills written down in diaries from the last ten years and I've been scouring them to devise new drills. It's not hard, but Lolo and Toto make it more challenging by having some very good drills.

Contrary to the common perception of French coaching standards, they're very organized. Often in training the players have been split into three groups of, say, twelve, so the two Laurents and I would have a dozen each, and then we rotate the groups. They would be working on anything from passing and footwork to two-on-ones and clean-out techniques, and I have my directives from Lolo and Toto.

If I'm not sure how to relay something to the players, the best thing to do is say, 'Comment dit-on en français?' I've picked up huge amounts of lingo already. It's a great way to learn a language, being thrown into a job like this, with fifty-plus people talking to you every day.

I get a buzz from doing the drills. They go so quickly, and I like the hands-on part the best. I was talking to Johnny about this and he asked me if I would be interested in a Conor O'Shea/David Humphreys type role. 'Yeah, maybe in time,' I said. 'But, like, I actually love the challenge of coming up with something on the pitch.' Clearly some serious attributes are needed to be a director of rugby, but because I've just stopped playing, I think I have technical ability which can be passed on.

I've enjoyed these first few weeks, but I think it will be more real when Jess and the kids arrive. I've eaten in the Sushi Bar on my own in the 'centre ville' at least a dozen times. There has been a lot of 'Une table pour une personne, s'il vous plaît' over the last month or so. I have the same order too: 'le dragon'. It's a California roll with tempura prawns, avocado and asparagus. I prefer spending most nights on my own anyway. As a coach I can't be hanging around with players. I have to draw the line now. There's also no point in being friendly with everyone every night, and then when Jess and the kids arrive spending all my time with them. You can't just drop everyone like a hot potato.

Just for the moment, though, it seems like a surreal world, going home to an empty house with nothing there. One of my suitcases is still unpacked at the bottom of the stairs.

CHAPTER 15

A New Season

We flew down from Orly to Toulon for our first pre-season friendly – arriving to spectacular views – and from there to the hotel. It felt odd. It was piping hot and I wore the match shorts and socks for the warm-up, and all the boys were slagging me. 'Tu es joueur? Tu es joueur?'

Laurent Travers had introduced a 'no card playing' rule on match days and I don't think some of the Racing players were too happy about this, not least because an 8.30 p.m. kick-off made for a long day. Another rule is that mobile phones are switched off from three and a half hours before kick-off.

We were scheduled to assemble at seven p.m. in the hotel, but all the French players were already in the room by 6.40 and ready to go. In Ireland, some might turn up about ten minutes ahead of time and the bulk of us about five minutes beforehand.

I was surprised by the pep talk when we got to the ground. It was quite serious for a friendly. One end behind the posts wasn't open but the rest of the Felix Mayol was sold out, although clearly a few season ticket holders were still on holiday, and all the boys were scrambling for tickets.

We were staying in the Hotel Ibis which is beside the Felix Mayol, and the bus passed through a corridor of supporters. I walked to the ground with Laurent Travers and the Toulon crowd were unbelievably respectful. 'O'Garaaaa!' 'Bienvenu, O'Garaaaa!' That's why you play rugby. But for a pre-season game it was crazy. They all seemed to know I was with Racing.

Jonny Wilkinson was on the pitch practising with one of the Toulon coaches, Pierre Mignoni, when I arrived. The last time I was at the Felix Mayol with Munster, three years earlier, I was yellow-carded for fighting with Mignoni. I didn't speak to Jonny until after the game because even though it was a friendly, I'd respect his routine.

He played the full eighty, and there was good intensity. It was physical, and defences were on top. They beat us 14–6 with two penalty tries against our scrum, and with seven international props on the books the management weren't happy with that.

There were other problems with our defensive plays. Racing have one guard either side of the ruck, and the guard can go after the opposition 9. I am more used to a system in which the guard never moves and takes any runners inside the 9, with the second defender taking the 9.

Afterwards the boys went for a drink, which, oddly, held no appeal for me. Usually after playing a game I'd have to fight that back. I did fitness after the game and I felt good afterwards. I needed it. I'd been so busy that I'd neglected that side of things. Then again, Racing aren't paying me to train myself.

I doubt coaching will ever give me the same thrill and buzz that playing did, but I'm now prepared for that. I learned that straight away from the first few games. Playing was some adrenalin rush, especially as a 10, and especially if it came down to the last kick at goal. As a player, that's what I lived for. You become better equipped to handle pressure the more you're exposed to it, and I liked that about the game. Getting my team over the line was a source of huge internal satisfaction, and that happened many times for Munster and for Ireland.

That will never be repeated, but you have to expect that, move on, and find a different motivation. I don't think I'll be impatient with players, partly because I'm starting off as a coach in France and the French like to do things slowly anyway, and partly because I don't think I am an impatient person. I have really high standards and expect them in others, but I'd be prepared to compromise. I also realize that 'you can't beat the mob'; but if the mob don't have high standards then the team aren't going to win anything, in which case you have to move on.

Of course I'll miss playing. Even in that first pre-season friendly when the boys were warming up I experienced a shot of adrenalin. I felt like I could play. There'll be other games when I have the same feelings, perhaps even more powerfully, but this will be counteracted by a sense of contentment, achievement and happiness, and a note of realism: I know that it can't go on for ever.

I won't have as many sleepless nights or as much pain in my body, but I think that's all part of missing it too. There's a great feeling you get from pushing your body to the max. I'm sure this can be experienced through participating in events like a triathlon, but there's something special about doing it in a group environment, and achieving something when everyone is pinned to the ropes with nothing more to give but somehow coming through. It's just a very powerful feeling. I'll miss that all right.

The squad assembled at the training centre the following Sunday, before departing for a week-long training camp in Lausanne, culminating in a match against Harlequins in Geneva. It was a busy, hard week's training. Performances would improve because there would be more rest time, and fellas would be hungrier for games. At the start of pre-season the boys seemed to be on the pitch every day. The heavy workload was necessary with new coaches, new patterns, new combinations and new players, so Lausanne was good. In fact the whole week was an eye-opener.

On that Sunday we all had to arrive at the club with a goldfish. I had to find a pet shop that very morning, buy one, arrive with it in a plastic bag and hand it over without knowing what was going to happen next. It transpired that the ensuing game of spin-the-wheel involved certain punishments, and one of them was 'poisson'. The nominated player had to pick out his goldfish and . . . down the hatch. The alternative was chilli peppers. That was my punishment, to chew and swallow a chilli. I nearly died. I genuinely thought I was having a nervous reaction because my lips swelled up and my face was pumping hot. I chose a yellow one thinking it wouldn't be too bad. Apparently they're the second strongest! I was in awful, awful shape. The chef sorted me out by telling me pineapple is the best cure for a reaction to spicy food. So, for any people out there who are suffering after eating spicy food, get some pineapple into you! It brings the temperature down. Well, two big pineapples did the trick for me anyway. I was in wicked shape.

In Lausanne the facilities were basic and the pitch average but it was a good week. We were all tight together. On the Saturday we took a bus to the Stade de Genève where Munster had played Bourgoin in 2006/07, and the pitch was crap. I presume the costs for each club were paid, that's why they held it in Geneva, but I'd say about five thousand were at it. Racing won after an average first half but were good in the second half.

Only since I've come to Racing have I appreciated the level of respect for Munster in France. Before we played Racing in the Stade de France last October I remember thinking 'this is going to be really tough'. After chatting with a few Racing people it transpires they were fearful of Munster. They respected Munster probably way more than we respected them, which is interesting. Sitting at my desk one day I thought, 'If only some of the younger Munster lads could dip into what I know now.' I think they'd go back to Munster with such a different attitude – appreciating how lucky they are, determined to grasp the opportunity and make the most of their time, because it is so special.

The Munster lads compiled a DVD as a farewell presentation to me. They actually tried to pin me down on four different occasions but I wouldn't go to a presentation, in part because at the time I probably didn't want to accept it was over, but mainly because I didn't want to meet them all as I would have ended up in tears. So I just avoided them. The DVD arrived in the post on the Thursday morning before we went on holiday. Our video analyst, George Murray, had compiled some of my better moments intermingled with some thoughts from a few of the boys. Sure enough, I just broke down. It was too much. Too emotional. Too good.

Retirement is very final, and when you care about something

so much, that makes it massively emotional. But in my head I'm going back there some day. That's why I'm doing everything possible to make myself a better coach – in order to return to Munster. Then I'll say hello again as opposed to saying goodbye.

One thing I can't go back to is pulling on a green jersey and representing my country. I was hugely disappointed that my Ireland career ended with my being dropped from the squad for the first time. At the time you see it as a personal attack, though when sense prevails you see that it was a sporting decision. You accept it and move on.

I have since received over a thousand letters on the subject. It's been staggering. Most of them have simply been addressed 'Ronan O'Gara, rugby player, Cork' or 'Ronan O'Gara, Douglas, Cork'. There's something special about reading a handwritten letter. It's more real. More meaningful. Some of them expressed anger about the way my career finished with Ireland, but most were along the lines of 'thanks for the memories and best wishes and good health to you and your family'. Some of the media are very quick to pick out the faults but some can only see the good in someone. There are good people out there.

Another thing I'm realizing quickly is that preparing for a match as a coach is hugely different to preparation for a game as a player. The Munster dressing-room could be a superstitious place before someone piped up with the observation that super-stitions hold you back and affect performance. Some players' routines were subconsciously affected by it and they did things differently, but I was more of a feel person, more of an instinctive player. I suppose if I had my time back I would apply one lesson I definitely learned in my latter years, namely 'less is more'. In Munster we always had to be the hardest trainers and the best trainers, yet sometimes I was so absolutely shattered that there wasn't a spurt in me. You have to keep constantly adapting and looking at what works for you.

I couldn't start my mental preparation for a match on the day of the game. I wasn't a freak of an athlete or anything like that, my head was one of my best attributes, so I had to use it to get the best out of myself and hopefully get the best out of our team. I had to start thinking and getting the plays ready early in the week.

In contrast to this, I'm barely crawling as a coach. Everything is new to me at the moment. I have no relevant experience to apply to any given situation. I obviously know an awful lot about rugby, but not much about coaching. I'm enjoying it so far, though, and I think that's because Toto and Lolo are secure in their own abilities and are therefore willing to hand over responsibility. They've been open to ideas and suggestions. I haven't been pawned off. They're actually interested in what I have to say and they write it down. They might even repeat one or two of my points, so I'm doing more than merely watching them. If that was all there was for me here I'd move on. I feel involved, and feeling involved is critical.

I suffered from pre-match nerves throughout my career. For the first five years or so I felt I had to keep proving myself when not everyone perhaps rated me. Then comes the stage when you know you're a good player, and with that comes increased responsibility, and with increased standards comes the requirement to do it consistently. So I never let up. I always took it very, very seriously, but I'm proud of that. I wouldn't change anything, and I got the ultimate return from Munster and Ireland; for them I was prepared to make whatever sacrifice was required. I put everything into it in order to get as much as I could out of it.

I hadn't expected nerves would be a factor as a coach, but I certainly didn't sleep well at first. When you're a player and you're on the pitch, you have direct influence over the way things are going. The minute you stop playing you realize how comparatively useless you are. You can tell someone, but there's nothing like doing it. Talk is cheap!

But I'm not starting out as a coach nervously or feeling insecure. I know it will take years and years to become a head coach. I have, however, a pretty good handle on being a backs coach and a kicking coach. Maybe not for such an experienced team as Racing, but in everything you have to take small steps and put in solid foundations before moving on. It's not as if I'm a novice at rugby. I take comfort from the knowledge I've built up over the years as a player. I probably know as much as if not more than most, from a playing point of view, even if this knowledge doesn't naturally translate immediately into coaching. My playing career was mostly about getting myself right. When you're a coach it's about 'getting ourselves right'. The 'me' goes out of it.

One thing I learned on the pitch which I think is hugely under-appreciated is the power of encouragement. Positive words bring out the best in people, not just the players. I've seen proof of that with younger and older players in Munster. That was a team with heart, spirit, brotherhood, call it what you like, and this is something I'm trying to instil now in my early days as a coach. I will see that the boys are encouraged, especially the French because they are notoriously moody. They *need* to be encouraged.

*

On Saturday 17 August, the opening weekend of the Top 14 season, we played Brive in La Rochelle on the west coast of France. I drove into our training centre and parked the car in Bay 28, then took the bus to Montparnasse. From there it was three and a half hours on the midday TGV to La Rochelle. Taking the train to a match – it took me back to my AIL days with Con. Great days. Great craic. Cans to beat the band on the return journey. This was comparatively very tame.

We had two carriages on the TGV: twenty players in one and six plus the coaching staff in the other. Normally I wouldn't have even thought about it – I'd have been in the carriage with all the players. I still have to stop myself in training. I instinctively head to the side of the pitch where the players are; the coaches go left. And I'm very slow to pick up cones and get my arse in gear. That was always done for me, but now it's one of my duties.

On the TGV I sat opposite Lolo and chatted with him. Laurent Labit's a lovely fella. He just is, you just get a feeling off a fella. My French is good enough to hold a rugby conversation, although sometimes he shoots off and I have to slow him down. 'Doucement, Lolo, s'il te plaît,' I say. We talked about everything really, then myself and Johnny went for a 'doubler' – a double espresso. We're on to the double espressos already! He was in the players' carriage but he passed through and gave me the nod. So the two of us went for a coffee and a chat with Benjamin Dambielle, the reserve 10 and 15. Johnny was in good form. I think he loves it here.

Going to a match didn't feel too different at all, which was odd. I was still going to a match. I rang Jess about it and said, 'Jesus, I thought the minute I retired that feeling would be gone, but it doesn't seem too much different.'

We took another bus to the Mercure Hotel, twenty minutes outside La Rochelle, and had a video session there at six p.m., followed by the Captain's Run at 6.30. The meeting went through what we were to use off kick-offs, scrum plays, line-out plays and slow ball plays, and reminded the players about playing the game in the right areas. Then we went to the Rochelle stadium and did a gentle, slow warm-up, followed by seven minutes of plays for the starting team – two scrums, two line-outs, receive a kick-off – and then seven minutes for the reserves.

Back for dinner at eight o'clock. After that some of us sat around and watched a bit of the Friday night season-opener between Montpellier and Toulon. I was rooming with the Racing Metro 'Doc', Jean-Marc Laborderie. When you don't know a fella that well and the two single beds are more or less on top of each other, it can be a little strange, but it was grand. It was like I was back starting all over again, going into the Irish squad at the age of twenty-two.

Jean-Marc's good company, and interesting. He's been in Dubai with a professional soccer team for the last two years, but he's back now. He liked his time there. The challenge, however, wasn't good enough for him. He is very competitive and said the money was huge but the level of competition very average.

We had more meetings in the morning. They love a meeting. Match day began with a 10.15 a.m. scrum video for the forwards, and at 10.45 we had a collective video. We looked at Brive – where they kick off, what they do off line-outs, what they do off scrums – then we took a bus to a soccer pitch for a walk around and a few games of forwards against backs – an instincts game. You have to have your hands behind your back and you can't use them unless the ball comes directly to you.

Lunch was still the staple match-day diet of chicken and pasta. No other choice. 'Jesus, I can't believe it, more bloody chicken and pasta!' I said to myself. 'Two weeks in a row as well. Looks like some things aren't going to change.' Then 12.30 to 3.30 was 'chill-out time'. I went for a nap. I'd only slept from twelve till four the previous night, maybe because I was unused to rooming with the Doc, or maybe because I was a small bit excited about the match. In any event, I just didn't sleep, and I was shattered.

After sleeping for an hour and a half, I hung around and watched a bit of Clermont away to Biarritz. Clermont were well on top. At 4.15 we all went for a little stroll around the hotel together. I didn't know what they were doing so I asked Laurent Travers.

I said, 'What's this about?'

He just said: 'Tranquille.' Meaning it's calming, or peaceful.

Come to think of it, we did something similar on occasions with Ireland and Munster.

We soon returned for more presentations on Brive, and then got on to the bus to the ground. I sat three from the front. My new seat. I've no choice: it's first, second or third row for me now. No more sitting second row from the back, as I did my whole career for Ireland and Munster. The same spot. It's a different buzz at the front of the bus, a completely different dynamic. A different type of person. Everything. You can't just wander back. The back of the bus is for players and I'm not a player any more, so it's gone. That is painful, because of the fellas I'm missing. I always had Paulie and Drico for company. They were the two constants from Munster and Ireland.

I had the Doc beside me for this journey. We're good old pals now! The physio, Laurent Hubert, and the video analyst, Anthony Marhuenda, sat in the second row and the other two Laurents were on separate sides at the front, Lolo to the left, Toto to the right – a row each to themselves.

I knew Johnny would be out an hour before kick-off, I know his routine. So out we went and into punting, using a stretching aid. I'd never used one of those. I was cold and inflexible, which was another new pre-match feeling. I used to have my routine, as I got older, of running two laps, or two half-laps. This time I came out of the dressing-room and went straight into kicking.

I don't meddle with Johnny's kicking practice. What I did worked for me, but what works for Johnny works for Johnny. It's important to respect his head space. If you notice something you say so, though. It's very obvious too when you're watching someone. Because we don't have eyes on ourselves it's helpful to have an extra pair. Sometimes there's very little to be said, other times there is a bit to be said, but it's always interesting for me and for him too, because the day you think you have the kicking nailed is the day you fall on your arse. It's about continual assessment, from week to week.

He kicked very well in the warm-up. He takes sixteen to twenty kicks in practice before a game. I used to take around six; for me ten would be an awful lot. I found it very hard to maintain that focus over twenty kicks and I also struggled to distinguish between game and training. I preferred doing the bare minimum and not being overworked. When I took six or eight kicks, I felt under more pressure to nail each of them, which is what I wanted; if I hit sixteen to twenty I was allowing myself leeway to miss one or two. I've done it that way myself in the past, thinking training is the same as the game, but it never is, which is why I had to put pressure on myself, even in the warm-up.

Johnny picks out spots too. We're very similar in that regard. Johnny actually hadn't done much kicking at goal coming into the first game of the season because Leigh Halfpenny was the goal-kicker for the Lions in Australia. He'd had plenty of practice, however, so now we were back in Tarzan and Jane territory: train like Jane, play like Tarzan.

Jacky Lorenzetti had decided to move the game to La Rochelle, a popular tourist port town, as he reckoned Racing would have more support there in mid-August than in Paris. As almost eight thousand fans, mostly wearing ciel et blanc (sky blue and white), packed into Stade Marcel-Deflandre, he was probably right.

The stadium is about a three-iron from the coast, and although it was around twenty-five degrees when the game kicked off at 6.30, there was a stiff breeze blowing in from the sea. It dawned on me during the game that it was a good toss to win. Brive won it, gave us first use of the wind, and we were too rusty to make good use of it in the first half.

Johnny spiralled a couple of kicks beautifully, and his cross-kick set up our first try. He converted it, then nailed a penalty to make it 10–5 before missing his third kick, from about forty-eight metres out. The wind was blowing strongly from right to left and he just wrapped it a little bit. His next one went directly over the top of the right-hand post. We had discussed it, and I told him 'two metres in from the right-hand post' was the line, but he just pushed it a small bit to the right. He landed a good kick into the breeze at the start of the second half, but then he missed his next one by about ten metres. It wasn't anywhere near the posts, and soon after that he was replaced by Jonathan Wisniewski, although he was always going to be taken off around the hour mark. Wisniewski landed his two penalties to give us a 19–14 win. It happens to all of us. Maybe Johnny was a small bit uptight and quickened it.

My role wasn't all about Johnny. I was involved in the warm-up, encouraging the players, but at the same time I know my place. Lolo is the head backs coach. 'Your time will arrive if you keep your dignity,' I thought. I tried to watch a little bit of the game from behind the posts. It's a great place to watch – you can see where the space is – but I had to move back so that put a stop to that. The fourth official was all over me. The president's adviser, Arnand Tourtoulou, was sent down to tell me I had an official warning or something.

Four of us were running on with the water bottles in addition to the two water breaks in each half. The boys were soaking wet. It seemed to be taking a lot out of them, and it was an average game. Nothing exciting about it really. Let's call a spade a spade. By the end I was just waiting for the whistle to go because I was bored. Sometimes you've just got to take the four points and move on.

In fairness to Wisniewski, he's a bloody good goal-kicker and, as we know, goal-kicking is highly important. It's going to be a big season for Johnny. He needs to be goal-kicking well for Racing and Ireland, and I am partly responsible. I carry an awful lot of his load. Never in my life have I wanted another goal-kicker to be so good as I want Johnny to be now. It's part of my brief, and I take that seriously, which was why I was pissed off in La Rochelle, because Johnny didn't kick well. But that is the way I am. Johnny's been kicking a long time, and his percentages have been very good for a few years. A third of the way through this season now, he has the best kicking statistics in the Top 14.

As for me, this is a different type of pressure. I think there was definitely a sense of relief overall when I knew in my head I was done. Less responsibility, I suppose, because it meant so much, but it's amazing how quickly things move on and we find new pressures. I found some in that first game, because I would be an awful lot more at ease with myself if I had missed the kicks. When you're coaching and you haven't missed them, it's painful. Maybe I'll develop a little more sympathy for coaches now.

Calling myself a coach to other people felt a little odd at first, but I'm very comfortable with it now. It feels natural. Maybe if I was at home I'd have more doubts about this venture, but over here I don't really know anyone, I haven't read anything and I haven't had any doubts. That is a pleasant change, as I had plenty of them as a player.

Then again, I'm not under huge pressure yet. I'm part of a team and learning how I can help Racing to reach their potential. I've been through every experience as a player so I'm sure I can help them.

Hopefully I will remain composed, even though people expect me to have really high standards. I've seen people becoming flustered and losing the head, and it doesn't do anything to improve their performance. It actually inflates or accelerates the problem. I suppose I remained cool as a player so I want to do that as a coach too. There's always a next game.

After Johnny had been replaced against Brive, I told him: 'Johnny, I've had twenty days like that and it's important you don't do it next week, because good players don't do it two weeks in a row.' Johnny is twenty-eight now, and an experienced player who has been through a lot, so if we can't say it to each other as it is, then we're going nowhere.

Jess and the kids arrived in Paris on 21 August and it felt like it had been a year since I'd seen them. The house just didn't feel like a home before they arrived. I hadn't used the kitchen, the fridge or the cooker. No reason to. Why would I eat on my own? I don't do things on my own. I'm used to family life. Again my bag had stayed unpacked at the bottom of the stairs. Mum and Dad came over too, on the ferry from Rosslare to Cherbourg, and brought over my old Samsung TV, from my good old days of promoting Samsung.

Their arrival marked the start of a new adventure. Family is real life. It's more important than rugby. It's what I'm looking forward to, and it'll make the rugby more enjoyable, because we all have to leave the game sometimes. So far for me it's been rugby and nothing else. But I'll have to find another family day, because Sundays here begin at nine a.m. in a video session with Lolo and Toto. It's actually not too hard: we watch the match, make observations and comments, note down potential improvements, highlight what's good and not so good, cut the video and select a few clips for the backs, the forwards and the squad overall. That's it, essentially. But Sunday morning as a player used to be real gold dust family time. Wrecked.

I had to do it this way. I had to spend the first seven weeks on my own without my wife and kids. It had to be done this way because first impressions last, hopefully, and I've thrown myself into it. I've been ever-present. It's not as if I've been trying to skive off as if there's nothing to do. I've embraced it, and the two

Laurents work bloody hard. That's been interesting to see, and you can't beat hard work, no matter what game you're in.

But it also has to work for Jess and the kids or it doesn't work. She might hate it, and if she does she's going to have to go home, and I don't know what that will mean for me, whether or not I would finish out the year. So far, though, she's made a go of everything.

I want to stay committed to this as long as I'm contracted to it. Coaches who announce in advance that they are leaving or retiring run the risk of becoming a lame-duck manager or coach. I never became a lame-duck player, in part because I saw out my last contract and didn't announce my retirement until I'd played out my last game in my last full season.

I have high hopes for Racing. Sometimes rugby is so simple. A lot of the moves work, no matter how, because they're executed by good players, but if you don't keep the ball, it doesn't matter. We go on about coaches and moves and facilities and the importance of supporters, and all of them are important, but if a team doesn't have three or four great players, it won't go anywhere.

I'm not worried about what the future holds. I don't worry about rugby any more. Not since Darbs passed away. I don't worry about such things; it's not worth it. I'm lucky. It's good to be alive, to be drinking espressos in France, to be living and learning. I never forget Munster either. With every passing day I'm more appreciative of having played for only one club. It's a nice thing to be able to say. It's a nice thing to be able to look back on, and when I eventually do up a small rugby room in my house, the room will reflect that.

Wherever that house is going to be.

Ronan O'Gara

Career Highlights

Cork Constitution
Munster Senior League (1998)
All-Ireland League (1999)

Munster
240 appearances*
2,625 points*
(15 tries, 368 conversions, 556 penalties, 27 drop goals)

Heineken Cup

Winner 2006, 2008
Finalist 2000, 2002
110 appearances*
1,365 points*
ERC European Player award (2010)

Inter-provincial championship winner 1999, 2000, 2001
Celtic League winner 2003, 2009, 2011
Celtic Cup winner 2005

Ireland
128 caps*
1,083 points*
(16 tries, 176 conversions, 202 penalties, 15 drop goals)

Six Nations

Grand Slam winner 2009
Triple Crown winner 2004, 2006, 2007, 2009
63 appearances*
557 points*
Top points scorer 2005, 2006, 2007, 2009

British & Irish Lions
16 appearances (2 caps)
124 points
(3 tries, 32 conversions, 15 penalties)
Tourist 2001 (Australia), 2005 (New Zealand), 2009 (South Africa)

* record at retirement

ACKNOWLEDGEMENTS

My career would not have been possible without so many people, and thanks are due to each and every person whom I have had the fortune to be associated with. Many of their names are in the text of this book, from lifelong team-mates to valued friends.

Special thanks are of course due to my parents, Jess and the kids, and those whose advice I have relied upon over the years, notably Michael O'Flynn. Nothing would have been possible without all of you.

Thanks also to those involved in putting this book together: Gerry Thornley for putting my thoughts and actions into words on the tightest of schedules; Jonathan Harris for putting the deal together; Eoin McHugh, Giles Elliott and everyone at Transworld Ireland.

Ronan O'Gara
Paris, October 2013

First off, thanks to Rog. The chance to work with such a fascinating legend on this project was every bit as compelling as I imagined it would be, and was also very enjoyable. Thanks too to Eoin, Giles and all the staff at Transworld for their help, guidance and professionalism.

This book simply would not have been completed without Yannick allowing Bar Basque in Soustons to become my 'office' or without the unstinting input from the 'team': my mum Petria, sister Yseult, wife Una and 'kids' Dylan, Evan and Shana. Profound thanks to all.

Gerry Thornley
Dublin, October 2013

PICTURE ACKNOWLEDGEMENTS

Honorary doctorate photograph © Diane Cusack Photography, with thanks.

All other photographs © Inpho Photography, with thanks to Billy Stickland and his team, as follows:

First section (© INPHO/name; top to bottom, left to right)
Page one: Lorraine O'Sullivan; Andrew Paton; Billy Stickland
Page two: Morgan Treacy (all)
Page three: Billy Stickland; Lorraine O'Sullivan; Dan Sheridan
Page four: Cathal Noonan; Dan Sheridan (x 2)
Page five: Billy Stickland; James Crombie
Page six: Dan Sheridan (both)
Page seven: Billy Stickland (both)
Page eight: Billy Stickland; Dan Sheridan

Second section (© INPHO/name; top to bottom, left to right)
Page one: Dan Sheridan; Billy Stickland; Dan Sheridan
Page two: Getty Images; Billy Stickland; Dan Sheridan
Page three: James Crombie; Dan Sheridan; Morgan Treacy; Dan
  Sheridan

Page four: Dan Sheridan; Billy Stickland; Dan Sheridan
Page five: Billy Stickland (x 2); Dan Sheridan
Page six: Billy Stickland (all)
Page seven: Billy Stickland; James Crombie (x 2); Billy Stickland
Page eight: Billy Stickland; Harold Cunningham

Index

ABOUT THE AUTHORS

Ronan O'Gara was born in 1977 in Sacramento, California, and educated at Presentation Brothers College and University College Cork, captaining Pres to the Munster Junior and Senior Schools Cup and winning an All-Ireland Under-20 winners' medal with UCC in 1996. In 1998 he helped the Ireland Under-21 team to the Triple Crown and the following year guided Cork Constitution to the AIB League title, before making his full international debut against Scotland in 2000.

O'Gara made his Munster debut in 1997 and was the inspirational force behind their Heineken Cup victories in 2006 and 2008, as well as three Celtic Leagues and a Celtic Cup. He played in three World Cups for Ireland, won the Triple Crown in 2004, 2006 and 2007, then the Grand Slam in 2009, kicking the winning drop-goal against Wales. He was a member of the British & Irish Lions touring teams in 2001, 2005 and 2009, captaining the Lions as well as Munster and Ireland during the course of his career.

On announcing his retirement in May 2013, O'Gara was the most capped player in Munster (240 appearances) and Ireland (128 caps) history, the leading points scorer for Munster (2,625) and Ireland (1,083) and in the Heineken Cup (1,365 points), for which he was awarded the ERC European Player Award in 2010. O'Gara is now assistant coach at Paris-based team Racing Metro.

Gerry Thornley, who collaborated with Ronan O'Gara on this book, has been the rugby correspondent of the *Irish Times* since 1997 and is a regular contributor and analyst on both television and radio. His previous book *Trevor Brennan: Heart and Soul* won the William Hill Irish Sports Book of the Year in 2007.